SILK
AND THE
SWORD

SILK
AND THE
SWORD

THE WOMEN OF THE
NORMAN CONQUEST

SHARON BENNETT CONNOLLY

AMBERLEY

For James and Lewis, with all my love.

First published 2018

Amberley Publishing
The Hill, Stroud
Gloucestershire, GL5 4EP

www.amberley-books.com

British Library Cataloguing in Publication Data.
A catalogue record for this book is available from the British Library.

ISBN 978 1 4456 7875 7 (hardback)
ISBN 978 1 4456 7876 4 (ebook)

Typesetting and Origination by Amberley Publishing.
Printed in the UK.

Contents

Acknowledgements

Writing my second book has been an incredible experience and I would like to thank everyone who has helped and encouraged me throughout the process. I would like to thank the staff at Amberley, especially my editor Shaun Barrington, for giving me the opportunity and Cathy Stagg for her help thoughout editing.

I would particularly like to thank Amy Licence, whose help, advice and friendship has been invaluable to me in my journey to become an author. I am also grateful to my fellow Amberley authors, Kristie Dean, Annie Whitehead and Susan Higginbotham, who have offered advice and encouragement throughout. Thanks to the wonderful Anna Belfrage, for all the little messages of support and discussions about our favourite women throughout history. And to Paula Lofting, for our discussions on the mysterious woman in the *Bayeux Tapestry*. Some particular thanks must go to Dr Ann Williams, an expert on the period, who was kind enough to share an, as yet, unpublished article on her research into Gytha and the Godwin family.

Writing can be a lonely experience, you spend your time reading books for research, or sitting, staring at the computer screen, trying to think of something to write. But social media has changed all that, there are always friends just a 'click' away to give you some diversion or encouragement. I would therefore like to thank the readers of my blog, *History ... the Interesting Bits* for their wonderful support and feedback. A special thank you goes, too, to my friends in the online community, whose amusing anecdotes and memes have given me that boost when I needed it, particularly Karrie Stone, Tim Byard-Jones,

Acknowledgements

Karen Clark, Geanine Teramani-Cruz, Anne Marie Bouchard, Harry Basnett, Derek Birks and every one of my Facebook friends and Twitter followers. Also, the online author community has proved invaluable to me. So I would like to extend a special thank you to S.J.A. Turney, Tony Riches, Sarah Bryson, Matthew Harffy, Dr Janina Ramirez, Mary Anne Yard and Prue Batten for all your support and encouragement with this book and the last.

And thank you to the various historical sites I have visited, including Conisbrough Castle, Lewes and Pevensey Castles, Lincoln Cathedral, the battlefield near Hastings, and all the wonderful staff who have been happy to talk about all things 1066. I would like to include some thank yous to those who supported the release of my first book, *Heroines of the Medieval World*. Particular thanks have to go to Liam Cooke and Gavin Smithies at Conisbrough Castle, for hosting the book launch; to Sasha and Gill at Lindum Books, for hosting my author talks and being so supportive of a debut author; and to Victoria, Nicola and everyone at Gainsborough Old Hall, for hosting my book signing and being my place of refuge when I need to get away from the computer.

Particular thanks go to my mum (Angela Bennett), Karen Mercer, Anne Marie Bouchard and Dennis Jarvis for their kind permission to use their wonderful photos, and to Daniel Gleave for taking a special trip to Westminster Abbey, just to get a photo for my book! A thank you must also go to my friends closer to home, particularly Sharon Gleave, Jill Gaskell, Di Richardson, and all my local friends, for their wonderful support and for dragging me out for a coffee every once in a while. I reserve a special thanks to my family, especially my sister, Suzanne Cassidy, whose support has been incredible and very much appreciated. And to my mum and dad for all their love and encouragement, and for their own passion for history. A special thank you also goes to my research assistant and son, Lewis Connolly, who has travelled to various wonderful places with me in the process of making this book a reality. And to my husband, James, thank you for putting up with all the history talks. I couldn't have done it without all of you.

I also owe a debt of gratitude to the great historians who have gone before me, who gallantly edited and translated the great chronicles of the eleventh century, so that they are accessible and readable for all of us who have an interest in the period.

Family Trees

1. Genealogy of Cnut (simplified)

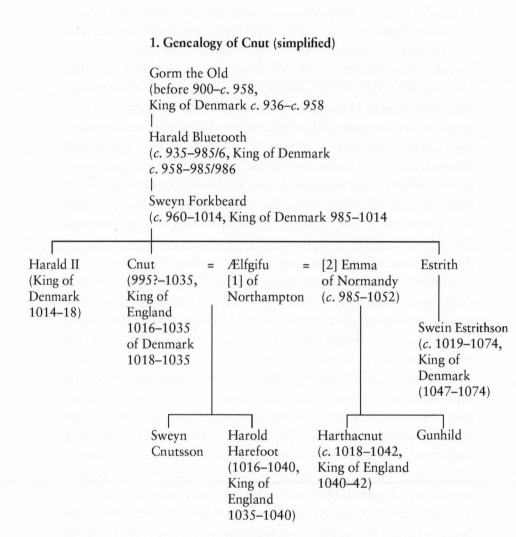

Gorm the Old
(before 900–*c. 958*,
King of Denmark *c. 936–c. 958*

Harald Bluetooth
(*c. 935–985/6*, King of Denmark
c. 958–985/986

Sweyn Forkbeard
(*c. 960–1014*, King of Denmark 985–1014

Harald II
(King of
Denmark
1014–18)

Cnut   =   Ælfgifu   =   [2] Emma   Estrith
(995?–1035,   [1] of   of Normandy
King of   Northampton   (*c. 985–1052*)
England
1016–1035   Swein Estrithson
of Denmark   (*c. 1019–1074*,
1018–1035   King of
Denmark
(1047–1074)

Sweyn   Harold   Harthacnut   Gunhild
Cnutsson   Harefoot   (*c. 1018–1042*,
(1016–1040,   King of England
King of   1040–42)
England
1035–1040)

2. Genealogy of Edmund Ironside (simplified)

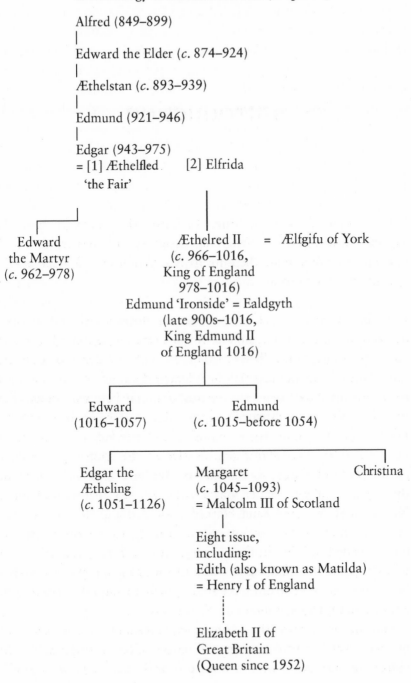

Alfred (849–899)
|
Edward the Elder (*c.* 874–924)
|
Æthelstan (*c.* 893–939)
|
Edmund (921–946)
|
Edgar (943–975)
= [1] Æthelfled   [2] Elfrida
  'the Fair'

Edward
the Martyr
(*c.* 962–978)

Æthelred II   = Ælfgifu of York
(*c.* 966–1016,
King of England
978–1016)
Edmund 'Ironside' = Ealdgyth
(late 900s–1016,
King Edmund II
of England 1016)

Edward
(1016–1057)

Edmund
(*c.* 1015–before 1054)

Edgar the
Ætheling
(*c.* 1051–1126)

Margaret
(*c.* 1045–1093)
= Malcolm III of Scotland
|
Eight issue,
including:
Edith (also known as Matilda)
= Henry I of England

Elizabeth II of
Great Britain
(Queen since 1952)

Christina

Introduction

In the year of our Lord 1066, the Lord, who ruleth all things, accomplished what he had long designed with respect to the English nation; giving them up to destruction by the fierce and crafty race of the Normans.[1]

The year 1066 was when the fates of three kings and a duke decided the future of England. It was a year of invasion, of war and conquest – and death. The year started with the death of Edward the Confessor in January 1066. Edward died leaving no son and therefore no direct heir. The nearest familial heir was Edgar the Ætheling, the son of Edward's nephew, Edward the Exile. However, Edgar was just a teenager, and England needed a strong hand on the rudder. The *Witan* quickly elected the country's strongest baron, Harold Godwinson, Earl of Wessex, to take charge of the realm. And no sooner was Edward's body in his tomb than Harold was crowned King Harold II of England. It should have been a smooth transition of power, leading to a long reign and much-needed stability in the country. However, England was riven with deep divisions among its nobility and, to make matters worse, both Edward and Harold were said to have promised the crown to another man, Duke William of Normandy.

Into this mix came a third contender, Harald Hardrada. A former member of the revered Varangian Guard in Constantinople, Harald Hardrada was King of Norway and with the help of Harold's disaffected brother, Tostig, saw an opportunity to make England a

Norse kingdom once again. A forty-year-old promise between the kings of England and Denmark gave Harald the excuse to stake his claim on England and launch his own invasion.

The history books have always concentrated on the battles and the lives of the men involved. You would be forgiven for thinking that women had no place in these male-dominated, cataclysmic events. Most studies of the period entirely ignore the contributions of women, or sideline them to only a mention on the retelling of the events of that fateful year. However, if you look deep into the story of 1066, of the years preceding it and the years which followed, it is clear that several women had pivotal roles in the history of the era. From the enigmatic and influential Emma of Normandy in the first-half of the eleventh century, to William the Conqueror's duchess and queen, Matilda, and Margaret, the sainted Queen of Scotland, at the century's close, women were at the centre of events. Their contributions gave rise to spectacular legends, from the story of Lady Godiva to the miracles associated with St Margaret. Their actions and family loyalties helped to shape the country that England would become.

The stories of these women are far from straightforward; their lives were just as complex and fascinating as the great men of their time. In peeling away the legend from the known facts and using the chronicles from the time, we can rebuild the lives of the women who played significant roles in the story of 1066. Harold II of England had been with Edith Swanneck for twenty years but in 1066, in order to strengthen his hold on the throne, he married Ealdgyth, sister of two earls. William of Normandy's duchess, Matilda of Flanders had, supposedly, only agreed to marry the Duke after he'd pulled her pigtails and thrown her in the mud. Harald Hardrada had two wives – apparently at the same time. All of these women had their own duties and responsibilities and used their influence over those around them to help shape the future of England.

It is also important to take note of the fact that 1066 was not a year in isolation. It was the culmination of events from ten years before, fifty years before and even a hundred years before. The characters who lived at the turn of the century made decisions that would, in a butterfly effect, influence events sixty-six years later.

The first half of the century effectively laid the foundations for the second half, indeed for the entire futures of England, Normandy, Norway and Denmark. The marriage of Æthelred II and Emma of Normandy being one such example; if it was not for that marriage Edward the Confessor would never have been born, Normandy would not have had such an interest in England, and Emma may not have married Cnut and given birth to Harthacnut, which also gave the Danes a vested interest in England.

Conversely, 1066 is not just a year that resulted from its past, it is also a year that moulds the future by creating a Norman England. And the women, again, played prominent roles in the shaping of that future. As mothers they were, effectively, the symbols of that new England, but they were so much more. The industry of St Margaret, Queen of Scotland, helped to shape the style of queenship and of religion in Scotland for generations to come. Matilda of Flanders, in her role as regent for her husband's lands, proved that women were capable of so much more than childbearing. Although they could not play a military role, nor be visible on the political stage, that does not mean that the women associated with these great kings, princes and barons had no influence on events, policies and their outcomes. Their influence, of course, is more subtle, but we can often see the touch of the queen, or lady, on events of the time. Indeed, many of them were able to guide the direction of policy, some more overtly than others, but all left their mark on events and history to a greater or lesser extent.

We have the chronicles of the time, which sometimes do make mention of the women involved. The *Anglo-Saxon Chronicle* is a wonderful source, a collection of six chronicles from various areas of England; it is at times annoyingly short on detail and sometimes contradictory. However, it is a fabulous resource telling us England's story, year by year. We also have later chronicles, such as Henry of Huntingdon writing a hundred years after the events – although he is prone to seeding his facts with gossip and rumour. Some of these women also took the story into their own hands, helping to pass on their lives to future generations. While Emma commissioned the *Emma Encomium Reginae,* which told her story as well as the story of those around her, Edith of Wessex commissioned the *Vitae Edwardi regis*, recounting the life of her husband, Edward the Confessor, in a positive light and emphasising his eligibility for sainthood. The stories in these books are told with a friendly bias towards their patronesses, but they help to provide an insight into the lives and thoughts of their characters and the times they lived in.

One issue we have with the chronicles is the fact that there is no consistency with the spelling of names; uniformity in spelling was non-existent in the eleventh century and many names were spelled several different ways, so I have attempted to keep every name in the form in which we have become familiar, while letting you know of the alternatives, when I can. Harold II's second wife, for instance, is variously identified as Aldgyth, Ealdgyth, Eadgyth and Edith. Emma of Normandy is slightly different, in that her name was changed to Ælfgifu when she married Æthelred II. Ælfgifu can also be spelt as Ælfgyfu, Ælfgiva and Ælfgyva, and to complicate matters further, in the *Anglo-Saxon Chronicle* neither of Emma's actual names are used as frequently as the appellation 'The Lady'.[2]

I have tried to simplify matters by using the name we most associate with these ladies today. So, Emma/Ælfgifu/The Lady will appear as Emma, which will help to distinguish her from the first wives of Æthelred II and King Cnut (Emma's two husbands), who were also called Ælfgifu. And Godgifu, the wife of Earl Leofric of Mercia, will be called Lady Godiva, as that is how most of us identify her today. I have also tried to use different spellings for each of the main characters, even when their names are the same, in the hope of avoiding confusion where possible; so, for instance, King Harold II is spelt with an 'o', where Harald Hardrada is spelt with an 'a'.

So, who were these women? What was their real story? And what happened to them after 1066? From Emma of Normandy, wife of both King Cnut and Æthelred II, to Saint Margaret, a descendant of Alfred the Great himself, we will trace the fortunes of the women who had a role to play before, during and after the momentous year of 1066. Thoughout these tumultuous times, women played a prominent part, in support of their husbands, their sons and of their people, be they English, Norman, Danish or Norwegian. Their contributions were so much more than a supporting role, and it is time that their stories were told, and the influence they had on events, was examined in detail.

There is no getting away from the fact that the events of 1066 were orchestrated and executed by men, they were directed by the ambitions of Harold II, William of Normandy, Harald Hardrada and a host of other men, all ambitious for success and the ultimate prize: England. However, what should not be downplayed is the contributions of the women; their lives and roles were not insignificant and should be highlighted, rather than sidelined. My intention is to tell the story of the Norman Conquest, while providing the women with a platform for their stories, from the dawn of the eleventh century to its close.

PART ONE

BEFORE THE
NORMAN CONQUEST

1

The Battles for England

The years leading up to the Norman Conquest of 1066 were far from peaceful for any of the three protagonists involved. The kings and duke had faced their own challenges in their individual countries, with varying degrees of success. In order to look at the women who were involved and how events affected them, it may help to first look at the events which preceded the most famous year in English history. England's main enemy in 1066 were the Normans; however, before 1066 her struggles were primarily with the Danes.

Even though England before 1066 had had a number of years of relative peace, under the rule of Edward the Confessor, the eleventh century as a whole had been anything but peaceful. England had suffered from years of unrest whilst the royal house of Wessex fought with the Danish royal house, of Sweyn Forkbeard and Cnut, for supremacy over the country.

At the turn of the millennium, Æthelred II was on the English throne. Æthelred has come to be known to history as 'the Unready', suggesting he was ill counselled or badly advised, rather than that he couldn't get dressed in the morning. It was a play on words on his name; 'Æthelred' meant well-advised, while 'unraed' meant ill-advised, referring to his apparent ineptitude when it came to ruling the country. He was the great-great-grandson of Alfred the Great, King of Wessex, and had come to the throne, aged just ten or eleven, following the murder of his older half-brother, Edward the Martyr, in 978. Although he had the blood of Alfred the Great and Edward the Elder running through his veins, Æthelred failed spectacularly in living up to their standards of kingship. Since before the turn of the century, marauding Norsemen had been raiding deep into England, using nearby Normandy as a base from which to launch their attacks. This caused such discord between Æthelred and Normandy's ruler, Richard I, that the intervention of the pope was needed to broker a peace in 990–991. The treaty appeared to ease tensions until the year 1000, when a Danish army again settled in Normandy for the winter and used it as a launching point for an invasion of England in 1001.

A more permanent peace was then arranged, in which the new Duke of Normandy, Richard II, gave his sister, Emma, in marriage to the recently widowed King of England. Despite the fact the marriage put the seal on the alliance with Normandy, it did nothing to alleviate England's problems with the Danes. At the end of the tenth century, Æthelred had been paying tribute, or *Dane-geld*, to the Danes at regular intervals 'because of the great terror they were causing along the coast'.[1] Although the first payment was just 10,000 pounds, in 991 it escalated periodically – until the tribute had reached 24,000 pounds in the opening months of 1002.[2] However, in November 1002, the same year as his marriage to Emma, Æthelred changed tactics. Dire warnings that the Danes threatened his life and kingdom, and frustration at the years of Viking attacks, forced the king into action and Æthelred ordered that all Danish men in England be killed – the St Brice's Day Massacre.

Although historians believe there was a significant loss of life in the massacre, which happened on 13 November 1002, it was probably not a full-scale extermination of Danes in England. It may not have extended into the Danelaw, where the Scandinavian population was mostly concentrated, and which covered the lands north and east of the Thames and across the north of England. Unfortunately for Æthelred, one of the victims of the massacre was Gunhilde, sister of King Sweyn I Forkbeard of Denmark. For Sweyn, this was the catalyst to launch an invasion. He led an army into England in 1003 and, throughout 1004, King Sweyn and his fleet campaigned in East Anglia, coming up against fierce opposition from Ulfcytel, a notable East Anglian warrior.

Even though the English were unable to force Sweyn's withdrawal, a natural disaster did. A great famine swept across Europe in 1005, and the British Isles were not immune; unable to feed his army, Sweyn was forced to return to his homeland.

However, the Danes returned, year in, year out, with alarming regularity and Æthelred II was to spend the last ten years of his reign fighting them, trying to hold off their advance. In 1007, the tribute paid to Sweyn amounted to 30,000 pounds. In 1008 Æthelred ordered an extensive shipbuilding programme and by 1009 the ships were ready, said to be more numerous than England had ever previously seen. They were based at Sandwich, ready to defend against any invasion force. However, *The Anglo-Saxon Chronicle* says that 'Brihtric, brother of Alderman Edric [Eadric Streona], betrayed Wulfnoth, the South-Saxon knight, father of Earl Godwin, to the king; and he went into exile, and enticed the navy, till he had with him twenty ships; with which he plundered everywhere by the south coast, and wrought every kind of mischief.'[3] Having been accused of treachery, apparently falsely, Wulfnoth sailed away with his twenty ships. Brihtric, according to the *Anglo-Saxon Chronicle*, went after Wulfnoth with eighty ships, but they met with bad weather and were driven aground, only for Wulfnoth to come upon them and set the ships alight. With most of his fleet destroyed, Æthelred gave up on his navy and the Danes were soon back, under the command of the formidable Thurkill the Tall, Earl of East Anglia. As the Danes raided through Sussex, Hampshire and Berkshire, Æthelred raised a vast army and attempted to bring the Danes to battle, but was somehow thwarted by Ealdorman Eadric Streona, one of Æthelred's chief advisors. Thurkill's force settled down in winter quarters on the Thames, before raiding and burning Oxford in the new year. The year 1010 also saw the return of Sweyn, who arrived in East Anglia shortly after Easter, burning and pillaging as he went: Cambridge, Oxford, Northampton and Bedford were all burned by his raiding army. Æthelred's main failing was that he was unable to show a united front against the invaders, each of his leading men looking to their own interests, rather than the country as a whole. Sweyn raided where he wished, the English were unable to mount a united force to fight him, 'no shire, moreover, would stand by another.'[4]

By 1011 Sweyn controlled vast swathes of England, from East Anglia and Essex to Kent and Sussex, as well as half of Huntingdonshire and much of Northamptonshire and Wiltshire. *The Anglo-Saxon Chronicle* blames the indecisiveness of England's leaders, saying they had not offered tribute in time, nor mounted a fighting force to resist the invaders. Sweyn and Thurkill's forces took what they wanted, including hostages such as Archbishop Ælfheah (Alphege), Archbishop of Canterbury; the archbishop's refusal to pay a ransom led to his murder and martyrdom in April 1012. *The Anglo-Saxon Chronicle* stated:

> All these calamities fell upon us through evil counsel, because tribute was not offered to them at the right time, nor yet were they resisted: but, when they had done the most evil, then was peace made with them. And notwithstanding all this peace and tribute, they went everywhere in companies, harried our wretched people, robbed and slew them.[5]

When the tribute, amounting to 48,000 pounds (although *E* and *F* of *The Anglo-Saxon Chronicle* say the amount was 8,000 pounds) was finally paid, the Danish force disbanded, most of them returning to Denmark. However, not all of the Danes returned home. Sensing an opportunity, Thurkill changed sides, bringing his forty-five ships into the service of King Æthelred, promising to use them to defend England. Unfortunately, the huge tribute payment had brought little respite and in August of 1013 Sweyn was back, turning his ships into the Humber and landing at Gainsborough. Earl Uhtred the Bold of Northumbria submitted to him and, with a domino effect, Lindsey and the Five Boroughs submitted soon after. Once his army was provisioned, Sweyn Forkbeard turned south, where London – with King Æthelred in residence and strengthened by the support of Thurkill – held out against him. However, Sweyn's conquering rampage continued and London was soon the only city still holding out, the English everywhere else acknowledging him as King of England. Those in London finally submitted to Sweyn, for fear of the reprisals he might inflict should they continue to resist; they gave up hostages, tribute and supplies for his army. Æthelred's wife, Emma, and their three young children were sent to safety in

Normandy, while Thurkill helped to sneak the king out of London, before retreating to Greenwich. Æthelred spent Christmas on the Isle of Wight, before the defeated king joined his young family in exile in Normandy at the start of 1014.

Sweyn's tenure as King of England was short-lived, however, and he died on 3 February 1014, after a fall from his horse in his capital of Gainsborough. Although the Danish fleet chose Sweyn's eighteen-year-old son, Cnut, to succeed him as king, he did not have the confidence of others. The Danes in Denmark chose Cnut's brother, Harald, and the English leaders, church and secular, insisted that Æthelred should be restored to his throne. The English declared Æthelred was their natural lord so long, of course, as he governed better than he had previously done. Æthelred sent his son, Edward, with his messengers, to the English, to promise that he would be a better king than he had been and that anything done against him in the past would be forgiven, provided they unanimously accepted him as their king. Æthelred returned to England during Lent and was acclaimed everywhere with enthusiasm and renewed hope. He immediately advanced on Cnut at Gainsborough with a large army, burning and plundering as they went, killing anyone they came across. Cnut escaped by putting to sea with his fleet, stopping briefly at Sandwich to put ashore the hostages who had been given to his father, having cut off their hands, ears and noses.[6] The year only got worse when Æthelred ordered that the raiding army, Thurkill's army, camped at Greenwich, should be paid 21,000 pounds to ensure their continued loyalty; a waste of money given that Thurkill soon took his fleet to Denmark and pledged himself to Cnut. A natural disaster added to England's woes, when a 'great sea-flood' overwhelmed many towns and killed countless people.[7]

England's troubles continued into 1015; a great council at Oxford saw two Mercian thegns, Sigeferth and Morcar, murdered on the orders of Æthelred's most powerful Ealdorman, Eadric Streona. Æthelred took advantage of their deaths by seizing all their lands, as well as the wife of Sigeferth, who was held at a convent in Malmesbury. It was at this point that Æthelred's oldest surviving son, Edmund Ironside, turned against his father, rescued Sigeferth's wife and married her himself, thus claiming the lands of the murdered thegn. Æthelred's health was now failing and as his father lay sick at Corsham, it was Edmund who took up the fight against the Danes. Edmund was in the north when Cnut landed at Sandwich and proceeded through southern England. Despite their animosity, Eadric Streona and Edmund joined forces to march against the Danes. However, it seems that Eadric Streona was planning to betray Edmund and, taking forty ships with him, he changed sides and submitted to Cnut. With such reduced forces, Edmund was unable to continue the campaign and forced to withdraw; Wessex fell to Cnut without a fight and the West Saxons submitted to him.

The year 1016 opened, therefore, with an invasion into Mercia by Cnut, and Eadric Streona with him. Edmund gathered an army to face them, but without the regal authority of his father and the support of London, he was ineffectual, and the army soon dispersed. A second army was raised, this time benefitting from the presence of King Æthelred, but it also proved incapable of mounting a staunch defence and the king, fearing betrayal, returned to London. Edmund then went north, joining forces with Earl Uhtred the Bold of Northumbria and attacking south into Staffordshire and Shropshire; however, their plans were thwarted when Cnut advanced on York and Uhtred was forced to submit to Cnut or lose his earldom. On the advice of Eadric Streona, Uhtred was treacherously slain by Cnut, along with forty of his men. Cnut's brother-in-law, Erik of Hlathir, was made Earl of Northumbria instead of Uhtred.

Edmund retreated to London, where his father lay desperately ill. Cnut took to his ships and also sailed down the coast to London. Before he arrived, King Æthelred II died there on 23 April, St George's Day, 1016, 'having held his kingdom in much tribulation and difficulty as long as his life continued'.[8] As his oldest son, Æthelstan, had died from illness or injury in June 1014, Edmund was chosen by the peers and citizens in London as his father's successor. A summer of fighting ensued, with Edmund facing the Danes on numerous occasions and gaining sufficient victories as to revive the hope that England may yet be saved and to convince Eadric Streona to change sides once again. He submitted to Edmund before the final showdown at Assandun (possibly Ashingdon in Essex), on 18 October, when Cnut achieved

an overwhelming victory. The treacherous – and cowardly – Eadric
Streona fled the field, while many notable Englishmen were slain,
including Bishop Ednoth, Ealdorman Godwin of Lindsey, and
Ulfcytel of East Anglia. Cnut then advanced into Gloucestershire
in pursuit of Edmund but was advised by his counsellors to
make peace. An agreement was reached whereby the country was
divided between the two leaders; Edmund would take Wessex and
everything south of the River Thames and Cnut would control
Mercia and everything north of the Thames. Whether such a peace
would have lasted, we know not, for on 30 November 1016,
Edmund died, aged only twenty-two. Although there have been
suggestions of a gruesome murder, involving sharp objects thrust
into his bowels as he sat on the latrine, the chronicles of the time
make no mention of foul play. It is therefore more likely that
Edmund died from illness, or as a result of wounds received during
the summer of fighting, and that his death was merely a welcome
gift to his enemies.

With Edmund's death, Cnut was undisputed ruler of England.
He divided the country into four parts, taking Wessex for himself
while East Anglia went to Thurkill, Mercia to Eadric Streona and
Northumbria to Erik of Hlathir. However, Eadric Streona, it seems,
had outlived his usefulness – or turned traitor once too often – for
in 1017 he was killed in London, on Cnut's orders. Mercia then
passed first to Leofwine, Ealdorman of the Hwicce, and then to his
son Leofric, husband of the famous Lady Godiva. Within months
the last surviving son of Æthelred and his first wife Ælfgifu, Edwy,
called 'king of the churls' in the *Anglo-Saxon Chronicle,* was also
killed on the new king's orders.[9] Edmund Ironside's two infant
sons, Edward and Edmund, were sent into exile and given refuge by
the King of Sweden, who ignored Cnut's orders that they should be
killed. By August, Cnut had sent for Emma, the widow of Æthelred
II and mother of the late king's only surviving sons, Edward and
Alfred (the æthelings), who were in exile in Normandy. Marrying
Emma, now in her early thirties, brought with it amicable relations
with Normandy, had the added benefit of nullifying the threat posed
by the æthelings in exile there, and earned Cnut further acceptance
by engendering ties to the old English court. Cnut immediately set
about a process of consolidation and pacification. By 1018 he had

paid off and disbanded his Danish fleet and set about the matter of government. He built churches and honoured the traditional English saints, such as St Edmund, slain by the Danes in 869. In 1023, with great pomp and ceremony, Cnut translated the remains of St Ælfheah (St Alphege), the Archbishop of Canterbury, killed while a Danish hostage in 1011, from St Paul's in London to his cathedral at Canterbury.

In 1026 Cnut had made a pilgrimage to Rome and attended the coronation of Holy Roman Emperor Conrad II on Easter Day, 1027, before returning home. At the same time, his daughter by Emma, Gunhilda, was betrothed to Conrad's son and eventual successor, Henry. She would be Holy Roman Empress from 1036 until her death in 1038. Cnut's power and prestige were now so great that even Scotland, though not totally submitting to him, paid him homage. Already ruler of Denmark alongside his brother Harald, Cnut became sole king on Harald's death in 1018. Thus England was part of a larger Anglo-Scandinavian empire that was to expand further in 1028 when Cnut set his sights on Norway. Although he arrived on the Norwegian coast with fifty ships, they proved unnecessary. The Norwegians, discontented with the rule of their king, Olaf, and his habit of arresting their wives for sorcery, deserted him and he was unable to mount any effective resistance against Cnut. Without having to fight, therefore, Cnut was acknowledged as their ruler, and Norway's former king, Olaf (later St Olaf) was sent into exile. When Olaf tried to return to his kingdom in 1030, he was killed at the Battle of Stiklestad. Following Olaf's defeat and death, Cnut sent his concubine, or hand-fasted wife, Ælfgifu of Northampton, to rule Norway as regent for their fourteen-year-old son, Swein. However, Ælfgifu proved to be a heavy-handed ruler and in 1035 the disaffected Norwegians sought to place Olaf's illegitimate eleven-year-old son, Magnus, on the throne. When Magnus was brought to Norway, the majority of Norwegians sided with him, so there was no option for Swein and his mother but to flee to Denmark, where Swein died shortly afterwards.

King of England, Denmark and Norway, Cnut the Great died on 12 November 1035; he was buried at Winchester. Cnut had proved to be an able and competent ruler, giving England almost twenty years of relative peace following decades of raiding and conflict. However, his empire did not survive his demise and was soon divided between his three sons. With Swein ruling in Norway (although not for long), Harthacnut, Cnut's only son with Emma of Normandy, controlled Denmark and Harold Harefoot, another son from Cnut's relationship with Ælfgifu of Northampton, claimed England. Harthacnut was, supposedly, Cnut's acknowledged heir and Emma of Normandy tried to take control of England for her son. However, when it became clear that Harthacnut was in no hurry to leave Denmark and return to England, the English lords accepted his half-brother, Harold, as regent at a great council at Oxford. Earl Godwin of Wessex, who had resisted accepting Harold, also submitted, eventually. For a time and with the support of Earl Godwin, Emma was allowed to hold Wessex for Harthacnut.

Even though Harold and Swein claimed their kingdoms as the sons of Cnut, there were rumours at the time, cited in the *Anglo-Saxon Chronicle*, that questioned their parentage, especially Harold's: 'Some men said of Harold, that he was the son of King Cnut and of Ælfgifu the daughter of Ealdorman Ælfhelm; but it was thought very incredible by many men.'[10] Whether or not there is any truth to the rumours, we cannot now know. As it was, in 1036 Harold was accepted as England's ruler, Harthacnut was ruling in Denmark and Emma was living on her estates in Winchester, when her son Alfred came to England. Alfred the ætheling was probably approaching thirty years of age. He was the younger son of Emma and Æthelred II and had been living in exile in Normandy for the last twenty-five years. In 1036 he arrived in England, supposedly to visit his mother. Before he had the chance to see Emma, the ætheling was seized at Guildford and taken to Ely. The sources are confusing about what exactly happened. Some state that Earl Godwin welcomed Alfred, and swore fealty to him, but was then ambushed and the young ætheling taken from him – while others suggest that Godwin betrayed Alfred and handed him over to King Harold. Either way, Alfred was taken and blinded (a symbolic gesture aimed at destroying his worth as a king) and was either killed on Harold's orders, or succumbed to his wounds, with or without the connivance of Godwin, in late 1036 or early 1037. So one potential threat to Harold's crown was thus eliminated and buried in Ely.

In 1037 with Harthacnut still lingering in Denmark, Harold was officially chosen as King of England and crowned at Oxford. One of his first acts as undisputed king was to evict Queen Emma. She was driven from her estates, and the country, and she sought shelter in Flanders. Count Baldwin gave her a house in Bruges and supported and protected her for the next couple of years. In 1039 Emma was finally reunited with Harthacnut, who arrived in Flanders with a large fleet, and they spent the winter in Bruges, planning for their return to England. Before they could launch an invasion, news reached them that Harold I Harefoot was dead. He had had an essentially uneventful reign and died at Oxford on 17 March 1040. Harold had never married and had no legitimate son to succeed him; although he supposedly had a concubine, named Ælfgifu, by whom he is said to have had a son, Ælfwine, who founded the monastery of Sainte-Foi at Conques in Aquitaine.[11]

And so it was that Harthacnut sailed into Sandwich shortly before midsummer and was accepted as king by the English and Danes alike. He soon showed his vindictiveness by having his half-brother, Harold, disinterred. The dead king was beheaded before his body was thrown in a ditch. Harthacnut was a very unpopular king, he taxed his people heavily and turned almost everyone against him. In 1041 he ordered that Worcestershire should be laid waste after the murder of two of his tax collectors. One good move appears to have been that in 1041, his half-brother Edward, son of Emma by her first husband, Æthelred, was allowed to return to England. Edward's childhood is shrouded in mystery. There was some suggestion that he had been given to the monastery at Ely as a child, however, the reference is from a twelfth-century chronicle and is possibly a fabrication to add relevance to a charter. Although he never became a monk and had no literary reputation, Edward was renowned for his piety, earning the epithet The Confessor. It was Edward who came over to England, following the death of Sweyn Forkbeard, with promises from his father, Æthelred, that he would rule wisely should he again be given the throne. The Danish sagas say that

Edward stayed in England and fought alongside his brother, Edmund Ironside, and only returned to Normandy following Edmund's death and the accession of Cnut.[12]

Edward's exile in Normandy served to protect him, but also meant that he could be used as a bargaining chip against England's rulers. His strong claim to the throne meant he was a threat to Cnut, who tried to neutralise this by marrying Edward's mother, Emma. This may go some way to explain Edward's animosity to his mother, who does not appear to have been close to her oldest son. According to Emma in her own book, the *Encomium Emmae Reginae,* when she was in exile in Bruges Edward visited his mother and declined to mount a claim for the English throne in favour of Harthacnut.[13] However, this may well have been out of practicality, rather than any desire to give up his inheritance; Harthacnut had a fleet and an army, whereas Edward did not. And so it was that Harthacnut had sailed to England in 1040 and claimed the crown, before inviting his half-brother to join him the following year.

Edward was made a co-ruler of England and lived at his brother's court. This contributed to a smooth transition of power the following year, 1042, when Harthacnut had a seizure while drinking at a wedding in Lambeth; the king, 'as he stood drinking: fell suddenly to the earth with a tremendous struggle but those who were nigh at hand took him up; and he spoke not a word afterwards ...'[14] Harthacnut died on 8 June and was buried with his father at Winchester, mourned by his mother but few others. Like his half-brother, Harold, before him, Harthacnut had never married and had no child to succeed him. Before Harthacnut was cold in his grave, Edward was chosen as the new King of England. Despite the fact the Scandinavian kings, Magnus of Norway and Swein Estrithson of Denmark, both considered themselves eligible for the English throne, it was the support of Godwin, Earl of Wessex, which tipped the scales in Edward's favour. At the grand age – for a Saxon king – of thirty-eight, Edward was crowned at Winchester on Easter Day (3 April) 1043 by the Archbishops of Canterbury and York, amid great celebrations. There followed more than twenty years of relative peace. Although Edward did have trouble with some of his more powerful barons and there was conflict with Wales and some Danish raiding parties, the threats from Scandinavia, on the whole, appear to have dissipated. On 23 January 1045 Edward took a wife, Edith. She was the daughter of Edward's most powerful earl, Godwin, Earl of Wessex, without whose support Edward would have struggled to maintain his authority at the outset of his reign.

Edward faced many problems in the early years. Having spent the majority of his life in exile, he was very much a stranger in his native land. He was following a usurping dynasty, which had eroded the natural power and prestige of the Crown, and the dubious reputation of his own father had eroded the loyalty to the ancient royal house of Cerdic, to which Edward belonged. The earls, such as Godwin in Wessex, possessed substantial power and influence, while the royal demesne, scattered and reduced as it was, could not provide him with a substantial power base. From the beginning of his reign Edward sought to impose his authority on Church and State, bringing onside the powerful earls; Godwin in Wessex, Leofric in Mercia and Siward in Northumbria. It was with these three that he rode to Winchester to punish his mother and deprive her of her possessions and chief adviser, Bishop Stigand, and reclaim the royal treasury. The act was more of a public show of disapproval than severe punishment and Emma was back in Edward's good graces within a year, although she never held the great influence over Edward that she had with Harthacnut.

Edward had powerful Continental allies in his brother-in-law Henry III, the Holy Roman Emperor, and his mother's family in Normandy, and his experiences in his youth meant he had an understanding of Continental politics. He was, however, reluctant to get involved in Danish politics, refusing to help Swein Estrithson when he was threatened by Magnus of Norway. In fact, Edward, perhaps understandably, appears to have had little liking for the Danes. He exiled Cnut's niece, Gunhild, and her children in 1046; as well as Osgod Clapa, a Dane with lands in the eastern shires. Clapa was later to return with almost thirty ships and raid into Essex. Danish pirates, Lothen and Yrling, also raided along the south-east ports, including Thanet and Sandwich.

Early in his reign Edward relied on a small number of Normans within his affinity, as counsellors. Having spent most of his life in Normandy, he was more comfortable with them. His household included his nephew, Ralph of Mantes, and a Norman abbot, Robert Champart of Jumièges, who, although not a threat to the great men of England, had the ability to influence Edward and control events through their intrigues. Although Edward promoted both monastic and clerical men into positions of influence, the clerical priests tended to get the more lucrative posts. Robert of Jumièges benefitted greatly from Edward's religious policies, he became Bishop of London in 1044 and was promoted to Archbishop of Canterbury in 1051. And when Earl Godwin's eldest son, Swein, was banished for his various crimes, it was Ralph of Mantes, promoted to Earl of Hereford, who was given the lands of Swein's forfeited earldom.

The crisis came to a head in 1051 when, at the beginning of September, Edward was visited by his brother-in-law, Eustace of Boulogne. On his journey home, Eustace had tried to force the people of Dover to give him hospitality. The ensuing argument in Dover, between Eustace's men and the men of the town, led to several deaths. The count complained to Edward, giving only his side of the story, according to the *Anglo-Saxon Chronicle*, and the king ordered Godwin, as Earl of Kent, to punish the town's burgesses for the offence caused.[15] Godwin refused, and Edward retaliated by summoning a council – and his army – to meet at Gloucester on 7 September. Earl Ralph brought up his troops and the earls Leofric and Siward summoned theirs, while Godwin and his sons, Swein and Harold, gathered together their own forces and ordered them to assemble at Beverstone, south of Gloucester. Accusations and counter-accusations were made, but neither side appeared eager for open conflict. Godwin demanded the surrender of Eustace but was in turn accused of conspiring to kill Edward. It was agreed that Godwin would stand trial in London on 21 September, Godwin and Swein each giving a son as hostage to their good faith. However, as the two forces made their way to the capital it was Godwin's army that began to disintegrate. After Edward declared that Godwin could have his peace and pardon only by restoring to the king his brother, Alfred, in whose death the earl had been implicated in 1036, Godwin decided on flight rather than fight. Godwin, his wife Gytha and sons Swein and Tostig embarked on a ship for Flanders, while his other sons, Harold and his younger brother, Leofwine, made their way to Ireland. They were outlawed and even Edward's wife, Edith, was sent to a convent, either Wherwell or Wilton, while the family's enemies pressed Edward to divorce her.

The exile proved to be short-lived, however, and by September of 1052 Godwin and his fleet had reached London, the sympathetic citizens allowing them to set up camp on the south bank of the Thames. Godwin's show of force was all that was necessary for the royalist forces to back down. Afraid of Godwin's reprisals, Robert of Jumièges and others escaped by London's East Gate. Earls Siward and Leofric were reluctant to offer support to the king, and so it was left to Bishop Stigand to negotiate a peace, despite the king raging against the affront to his authority. Edward had no choice but to submit. Godwin and Harold attended a king's council meeting, held just outside London, where they declared themselves innocent of the charges against them and were allowed back within the king's peace. Their possessions were returned to them and Edith was allowed to return to court as queen. Their accusers had fled back to Normandy, possibly taking the Godwinson hostages, the sons of Godwin and Swein, with them. Bishop Stigand was made Archbishop of Canterbury, now that Robert of Jumièges was outlawed.

Edward's reign was never smooth sailing, although this crisis of 1051/2 appears to have been the biggest threat to England's stability. It was even suggested by one chronicler that William, Duke of Normandy, visited Edward's court during the Godwins' exile, and that it was then that Edward promised William his throne. Although it is not impossible that Edward made such a promise, it is unlikely that it happened at that time, as the succession was his greatest gift, and he would have done better to keep his options open. Moreover, the visit is treated with some scepticism as most chroniclers don't mention it, so it is possible it never happened. The period after 1052, once the dust had settled, was one of relative peace and security. However, several deaths led to some changes and juggling of earldoms. Edward's mother, Emma of Normandy, died in March 1052, and his brother-in-law Swein, the black sheep of the Godwinsons, died at Constantinople in September of the same year, on his return from a pilgrimage to Jerusalem. His father, the formidable Earl Godwin, followed him to the grave within months, dying while attending the Easter court in April 1053. This meant Harold now succeeded to the earldom of Wessex, relinquishing the earldom of East Anglia to its previous incumbent, Ælfgar, the son of Leofric of Mercia. The delicate balance of power among the earldoms did not last long, however, as Siward, Earl of Northumbria, died in 1055 leaving his heir, Waltheof, a child and still too young to hold such a formidable position on the borders of Scotland. The earldom was given to Tostig Godwinson, the favourite brother of Queen Edith. Everything changed again in 1057 when the Earl of Mercia, Leofric, died. His earldom passed to his son, Ælfgar. The vacant earldom of East Anglia was then given to Gyrth, another of Earl Godwin's sons, and a new earldom was created in the south for yet another Godwinson, Leofwine. Thus, while Ælfgar held onto Mercia, the majority of the country was firmly in the grip of the Godwinson family. The brothers were seen to be able military commanders and so with Harold having firm hold on the vulnerable south coast and Tostig controlling the Scottish border, England could feel secure.

In 1056 Edward clearly started looking to the future and the succession. He and Edith had no children, and many believe that he had taken a vow of celibacy and never intended to father a child with Edith. Whatever the rumours as to the relationship of the king and queen, the fact was that Edward was childless and thus had no obvious heir to succeed him. In about 1054 he sent for Edward Ætheling, the son of his brother, Edmund Ironside. As an infant Edward had been banished from England with his brother, Edmund, on the accession of Cnut in 1016. The two young boys were sent to Sweden, where Cnut's half-brother, Olof Stötkonung, was king. Not wanting to kill them on English soil, Cnut intended that they be murdered in Sweden. However, Olof was an old ally of the boys' grandfather, Æthelred II, and spared the children, sending them to safety in Hungary. When Cnut's assassins almost caught up with them there, they were forced to flee for their lives, settling at the court of Yaroslav the Wise in Kiev, where Ingegerd, the daughter of King Olof of Sweden, was queen. In 1046 the brothers returned to Hungary to help the exiled Andrew of Hungary claim his throne. Edmund married a Hungarian princess shortly after and died sometime before 1054. Hearing that Edward was alive, Edward the Confessor sent for his nephew, with a view to making him his heir. Edward the Exile arrived in England in 1057 but died soon after, before he had even met with his uncle the king, and was buried in St Paul's in London. The *Anglo-Saxon Chronicle* bemoans his death, 'Alas! That was a rueful time, and injurious to all this nation – that he ended his life so soon after he came to England, to the misfortune of this miserable people.'[16] With Edward's death, his son, Edgar, became the ætheling, but Edgar was still very much a child, about five years of age and unlikely to inherit if King Edward died in the near future. The succession, therefore, remained unsettled, and, with Edward the Confessor now in his fifties, you can imagine the more powerful men in the country – and overseas – surreptitiously having one eye on the greatest prize of all, the throne.

Edward also showed an interest in the situations of neighbouring countries, especially Scotland and Wales. In 1054 Edward ordered his Northumbrian earl, Siward, to advance into Scotland. King Macbeth, of Shakespearean fame, was defeated by Siward just north of the Tay in Perthshire. Macbeth was replaced with the alternative claimant to the throne, Malcolm III Canmore, son of Duncan I. Malcolm went on to defeat and kill Macbeth in battle in 1057. Malcolm and Edward were on amicable terms and the Scots king attended Edward's court at Gloucester in 1059, although it seems he still had an eye to annexing Northumbria. Relations with Wales were less cordial. The Welsh border was a fluid, frequently violent area, subject to raids from both sides of the border. With several princes holding power in different areas of the country, Wales was often volatile, and Edward attempted to take control of the balance of power. In 1053, Rhys ap Rydderch, prince of south Wales, was causing trouble along the border with his frequent raids. Edward the Confessor demonstrated his ruthless side when he ordered the prince's assassination; Rhys's head was delivered to the king. Another Welsh prince, Gruffydd, made an alliance with Earl Ælfgar of Mercia, causing the earl to be exiled from England for a time. Earl Harold invaded Wales and gained the submission of the Welsh princes; in 1063 Gruffydd was finally betrayed and killed by his own men, who delivered his head to Harold. Thus neutralised,

Wales was divided and given to Gruffydd's two brothers, Blethgent and Rigwatle, who gave hostages to both the king and Earl Harold. They each swore oaths to King Edward, promising to aid him where needed, on sea or land, and to pay tribute 'as was paid long before to other kings'.[17] The Welsh, however, were never going to acquiesce peacefully and in 1065 Caradoc, the son of Gruffydd, launched an attack on the builders of a new stronghold, Portskewett. This estate on the Severn estuary was being constructed by Earl Harold, who had intended to take the king hunting there. Almost all of those involved in the building project were killed.[18]

These years before the Norman Conquest were dramatic, to say the least, marked by intrigue, war and betrayal. However, the years 1052 to 1066 were also seen as the golden age of Edward the Confessor. Edward himself is remembered as a pious king, his lasting achievement being the magnificent Westminster Abbey and he was the last English king to be made a saint; his shrine taking pride of place in his own foundation, Westminster Abbey. However, he made no extravagant reforms in the Church or Government, allowing both to run smoothly and recover from the excesses caused by the struggles for the Crown between the House of Wessex and the Danes. England was mainly peaceful, even if the time was also marred by power struggles between its earls. Overall, England was a prosperous nation, with foreign and domestic trade booming. All these events in the first half of the eleventh century were led by men, who made war and laws, and built England as a nation that would be fought over in 1066. However, some women also played significant roles in these events. As queen of Æthelred and Cnut, and mother to Harthacnut and Edward the Confessor, Emma of Normandy had a great influence on the direction of kingship in the first half of the century. She has come down to us as a formidable woman who helped to shape England and deserves recognition for her part in the country's story.

2

Emma of Normandy

Even though she was not alive in 1066, you cannot tell the story of the Norman Conquest without including Emma of Normandy, twice queen of England. Emma had a significant influence on the first half of the eleventh century; as the queen of both King Æthelred II (the Unready) and King Cnut, Emma set the standard for queenship in England for generations to come. Emma is, also, the only woman to link all three camps involved in the battles of 1066. A native of Normandy, she was first married to an English king and then to a Scandinavian one. Two of her sons, one by Cnut, Harthacnut, and one by Æthelred, Edward the Confessor, became kings of England, and her nephew, William, Duke of Normandy (William the Conqueror) was the eventual victor at the Battle of Hastings.

Although nothing is known of her childhood, Emma was probably born in the late 980s. She was the daughter of Richard (I), Count of Rouen, and his second wife, Gunnor. Richard had been Lord of Normandy since 942 and had earned the nickname Richard the Fearless. He was the son of William Longsword, *princeps* or chieftain of Normandy and his Breton concubine, Sprota, who had been captured in war and undergone a marriage in the Danish custom – a handfasting – with William, rather than a Christian marriage. Richard was also the grandson of the famous Rollo, the first Norse, or Viking, ruler of Normandy. William had recognised Richard as his heir from the moment of his birth and sent the boy to be educated variously at Fécamp and Bayeux, both strongholds of Scandinavian influence. Richard was only ten years old when his father was murdered by the Count of Flanders on 17 December 942, and the young boy suddenly became a valuable pawn for neighbouring lords.[1] Louis IV, King of France, initially supported Richard as his father's heir, installing Richard in his father's office and giving the young boy into the custody of the Count of Ponthieu to continue his education. However, Louis soon reneged and attempted to force Richard to renounce his title; he took possession of Normandy for himself. When Richard refused to give up his birthright, Louis moved the youngster to Laon, under strict confinement.

However, with the help of his father's regents for Normandy, including Bernard de Senlis, who had been a companion of the great Rollo, Richard managed to escape his imprisonment. When King Louis was subsequently captured after raiding into Norman territory in retaliation, Richard had the opportunity to demand hostages to hold against Louis IV recognising him as Duke of Normandy. Richard then started looking around for strong allies, forming a treaty with Hugh the Great, Count of Paris, one of France's great landholders and Louis' rival and enemy. The alliance included the marriage of Richard to Hugh's young daughter, Emma of Paris, in 960. Emma had an impressive pedigree. Her grandfather was King Robert I of France and her brother was Hugh Capet, who would, in 987, become the first Capetian king of France. In 955 Richard had been appointed guardian of the younger Hugh, by the boy's father. The marriage, however, was to be childless and Emma died in 968.

Richard had kept a number of concubines during his marriage with Emma, with whom he had several children – at least two boys and two girls. However, Richard also kept a woman of a higher status who was considered more than a mere concubine, a mistress, although it is not clear that this was during his marriage, or only after Emma's death. This mistress was Gunnor, who was said by chroniclers to come from 'the noblest house of the Danes', although this appears to have been an exaggeration; it is more than likely that she was the daughter of first generation Danish settlers in Normandy.[2] Gunnor was mother to at least four sons and three daughters by Richard, most of whom, if not all, were born out of wedlock. Richard and Gunnor eventually married according to the Christian rite, thus legitimising their children. The marriage meant there was now a clear order of succession for Normandy and gave the children by Gunnor precedence over any children by Richard's other concubines.

Emma of Normandy was one of the three daughters of Richard and Gunnor, the others being Hawise and Mathilde; Mathilde died only a couple of years into her marriage, possibly in childbirth. It is thought that Emma was the oldest daughter, although this assumption is based mainly on the fact that Emma had a more prestigious marriage than her sisters. However, it may also be that Emma was thought the daughter more able to live up to the challenge of marrying into England. Of her four brothers, Richard would succeed their father as Richard II, and Robert was Archbishop of Rouen between 989 and 1037. Two further full brothers were Mauger, who became Count of Corbeil, and Robert Danus, who died as a young man.

Richard is described as being 'tall, well built, handsome; he had a long beard.'[3] A strong leader, he ruled over Normandy for forty-four years, expanding the territories of the Norsemen and plundering much of northern France. He aided his fellow Danes by offering shelter to, and trading with, those who were raiding and plundering into England, causing tensions between the two countries. He was a devout Christian and a benevolent lord; he made sure he bought back any Normans who were captured during skirmishes they fought for him. He died at Fécamp on 20 November 996, aged sixty-four, and was succeeded by his oldest son by Gunnor, also named Richard. Gunnor survived her husband by more than twenty years and, although there is no record of her involvement in her husband's government, she does appear to have been active during her son's reign, consistently witnessing charters into the 1020s; as dowager-duchess, her name often appeared after that of her son, the duke, and always before her daughter-in-law and grandsons. She died in 1031.

Emma probably had little contact with her mother. Although she would have been raised in her father's court, initially she would have been the responsibility of a wet nurse, before beginning her education under a governess. It was not the tradition among aristocratic families to foster daughters within other families, as it was with sons, and so the limited education Emma would have received would have been overseen within her father's court, which travelled chiefly between Rouen, Fécamp and Bayeux. It is unlikely that she and her sisters, and her brothers, even, were taught to read; reading and writing were skills left to scribes and clerics and were not considered essential in secular society. However, Emma would have been taught needlework and embroidery, court etiquette and diplomacy, and how to run a household, the skills she would need as a wife and mother. Emma was probably fluent in French and Danish, as the Normans seemed to live between the two worlds of Scandinavia and France.

In 1002 Emma's life drastically changed when she was given as a bride to Æthelred II, King of England. Æthelred was the youngest son of King Edgar the Peaceable and his last wife, Ælfthryth. The grandson of Edward the Elder, and great-grandson of Alfred the Great, Edgar was king from 959 until his death in 975. His wife, Ælfthryth, was probably born around 945; she was the daughter of Ealdorman Ordgar of Devon, her mother an unknown woman who is said to have been descended from the royal family. She was first married at the age of about eleven to Æthelwold, the son of Æthelstan Half-King, Ealdorman of East Anglia. However, Æthelwold died in 962, probably in a hunting accident, although there were rumours of murder on the orders of his wife's supposed lover, King Edgar. Edgar's marital history was already chequered. Ælfthryth could be Edgar's second or third wife; she was certainly the third relationship by which children were born. Edgar's first wife, Æthelfled 'the Fair', was the mother of his eldest son, Edward (the Martyr), although there seems to be some question as to whether Edgar and Æthelfled were ever married, given that Edward was later relegated in precedence to his younger brother, Edmund, on charters. Following Æthelfled's death, Edgar had a relationship with Wulfryth from which a daughter, Edith, was born in 963/964. The sources are uncertain as to whether or not Edgar and Wulfryth married, and some even suggest that she was a nun Edgar had seduced; although this may be confusion due to the fact that Wulfryth entered a nunnery shortly after Edith was born. Edith joined her mother in the abbey at Wilton, where Wulfryth eventually became abbess; in time both mother and daughter would be venerated locally as saints.

Ælfthryth and Edgar were married in 964 and were soon the parents of two sons; Edmund and Æthelred. Despite having an older half-brother, Edward, it is Edmund who was treated as Edgar's acknowledged heir; his name being above that of Edward's in a charter of 966, witnessed by both boys, which founded the New Minster at Winchester. Ælfthryth must have been distraught when, in 971 and still only a child of about seven, young Edmund died. On 11 May 973 Edgar had a coronation, at Bath Abbey, with Ælfthryth by his side. Edgar was about 30, and the venerated Archbishop Dunstan – later Saint Dunstan – of Canterbury officiated. Whether this was his first coronation or a second ceremony is still debated by historians, but it is the first known coronation of a Queen of England, Ælfthryth. A near contemporary account of the coronation depicts Ælfthryth feasting with many abbots and abbesses, wearing a silken gown sewn with pearls and precious stones.[4] The coronation was an important display for Edgar and Ælfthryth, used as a way to emphasise the legitimacy of their union, especially given Edgar's marital history, and the superior claims of their children as Edgar's heirs.

Ælfthryth's security was destroyed just three years later, when Edgar died at the young age of thirty-two. With their eldest son dead and the youngest only seven years old, the crown went to Edgar's eldest son, the twelve- or thirteen-year-old Edward. Edward faced opposition when Ælfthryth pressed Æthelred's claim, supported by several leading figures, including Bishop Æthelwold of Winchester and her first husband's brother, Æthelwine, ealdorman of East Anglia. However, with the backing of the revered (and future saint) Dunstan, it was Edward who was crowned. Following his coronation Edward honoured his father's promises to Ælfthryth, confirming the gift of jurisdiction over the whole of Dorset as her dower. As a consequence, Ælfthryth and her son, Æthelred, settled at Corfe, in the Purbeck Hills; it was a large estate surrounding a defensive mound, which would later become the Norman stronghold of Corfe Castle.

And it was at Corfe on 18 March 978 that Ælfthryth's reputation was irreparably damaged, following a visit from sixteen-year-old

King Edward. Whether Edward had been out hunting or was in the area specifically to visit his stepmother and half-brother seems to be uncertain. However, he did send a message that he would be calling on them and Ælfthryth's retainers were awaiting the young king at the gate, when he arrived with a small retinue. Still sitting in the saddle, he was handed a drink, then stabbed. It must have been a horrific sight, as the king's panicked horse bolted, racing off with Edward's foot stuck in the stirrup and with the dying king being dragged along behind his mount. The *Anglo-Saxon Chronicle* recorded:

> No worse deed than this was ever done by the English nation since they first sought the land of Britain. Men murdered him, but God hath magnified him. He was in life an earthly king. He is now after death a heavenly saint.[5]

Although Edward's brother, Æthelred, only about ten years old but now king of England, was above suspicion due to his age, Ælfthryth had no such protection. Some traditions go so far as to accuse Ælfthryth of wielding the dagger herself. However, while most believe she was complicit in the murder, it is by no means certain and it is entirely possible that court malcontents, who had migrated to Æthelred, were responsible for the murder. Ælfthryth rode out the ensuing furore and with her son as the new king, Ælfthryth was eventually exonerated of any complicity; the necessity of stabilising the country, establishing the new reign and rescuing England's reputation overrode the need for justice for Edward. Æthelred was crowned at Kingston, Surrey, on 4 May 979, a year after his brother's death and just a few months after the reburial of Edward's remains, with great ceremony, at Shaftesbury Abbey. A council was established to assist the young king in ruling the country, probably involving Queen Ælfthryth, who may have acted as regent during Æthelred's minority; it also included the aging Dunstan, Archbishop of Canterbury; Æthelwold, bishop of Winchester; and Ælfhere, ealdorman of Mercia. Even when Æthelred was old enough to rule alone, Ælfthryth did not entirely retire, and held considerable influence over her son and his family until her final years.

Æthelred was first married to Ælfgifu of York, sometime around 1085. Ælfgifu was most likely the daughter of a nobleman named Thored, who was Earl of Northumbria between *c.975* and *c.992*. The couple had more than ten children together, including at least six boys and four girls, of whom Æthelred's eventual successor in 1016, Edmund Ironside, was the third son. Ælfgifu seems to have had little influence over her husband and his court; she was not a witness to any of his charters during their marriage and, unlike Æthelred's mother, she was never crowned queen. It is even likely that her mother-in-law Ælfthryth raised a number of her children, including the royal couple's first-born son and ætheling, Æthelstan. Æthelstan died aged about twenty in 1014, two years before his father. Æthelred's mother, Ælfthryth, the dowager queen, did eventually retire from the limelight, to the abbey at Wherwell, sometime before the year 1000; she died there on 17 November in either 999, 1000 or 1001. By contrast, Ælfgifu's death went entirely unrecorded. We know she must have died by 1002, when Æthelred married Emma of Normandy as his second wife.

Ælfgifu's death gave Æthelred the opportunity to broker a lasting peace with neighbouring Normandy. For many years, marauding Danes had been using Normandy as a base from which to raid deep into England, causing tensions between Æthelred and Emma's father, Richard I. This had led to the intervention of the pope, who brokered a peace treaty between the two rulers in 990–991. The treaty appeared to ease tensions until the year 1000, when a Danish army again settled in Normandy for the winter, before returning to England in 1001. A new arrangement was made with the new Duke of Normandy, Richard II, which included the marriage of Richard's sister, Emma, to the recently widowed king of England. Little mention is made of the event in the chronicles, the *Anglo-Saxon Chronicle* merely states in the spring of 1002 'Richard's daughter came here to the land.'[6] Henry of Huntingdon, writing later, stated:

> In the year 1002, Emma, the flower of Normandy, came into England, and was crowned and received the title of queen.[7]

Emma and her attendants arrived in England in April 1002 and she was met at the coast by her future husband. In stately procession, she was escorted to Canterbury, where she would marry the king, and, significantly, be crowned queen, unlike Æthelred's first wife. Her name was changed to the more Saxon-friendly Ælfgifu – although it was the same name as Æthelred's first wife, it was also the name of Æthelred's revered grandmother, St Ælfgifu, who was the wife of King Edmund I, Edgar the Peaceable's father. At the time of their marriage Æthelred was in his mid-thirties, while Emma was probably about fifteen years old. The wedding and coronation would have been a welcome diversion from the recent Danish raids. As a fifteen-year-old in a new land and step-mother to a large family, things must have been very strange for Emma. They cannot have been made easier by having to get used to the new name from a strange language, Ælfgifu, as well as the language itself. Nor could it have been easy to acclimatise herself in her new surroundings, and learn that her father's allies, the Scandinavians, were her husband's greatest enemies and feared throughout her new land. This last must have been made harder by the knowledge that she was descended from those same Scandinavians and she may well have had to overcome some prejudice from her new subjects. Little is known of her life as Æthelred's wife and queen, although William of Malmesbury suggests the relationship was strained and they were never on friendly terms with each other.[8] Emma does appear to have been more visible than the king's first wife and was given a prominent place on the witness lists of the king's charters. She was, in fact, included on charters from the very beginning of her time as queen. In 1012 she was given a plot of land on the high street in Winchester by Æthelred, which would serve as her main residence in England for the next forty years.

Emma's children, however, were not given precedence in the succession over the children of Æthelred's first wife, despite the fact that, unlike Emma, she had never been crowned queen. In 1010 Æthelred still had at least five surviving sons from his first marriage, of whom the oldest, Æthelstan, was expected to succeed him. Emma had three surviving children by Æthelred; two sons and a daughter. Edward was born in 1003/04 at Islip in Oxfordshire, and may have been educated by the monks at Ely. He would go on to become King Edward the Confessor. Alfred was born sometime before 1012 and styled ætheling, or throne-worthy.

He was viciously murdered at Ely in Cambridgeshire in 1037, probably on the orders of his step-brother, King Harold I Harefoot, and was buried in Ely Cathedral. Emma's daughter, Gode (or Godgifu), was initially married to Drogo, Count of Mantes and the Vexin, who died in 1035. The couple had three sons: Ralph, a staunch supporter of his uncle, Edward the Confessor, he became Earl of Hereford and died in 1057; Walter III, Count of Mantes and the Vexin, died sometime after 1063; and Fulk, who was Bishop of Amiens from 1030 and died in 1058. Godgifu was married for a second time to Eustace II, Count of Boulogne, and died before 1049; although there is little evidence, it is possible that there was a child of the second marriage, as a grandson of Eustace was given as a hostage to William I in 1067.[9]

Even though Emma's marriage was to seal an alliance with Normandy and prevent the Danes from using that country as a launch pad for assaults on England, it did nothing to bring Æthelred's problems with the Danes to an end. In the final years of the tenth century, Æthelred had been paying tribute to the Danes at regular intervals, as mentioned in Chapter One, 'because of the great terror they were causing along the coast.'[10] The first payment had been 10,000 pounds in 991 but escalated to 24,000 pounds in the opening months of 1002. However, in November 1002, the same year as their marriage, having been warned that the Danes in England would take his life and kingdom, Æthelred changed tactics and ordered that all Danish men in England be killed. The St Brice's Day Massacre, however, was not a full-scale extermination and probably did not extend into the Danelaw, which extended north and east of the Thames and across the north of England. Æthelred justified the massacre in a charter of 1004, explaining the need to rebuild the church of St Frideswide:

> For it is fully agreed that to all dwelling in this country it will be well known that, since a decree was sent out by me with the counsel of my leading men and magnates, to the effect that all the Danes who had sprung up in this island, sprouting like cockle amongst the wheat, were to be destroyed by a most just extermination, and thus this decree was to be put into effect even as far as death, those Danes who dwelt in the afore-mentioned town, striving to escape

death, entered this sanctuary of Christ, having broken by force
the doors and bolts, and resolved to make refuge and defence for
themselves therein against the people of the town and the suburbs;
but when all the people in pursuit strove, forced by necessity, to
drive them out, and could not, they set fire to the planks and
burnt, as it seems, this church with its ornaments and its books.
Afterwards, with God's aid, it was renewed by me.[11]

Unfortunately for Æthelred, one of the victims of the massacre
was Gunhilde, sister of King Sweyn I Forkbeard of Denmark who,
in retaliation, then led an invasion of England in 1003. With the
support of his fleet, King Sweyn and his men campaigned mainly
along the coast of East Anglia until 1005, when the great famine
ravaging Europe reached the British Isles; the lack of food forced
them to withdraw to their own lands, if only temporarily. Emma
gets a mention in the 1003 entry of the *Anglo-Saxon Chronicle*,
in which she is referred to as 'the Lady': 'Here Exeter was broken
down through the French churl Hugh whom the Lady had set
as her reeve; and the raiding army completely did for the town
and took great war booty.'[12] However, from 1006 Viking raids
escalated and Æthelred spent the last ten years of his reign in an
almost constant state of war. His sons by his first marriage were
now old enough to join him in the fighting, three of whom died,
possibly killed in battle or from wounds received in the fighting,
before 1015 – including Æthelred's eldest son and heir, Æthelstan,
who died in June 1014. It must have been a terrifying time for
Emma with her young family, as by 1013 Sweyn Forkbeard had
gained the upper hand. With Æthelred's hold on England becoming
ever more precarious, Emma and her children were sent to safety
in her native Normandy. The *Anglo-Saxon Chronicle* records
'the Lady then turned across the sea to her brother Richard, and
Ælfsige, abbot of Peterborough with her. And the king sent Bishop
Ælfhun across the sea with the æthelings Edward and Alfred in
order that he should look after them.'[13] Æthelred spent Christmas
on the Isle of Wight before joining his family in Normandy, as
Sweyn consolidated his victory.

The English royal family were only able to return to England
following Sweyn's death from a fall from his horse in February of

1014. Sweyn's son, Cnut, became the new leader of the Danes in England, but the English determined that King Æthelred should be sent for 'declaring that no lord was dearer to them than their natural lord – if he would govern them more justly than he did before.'[14] According to the *Anglo-Saxon Chronicle* Æthelred then sent Edward back to England with his messengers, with promises that he would be a good lord to them and that he would improve the things which they hated. Danish kings were declared outlawed from England forever. As Æthelred and his family returned home, Cnut withdrew to Gainsborough, with his army. Before Cnut was able to launch any further attacks, Æthelred brought his whole army north into Lindsey, the area surrounding Gainsborough, raiding, burning and killing where he could. Cnut put to sea and headed down the coast with his fleet. He put in at Sandwich, where he maimed the hostages who had been held by his father, and put them ashore before sailing for Denmark.

The last years of Æthelred's life were fraught with conspiracy and in-fighting, brought to a head in 1015 by the machinations of Eadric Streona, ealdorman of Mercia, and a dominant member of the king's council. During a great assembly at Oxford, Streona had invited Sigeferth and Morcar, the two foremost thegns in the Seven Boroughs, to his chamber – where they were murdered. Not only did the king then seize all their property, but also Sigeferth's widow, who was taken to Malmesbury. The ætheling, Edmund, once the third son but now his father's heir after the deaths of his older brothers in the preceding years, then joined the fray, taking Sigeferth's widow as his own wife and taking control of the dead thegns' lands. Cnut landed on the south coast and started raiding into Wessex as Edmund challenged Eadric Streona. Although they initially put their differences aside, in the face of this new threat from Cnut, the alliance of Eadric and Edmund would not last. Ealdorman Eadric, therefore, turned to Cnut, pledging his allegiance to the Dane. Cnut stayed in the south-west until Christmas but started raiding into Mercia in the new year. Edmund organised resistance, with the help of Earl Uhtred of Northumbria, but was again on the back foot when Uhtred was forced to submit to Cnut in order to protect Northumbria, only to be murdered on Eadric Streona's advice.

King Æthelred, in the meantime, had been ailing. In the later part of 1015 he had lain sick at Cosham, a royal estate at the head of Portsmouth Harbour in Hampshire, as Edmund had taken on the responsibility of organising the resistance to Cnut. His health rallied in 1016, when he led an army out of London, but little was achieved, and he was soon back in the capital. It was as Cnut turned his sights on London, after Easter 1016, that Æthelred died. The king 'ended his days on St George's Day [23 April], and he had held his kingdom with great toil and difficulties as long as his life lasted.'[15] Emma's whereabouts throughout 1016 are unclear. It may well be that she was with Æthelred when he died, before retiring to her own estate near Winchester as the battle for the kingdom was fought. There is a story that she took Æthelred's body to the abbey at Wilton, to be buried beside his half-sister, St Edith. However, there is convincing evidence that he was buried in St Paul's Cathedral, London, with the tomb being lost when the cathedral was destroyed in the Great Fire of London in 1666.

Edmund, renowned as Edmund Ironside, was chosen to succeed his father as King Edmund II. His spirited defence of the kingdom was met with defeat at the Battle of Ashingdon on 18 October 1016, after which England was effectively divided in two, with Edmund controlling Wessex and Cnut ruling Mercia and Northumbria, until Edmund's death. Either before or shortly after Edmund died, on 30 November 1016, Emma's three children by Æthelred – Edward, Alfred and Gode – were sent to safety in Normandy, but whether their mother had accompanied them is unclear. By 1017 Cnut had succeeded as king. With Edwy, the only surviving adult son of Æthelred and his first wife, having been killed on Cnut's orders, and with Edmund Ironside's infant sons, Edward and Edmund, in exile on the Continent and Emma's children exiled in Normandy, there were few people left in England capable of opposing the new king. The *Anglo-Saxon Chronicle* records that 'before 1 August the king ordered the widow of the former king Æthelred, Richard's daughter, to be fetched to him as queen.'[16] Such a short, matter-of-fact statement leaves us wondering from where Emma was 'fetched', whether it was from Normandy, or from somewhere in England, nor do we know whether Emma came willingly or was brought to Cnut by force. The marriage between Cnut and

Emma was a sensible political move for both. For Emma, still only about thirty years of age, it gave her security and a way forward following Æthelred's death; she was now married to the victor, rather than the man always on the run, and she could continue to wear her crown. As for Cnut, almost ten years Emma's junior, he could use her political experience with the English nobility and church. The marriage was a chance for Cnut to prove that he wanted reconciliation with the old regime and served as a symbol of continuity when so much had changed. It would also help to neutralise the threat posed by Æthelred's sons by Emma, Edward and Alfred. Normandy's ruler, Duke Richard, was less likely to act in the interests of his nephews if it put his sister in danger. Moreover, Cnut may have thought that if he could get Emma on his side, especially if they had children together, it would deter her from promoting the interests of her exiled sons.

Emma was, in a way, the second wife of Cnut. Although, unlike with Æthelred, whom she married after his first wife died, Cnut's first wife was still very much among the living. It is not certain, of course, that Cnut had actually married Ælfgifu of Northampton. Although it is possible that Cnut repudiated Ælfgifu in order to marry Emma, it is highly unlikely that the couple had gone through a Christian marriage ceremony. It is possible that Ælfgifu was Cnut's concubine, or mistress, or, if they had been married, that she was a 'handfast' wife according to the Danish custom. There is no convincing evidence either way. All we know for certain is that Cnut and Ælfgifu did have at least two children together, Sweyn and Harold, who were considered illegitimate; although there were contemporary rumours, which will be explored later, that neither child was Cnut's son. How Emma felt about this other 'wife', we can only surmise, but she can't have been happy that Cnut's two sons by Ælfgifu were a threat to the succession of any children she may have by Cnut. Nor do we know how Emma may have felt about having to leave her three children by Æthelred far away in Normandy, even if it was to ensure their safety.

Cnut and Emma were to have two children who survived to adulthood. A son, Harthacnut, was born around 1018 and succeeded his half-brother, Harold I, as King of England in June 1040. A daughter, Gunhilda, was born around 1020 and was married to Henry III, Emperor of Germany, on 10 June 1036, taking the name Kunigunde on her marriage. She had one daughter, Beatrice, who was born in 1037 and became abbess of Quedlinburg, before she died in Italy, in July 1038, of the pestilence. Cnut and Emma had a second daughter whose name is unknown, who died aged about eight and was buried in Bosham Church, Sussex, where her grave is marked by an engraving of a black raven, a symbol of the Danes.[17]

Emma enjoyed high status at Cnut's court, she was more valuable to Cnut than she had ever been to Æthelred and she and Cnut often appear together in surviving records, perhaps demonstrating how each supported the other. The 1023 entry of the *Anglo-Saxon Chronicle* mentions Emma's involvement in the accompanying ceremonies when Cnut had the body of St Ælfheah (St Alphege) conveyed to Canterbury, stating '… on the third day came Emma the Lady with her royal child Harthacnut, and then with great pomp and rejoicing and hymns of praise they all conveyed the holy archbishop into Canterbury, and honourably thus brought [him] on 11 June into Christ Church.'[18] In 1024 the *Anglo-Saxon Chronicle* records a loss that would have been personal for Emma and her children by Æthelred – the death of her brother, the Duke of Normandy, stating: 'Here Richard the Second died. Richard, his son, reigned about one year, and after him, Robert, his brother, reigned 8 years.'[19]

Cnut's star continued to rise, with his succession to the Danish throne following the death of his brother Harald, in 1018/19 and the conquest of Norway in 1028, replacing Olaf (later St Olaf) as its king. Cnut's first wife, Ælfgifu, was sent to Norway with their eldest son, Sweyn, to act as regent in Cnut's absence, but managed to alienate the Norwegians and was eventually chased out of the country.

Cnut was a very active ruler; the *Anglo-Saxon Chronicle* records how he spent his time moving between his three kingdoms as much as he could, and how he travelled to Scotland for a meeting with King Malcolm in order to receive his submission. A pious Christian, Cnut even went on pilgrimage to Rome in 1027, where he was present at the coronation of Holy Roman Emperor Conrad II. We do not know whether Emma travelled with him, however, given that they often appeared as a couple on charters, it is possible that she sometimes joined Cnut on his travels. While in Rome Cnut arranged for the marriage of his daughter by Emma, Gunhilda, who was about five years old, to Conrad II's son, Henry – the future Holy Roman Emperor Henry III. Although they were not married until later, it is possible that Gunhilda had travelled with her father and was left in the care of Conrad to be raised by her future husband's family. Whatever the case, the couple was married in 1036 and Gunhilda was Queen of Germany until her death in 1038.

Emma's life changed again in 1035 when, on 12 November, Cnut died at Shaftesbury. His body was taken to Winchester to be buried in the Old Minster. Writing a century later, Henry of Huntingdon succinctly summed up Cnut's reign:

Besides the various wars in which he gained so much glory, his nobleness and greatness of mind were eminently displayed on three occasions. First, when he married his daughter to the Roman Emperor with an immense dowry. Secondly, when, during his journey home, he reduced the oppressive tolls exacted from pilgrims on the roads through France by the redemption of one-half of them at his private expense. Thirdly, when at the summit of his power, he ordered a seat to be placed for him on the sea-shore when the tide was coming in; thus seated, he shouted to the flowing sea, 'Thou, too, art subject to my command, as the land on which I am seated is mine; and no one has ever resisted my commands with impunity. I command you, then not to flow over my land, nor presume to wet the feet and the robe of your lord.' The tide, however, continuing to rise as usual, dashed over his feet and legs without respect to his royal person. Then the king leaped backwards, saying: 'Let all men know how empty and worthless is the power of kings, for there is none worthy of the name, but He whom heaven, earth and sea obey by eternal laws.' From henceforth King Canute never wore his crown of gold, but placed it for a lasting memorial on the image of our Lord affixed to a cross, to the honour of God the almighty King: through whose mercy may the soul of Canute, the king, enjoy everlasting rest.[20]

Following her husband's death Emma established herself at her estate at Winchester, the *Anglo-Saxon Chronicle* saying, 'And the Lady Ælfgifu Emma settled inside there.' Although Cnut had probably intended for Harthacnut, his son by Emma, to succeed him, it was Harold Harefoot, Cnut's son by Ælfgifu of Northampton, who, despite opposition from leading magnates such as Earl Godwin, was chosen as regent as Harthacnut was in Denmark. The *Chronicle* adds 'And then it was decided that Ælfgifu, Harthacnut's mother, should settle in Winchester with the king her son's housecarls, and hold all Wessex in hand for him.'[21] Emma was not to be left in peace, however, as one of Harold's first acts concerned her. Emma was unable to resist, it seems, when Harold 'sent and had taken from her all the best treasures which King Cnut had, which she could not withhold; nevertheless she stayed on inside there as long as she could.'[22] The fact Emma held Cnut's treasury is testament to the high regard in which the late king had held his queen and was probably a practical solution to ensure the security of the treasury, given Cnut's frequent travels outside England.

In 1036, Emma faced further tragedy when her son Alfred arrived in England. According to Norman sources, it was Edward who had first tried to join their mother in Winchester in 1036, sailing up the Solent and winning a battle near Southampton before returning to Normandy with his plunder. It was after this that Alfred attempted to visit his mother in Winchester, but many feared he would make a play for the crown. Supporters of Harold Harefoot, apparently led by Earl Godwin sought to prevent this:

But then Godwine stopped him, and set him in captivity,
and drove off his companions, and some variously killed;
some of them were sold for money, some cruelly destroyed,
some of them were fettered, some of them were blinded,
some maimed, some scalped.
No more horrible deed was done in this country
since the Danes came and made peace here.
Now we must trust to the dear God
that they who, without blame, were so wretchedly destroyed
rejoice happily with Christ.

The ætheling still lived; he was threatened with every evil;
until it was decided that he be led
to Ely town, fettered thus.
As soon as he came on ship he was blinded,
and blind thus brought to the monks.
And there he dwelt as long as he lived.
Afterwards he was buried, as well befitted him,
full honourably, as he was entitled,
at the west end, very near at hand to the steeple,
in the south side-chapel. His soul is with *Christ*.[23]

Emma's own biography, the *Encomium Emmae Reginae* tells the story slightly differently, saying that Harold Harefoot forged a letter from Emma to her son, which claimed that the English would prefer Edward or Alfred as king, enticing Alfred to come to England and claim the crown.[24] It does seem likely that Alfred received such a letter, but it may well have come from Emma herself, who sought to lay the blame on Harold when the expedition failed so abysmally. When Alfred arrived in England, he was met by Earl Godwin, who swore fealty to Alfred and established him at Guildford, but then Harold attacked in the night and took Alfred to Ely, where he was tried, blinded, killed and buried. Other chronicles have Godwin sending Alfred to Harold, but the result is always the same; Alfred was blinded and either intentionally killed or died from wounds caused by his blinding.[25] Emma must have been relieved that at least Edward had remained safe in Normandy. Despite the fact she had not seen him for many years, the loss of Alfred must have been a cruel blow to his mother.

Emma's own situation got worse in 1037, when Harold was accepted as king of England by the *witan*, the council of England, as Harthacnut was lingering overlong in Denmark. As a consequence, Emma was forced to flee England and sought refuge at the court of Baldwin of Flanders, who received her honourably, gave her a house in Bruges, protected and entertained her. It may well be that Emma settled in Flanders because it was closer to Harthacnut in Denmark, but it may also be telling that she did not seek refuge in Normandy, where her oldest son, Edward, was living. Having received a letter of summons from his mother, Edward is said to have visited Emma in Bruges, ostensibly to disavow any interest in the English throne, although this would have been a moot point, given Edward's lack of funds and military resources. Edward's lack of interest in an expedition to England with his mother may also have been as a result of his feelings towards her. Emma is said to have doted on Harthacnut and was determined that he would be king, whereas Edward, on the other hand, felt that he had been abandoned by his mother and may have felt that she betrayed him by marrying Cnut. Nonetheless, it could be argued that Emma's adoration of her youngest son was a result of the fact that she had lost her three eldest children to a Norman exile and she was over-compensating by showering all her affection on Harthacnut.

It was from Flanders that Emma continued to work for her son Harthacnut and his claim to England's throne. In 1039 Harthacnut finally joined his mother, with a large fleet, and mother and son spent the winter as honoured guests of Count Baldwin. They had a stroke of luck in the spring of 1040, when Harold Harefoot died and Emma and Harthacnut were able to return to England, peacefully and triumphant. Although Harthacnut reigned for only two years, in that time Emma again enjoyed power and influence as the Queen Mother. Harthacnut had also made peace with his half-brother Edward, with whom he had been sharing a dual kingship in England from 1041. Harthacnut had a vindictive streak, which alienated him from his people. On his accession he 'ordered the dead Harold [Harthacnut's brother] to be dragged up and thrown into a ditch.'[26] A highly unpopular king due to the heavy burden of taxation he had levied on the country, Harthacnut died on 8 June 1042, of a convulsion while drinking at a wedding feast in Lambeth; he was buried beside his father at Winchester. Few, save his mother, mourned him; Emma is said to have given the head of St Valentine to the new minster at Winchester, for the sake of Harthacnut's soul. Despite the country's unfamiliarity with him, Edward was able to assume the throne with little opposition and was crowned in great splendour at Winchester on Easter Day (3 April) 1343 by the Archbishops of Canterbury and York. Edward's accession saw another change in status for Emma; although she was the revered Queen Mother during the reign of Harthacnut, Edward had no such respect for his mother. Following his coronation, the new king 'had brought into his hands all the lands which his mother owned and took from her all she owned in gold and in silver and in untold things, because earlier she had kept it from him too firmly.'[27]

The *D* manuscript of the *Anglo-Saxon Chronicle* tells of the same event, though a little more bluntly, clearly demonstrating Edward's feelings towards his mother: 'the king was so counselled that he – and Earl Leofric and Earl Godwin and Earl Siward and their band – rode from Gloucester to Winchester, on the Lady by surprise, and robbed her of all the treasures which she owned, which were untold, because earlier she was very hard on the king her son, in that she did less for him than he wanted before he became king, and also afterwards ...'[28] This last part of the statement refers to a rumour that suggested Emma had promised 'her' treasure in support of an invasion by Magnus, King of Norway, against her own son's claim to the throne. If true, it would certainly go further to explain Edward's antipathy towards her. This may also be testament to the trust in which Harthacnut held his mother, if the treasures involved also amounted to the English treasury, of which Emma had had custody at the end of Cnut's reign.

Emma's close friend and advisor, Stigand, newly consecrated as Bishop for East Anglia, shared in Emma's disgrace and was stripped of office and all that he owned. It may well be that Edward thought that Stigand had encouraged Emma in her perceived maltreatment of her only surviving son.

Several legends have arisen about Emma's apparent disgrace, including that she had committed treason by offering financial support to Magnus of Norway's proposed invasion of England. Another story, appearing two centuries later, suggested that Emma's relationship with Bishop Stigand was far more than that of her advisor and that he was, in fact, her lover – although the legend did get its bishops mixed up and named Ælfwine, rather than Stigand, as Emma's lover. The story continues that Emma chose to prove her innocence in a trial by ordeal, and that she walked barefoot over white-hot ploughshares. Even though the tale varies depending on the source, the result is the same; when she completed the ordeal unharmed, and was thus proven guiltless, she was reconciled with her contrite son, Edward.

Emma appears to have never recovered fully from the depredations placed on her. Both she and Stigand seem to have been reconciled with Edward's regime by 1044, however, she never again enjoyed the status to which she had become accustomed during the reigns of Cnut and Harthacnut. In that year she was witness to several charters, including a grant from the king of fifteen hides in Somerset to the Old Minster in Winchester; Emma's name – as Ælfgifu – appears second only to the king.[29] While Edward's initial harsh treatment could have been in response to a perceived threat from his mother, or revenge for her apparent abandonment of him, it may well be that Edward simply wanted to reduce his mother's influence and ensure that the country knew that he, and not his mother, was in control. Whatever the reason, Emma appears to have retired gracefully, if not entirely willingly, from the public eye following Edward's marriage to Edith of Wessex in 1045; suggesting that the court was not a comfortable place for two crowned and consecrated queens.

Emma's death is reported very briefly in the various manuscripts that comprise the *Anglo-Saxon Chronicle*, albeit with some confusion over the actual date, which is reported in the 1051 entry of the Abingdon (C) manuscript as 'And in the same year [1052] on 14 March passed away the Old Lady, mother of King Edward and Harthacnut, called Emma. And her body lies in the Old Minster [Winchester] with King Cnut.' However, the 1052 entry of the Worcester (D) manuscript states; 'Here on 6 March passed away the Lady Ælfgifu, widow of King Æthelred and King Cnut.' The Peterborough (E) 1052 entry simply states; 'Here in this year passed away Ælfgifu Emma, mother of King Edward and of King Harthacnut.'[30] Henry of Huntingdon, writing for an audience of Norman conquerors in the twelfth century, is more sensitive, stating; 'In the eleventh year of Edward's reign, Emma the Norman, mother and wife of kings, submitted to the fate common to all.'[31]

Emma is the only pre-Conquest queen of whom we have a surviving contemporary image. She is seen alongside Cnut in the *Liber Vitae* of Winchester's New Minster, in which the couple present a gold cross to the abbey.[31] Wearing a diadem and styled 'Regina', it is testament to the high status which Emma held in her own lifetime. Until her second widowhood she was the richest woman in England and renowned as a patron of the arts. She commissioned illuminated manuscripts from Peterborough and her own life story, the *Encomium Emmae Reginae*. Written in Latin and showing her in the most flattering terms, the *Encomium* gave Emma some control over her reputation in posterity and is a demonstration of how Emma wanted to be remembered. The frontispiece of the *Encomium*, especially, depicts Emma crowned and seated on a throne, flanked by the two sons who became kings, Edward and Harthacnut.

The story of Emma of Normandy mirrors England's struggle for a national identity in the first half of the eleventh century. Many of the events in which she was a major participant laid the foundations for events that were to follow. Although we cannot entirely blame Edward's lack of an heir on Emma herself, it could well be that his perceived rejection by her led to his distrust of women and the eventual succession crisis. Emma is also the thread that binds all the combatants of 1066 together. A Norman married to both a Saxon and a Dane, and the mother of a king from each, she herself represents the many nationalities and cultures which constituted eleventh-century England. The fact that, according to the *Anglo-Saxon Chronicle*, she had control of the treasury at the end of the reigns of both Cnut and Harthacnut suggests the extent of Emma's influence over these two kings and the country itself. It is proof of the high regard in which her second husband and youngest son held the twice-crowned queen.

3

Lady Godiva

Another lady of great influence in the first half of the eleventh century, and about whom a formidable folklore has grown over the centuries, is Godgifu, Countess of Mercia. She is more famously known as the Lady Godiva of legend, who rode naked through the streets of Coventry to persuade her husband to relieve the people of the burden of heavy taxes. Although she would have been known as Godgifu in her lifetime, we shall call her Godiva, the name we have all grown up with, and to distinguish her from several notable ladies of a similar name in this period.

There were at least three other prominent ladies of the early eleventh century with the name *Godgifu*. The most well-known was Godgifu, or Gode, full sister of Edward the Confessor and daughter of King Æthelred II and Queen Emma. She was married to Drogo, Count of Mantes and the Vexin, and had three sons by him before his death in 1035: Ralph, Earl of Hereford; Walter III, Count of Mantes and the Vexin; and Fulk, Bishop of Amiens. Godgifu then married Eustace II, Count of Boulogne, by whom she may have had a child, as a grandson of Eustace was given as a hostage to William I in 1067.[1] She died in 1049. Another contemporary Godgifu was a benefactress of Ely Abbey in the 1020s and a third Godgifu, also written as Godgyth, who died before 1055, was the wife of Earl Siward and a benefactress of Peterborough Abbey.[2] The name was, obviously, quite popular at the time; the Emmas of their day.

The origins of Lady Godiva herself are shrouded in mystery and the distance of time. We know nothing of her parentage or relations.

There is some suggestion that she had a brother, named Thorold, but this is based on a document of questionable provenance; a charter from Crowland Abbey in Lincolnshire names her as the sister of Thorold of Bucknall.[2] Thorold is said to have founded a Benedictine abbey on his manor at Spalding, Lincolnshire, which he then gave to the great abbey at Crowland. However, other sources argue that it was Bucknall, and not Spalding, which was given to Crowland Abbey.[3] The confusion with Godiva appears to come from the fact that the land at Spalding belonged to Godiva's son, Earl Ælfgar, before 1066, who was also a benefactor of Crowland Abbey. The situation is further confused by the fact the land later passed to Ivo Taillebois, who founded a church at Spalding as a satellite of the church of St Nicholas at Angers. Ivo's wife, Lucy, was the daughter of Turold, Sheriff of Lincoln. It is difficult to say whether Turold of Lincoln and Thorold of Bucknall are one and the same person, but it is possible; Turold and Thorold are both a derivative of the Scandinavian name Thorvaldr. Later legends even name Lucy as a daughter of Earl Ælfgar and therefore a granddaughter of Godiva. However, there is no surviving evidence to support this theory and the identity of Thorold and his relationship to Godiva is just as uncertain.

Godiva was probably married before 1010 and so it is possible that she was born in the early 990s. Although we know nothing of her family origins, we do know that her family cannot have been insignificant. She possessed considerable lands in the north-west of Mercia, suggesting that this is where she and her family were from. Mercia, in that time, covered almost all of the Midlands region, spreading from the Welsh borders across the centre of England. Her lands in Leicestershire, Warwickshire, Staffordshire and Shropshire, which amounted to sixty hides, may have constituted her own inheritance.[4] Godiva's family status is also attested by the fact that she made a very good marriage, to Leofric, who would later become Earl of Mercia.

Leofric was the son of Leofwine, who had been appointed Ealdorman of the Hwicce, an ancient kingdom within the earldom of Mercia, by Æthelred II in 994. While the family lands were given to victorious Danes on the accession of Cnut, Leofwine was allowed to keep his rank and title and may have succeeded the traitorous Eadric Streona as Ealdorman of Mercia after his death in 1017. However, this is far from certain, given that this was in the same year that Leofwine's oldest son, Northman, who may have been a retainer of Eadric Streona, was also murdered on the orders of King Cnut. Leofwine had two other sons; Edwin, who died at the Battle of Rhyd-y-Groes in 1039, and Godwine. The family had a reputation for despoiling the church in western Mercia; Leofwine, Leofric, Edwin and Godwine were all accused of stealing lands in Worcester that belonged to the Church. However, in the eastern part of the province, they were known religious benefactors. Earl Leofwine was recorded as a benefactor at Peterborough Abbey, and Northman is thought to have given to Twywell in Northamptonshire and to Thorney Abbey. The family's preferential treatment of the Church in eastern Mercia is possible evidence of their provenance from the region.

Leofric's marriage to Godiva, therefore, may have been a way of extending his family's influence into the western parts of Mercia. He was attesting charters as *minister* between 1019 and 1026, perhaps as sheriff under Hakon, Earl of Worcester. His father, Leofwine, probably died in 1023 or shortly after, as that was the last year in which he attested a charter. There is no clear indication as to whether Leofwine was ever Earl of Mercia, although Leofric certainly held that title through the reigns of four kings; Cnut, Harold Harefoot, Harthacnut and Edward the Confessor. Leofric's backing of Harold Harefoot over Harthacnut may have been a result of his son's marriage. Ælfgar is thought to have married Ælfgifu, who was possibly a kinswoman of Harold Harefoot's mother, Ælfgifu of Northampton, sometime in the 1020s. Such a relationship would explain Leofric's support for Harold Harefoot. Of course, so would the fact that Harthacnut was in no hurry to return from Denmark and Harold was on the spot and able to take charge.

Lady Godiva and Leofric appear to have had a partnership in their marriage. Their endowment of Coventry Abbey, according to John of Worcester, was made out of lands held by each of them. They also endowed the minster church of Stow St Mary, just to the north of Lincoln, and an Old English memorandum included both Leofric and Godiva in a request to Wulfwig, Bishop of

Dorchester-on-Thames 'to endow the monastery and assign lands
to it.'[5] Stow St Mary is a beautiful building at the centre of the
small village of Stow. Founded in the seventh century, it boasts the
faded graffiti carving of a Viking longboat on one of its inner walls.
The endowment included provision for secular canons, under the
supervision of the bishop. The endowment was made between
1053 and 1055. The memorandum specifically mentions the liturgy
to be used should be that of St Paul's, London, and accords the
division of income between the priests of Stow and the bishop.[6]
After the Conquest, Stow was in the hands of Wulfwig's successor,
Remegius of Fécamp, who became Bishop of Lincoln in 1067.
A later, spurious, charter, which was forged in Godiva's name,
grants land at Newark and Fledborough (in Nottinghamshire) and
Brampton and Marston (in Lincolnshire) to Stow. However, only
Brampton appears in Stow's possession in 1086, held by Remegius
as Bishop of Lincoln.[7]

The forging of church charters appears to have been a lucrative –
and prolific – business so it is often difficult to work out the extent
of Godiva's involvement in her husband's religious endowments.
For instance, there are two writs from the reign of King Edward the
Confessor which relate to Coventry Abbey; one includes her, but
is thought to be a forgery, whereas the one which is more likely to
be genuine makes no mention of Godiva. The *Evesham Chronicle*,
however, names both Leofric and Godiva (as Godgifu, of course)
as the founders of both Coventry Abbey and Holy Trinity Church
at Evesham. They also gave a crucifix, with the supporting figures
of the Virgin and St John the Evangelist, to Holy Trinity Church.
Coventry at this time was little more than a village and appears
to have belonged to Godiva herself. She also had land in various
other parts of Mercia, including Newark, which she may have
bought from her son, Ælfgar, as it was part of the comital lands
(the earldom). Her lands at Appleby in Derbyshire were leased
from Leofric, the Abbot of Peterborough, who was nephew and
namesake of her husband, Earl Leofric.[8]

A renowned benefactress of religious institutions, Orderic
Vitalis said that Godiva gave 'her whole store of gold and silver'
for the provision of ecclesiastical ornaments for the foundation
at Coventry.[9] Unfortunately, Orderic Vitalis does seem to have

confused Godiva and her daughter-in-law, Ælfgifu, and suggests that Godiva is married to Ælfgar and the mother of Edwin, Morcar and Ealdgyth, rather than their grandmother. John of Worcester, however, records Godiva's devotion to the Virgin and mentions her association with Leofric's endowments to churches and abbeys throughout the earldom, including Leominster, Much Wenlock, Chester, Coventry, Stow, Evesham and Worcester.[10] Despite the apparent inconsistencies and obvious confusion of Orderic Vitalis, it is clear that Godiva had a reputation as a patroness of the Church throughout Mercia during her own lifetime.

There is one example that counters this argument, however, which involves a joint grant by Leofric and Godiva, of Wolverley and Blackwell, Worcestershire. The *Second Worcester Cartulary*, compiled by Hemming on the orders of Bishop Wulfstan, claims that Leofric returned Wolverley and Blackwell, and promised that the manors at Belbroughton, Bell Hall, Chaddesley Corbett and Fairford, seized by his father Leofwine, would revert to the Church on his death. Hemming, however, claims that Godiva held onto the lands for herself, rather than returning them; although she is said to have given the Church expensive vestments and ornaments, and a promise not only to pay the annual revenues from these estates to the Church, but to return the lands on her own death.[11] That Edwin and Morcar seized the lands after their grandmother's death surely cannot be laid at Godiva's door?

Leofric was Earl of Mercia under four successive kings of England. He first appears in the written records as earl in 1032, although it is possible he was promoted to the rank sometime in the 1020s. He supported Harold Harefoot against Cnut's chosen successor, Harthacnut, possibly because his son Ælfgar was married to a kinswoman of Harold's mother, Ælfgifu of Northampton. However, this support may also have been as a result of his rival, Earl Godwin of Wessex, supporting Harthacnut and his mother, Queen Emma. Not a lot is known of King Harold Harefoot's three-year reign; the *Anglo-Saxon Chronicle* speaks of little but the weather – there was 'a great gale' in 1039 – and the deaths of bishops and abbots during this period. It does mention one incident, however, in the same year as the gale, during which the 'Welsh slew Edwin, brother of Earl Leofric, and Thurkil, and Elfget, and many good men with them.'[12] Edwin was killed at the Battle of Rhyd-y-Groes in Wales in 1039.

The rivalry with Earl Godwin continued into the reign of Harthacnut. Leofric participated in the attack on Worcester in 1041, a retaliatory punishment following the murder of two royal tax collectors in 1040, but it was Godwin who was tasked by Harthacnut with retrieving the body of King Harold Harefoot and tossing it into the marshes outside London. During the reign of Edward the Confessor the rivalry continued, with Leofric advising against sending aid to Godwin's nephew, Swein Estrithson, in support of his attempt on the Danish throne. Leofric also supported King Edward when he moved against Earl Godwin and his family in 1051, although he advised against outright conflict and an escalation into civil war; and it was Leofric's son, Ælfgar, who benefitted from the Godwinsons' exile by receiving Harold's earldom of East Anglia, even though he had to relinquish it on Harold's return. However, in 1053, when Harold succeeded to his father's earldom of Wessex, Ælfgar was again made Earl of East Anglia.

Leofric and Ælfgar must have felt outnumbered by the Godwinson family. With Harold as England's most prominent earl in Wessex, his sister married to the king, and various other brothers to occupy earldoms from the south to the north of the country, including Tostig in Northumbria from 1055. With Leofric and his only son controlling Mercia and East Anglia respectively, they were literally surrounded by Godwinsons. Leofric may also have had at least one brother to give him support; although Northman had been killed in 1017 and Edwin had died in battle in 1039, another brother, Godwine, who died sometime before 1059, may well have been around to even the odds against Earl Godwin's family's dominance. Leofric would also have two grandsons, but they were only children in the 1050s.

The Earl of Mercia was known for his generosity and piety, although this did not stop him appropriating ecclesiastical lands for his own benefit. His benefactions to various religious houses may well have had the dual purpose of providing patronage and gaining political support. For example, his patronage of Leominster may well have been to earn its powerful support for his secular authority over the region, against that of his rival in the area, Swein Godwinson. Although the policy failed to give Leofric the upper hand, it was far preferable to Swein's solution, which was to kidnap and marry the Abbess of Leominster – a crime which merited his banishment from England and resulted in the dissolution of the abbey and the birth of Swein's only son, Hakon.

Leofric died in 1057, on either 31 August or 30 September, at his manor of King's Bromley in Staffordshire. John of Worcester (also known as Florence of Worcester) said of him, this 'man of excellent memory died at a good old age, in his own manor called Bromley, and was buried with honour in Coventry, which monastery he had founded and well endowed.'[13] The 1057 entry of the *Anglo-Saxon Chronicle* reported; 'The same year died Earl Leofric, on the second before the calends of October; who was very wise before God, and also before the world; and who benefited all this nation.'[14] Godiva was to live on as a widow for at least ten more years. She would be there to see her son's inheritance of the earldom of Mercia. Although titles and land did often pass from father to son, it was not a foregone conclusion. Indeed, Ælfgar's rebellion in 1055 – which led to a subsequent exile – may well have been in fear of losing his inheritance, given that Edward the Confessor had just given the earldom of Northumbria to Tostig, son of Godwin, on the death of Earl Siward in place of his son and natural heir, Waltheof. Waltheof was still a child, however, and this may well have been a practical decision, in that it would be dangerous to leave such a powerful earldom – and the border with Scotland – in the control of a child. Ælfgar was banished again in 1058 but for a very short while, apparently, with the *Anglo-Saxon Chronicle* reporting: 'Earl Ælfgar was expelled but he soon came back again, with violence, through the help of Gruffydd.'[15]

We do not have the exact date of Godiva's death. Most historians seem to believe that she survived the Norman Conquest and died around 1067. She is mentioned as a pre-Conquest landholder in Domesday Book, but that doesn't necessarily mean that she was alive in 1066. Hemming, who compiled the Worcester cartulary, says that some of her lands passed directly to her grandsons, Edwin and Morcar, offering evidence that Godiva also outlived her son, Ælfgar, who probably died in 1062. If Godiva did live into 1067, then she would have seen the dangers that the Norman

Conquest brought to her family. Although her son was dead, her grandchildren were very much alive, and at the heart of events. By 1065 her grandsons were both earls. Morcar became Earl of Northumbria in 1065, chosen by the Northumbrians to replace the unpopular Tostig. His tenure, however, was of short duration and he was replaced by Copsig, an adherent of Tostig, by William the Conqueror. Edwin had succeeded his father as Earl of Mercia in 1062 but neither brother flourished under the rule of William the Conqueror. Their sister, Ealdgyth (who we shall talk about in detail later), married Harold Godwinson (Harold II) sometime in late 1065 or early 1066, and was the uncrowned Queen of England until Harold's death at Hastings in October 1066.

Godiva is believed to have died in 1067 and was most likely buried alongside her husband at Coventry; although the *Evesham Chronicle* claims that she was laid to rest in Holy Trinity, Evesham. In the thirteenth century, her death was remembered on 10 September, but we have no way of confirming the actual date.[16] After the Conquest, Godiva's lands were held by various personalities. Urse d'Albetot, Sheriff of Worcester, was in possession of Belbroughton; while Bell Hall was held by William Fitz Ansculf, who took over from Leofnoth, the brother of Leofric, a Mercian thegn who enjoyed a close relationship with the Earls of Mercia. Chaddesley Corbett, on the other hand, was held by Eadgifu (or Ealdgifu), a woman whose relationship to Godiva, if there was one, is unknown.

We have no contemporary description of Godiva, of her personality or appearance. Her patronage of such religious institutions as Stow St Mary and Coventry Abbey is testimony to her piety and generosity. Stories of this beneficence and devotion were known to later chroniclers, such as William of Malmesbury and Henry of Huntingdon. Henry of Huntingdon said of Godiva that her name 'meriting endless fame, was of distinguished worth, and founded the abbey at Coventry which she enriched with immense treasures of silver and gold. She also built the church at Stow, under the hill at Lincoln, and many others.'[17] Although Henry of Huntingdon's geography is a little skewed – Stow is a few miles north of Lincoln, rather than to the south, which 'under the hill' would suggest – it is obvious that Godiva's fame was still alive in the twelfth century.

Lady Godiva is, perhaps, the most famous Anglo-Saxon woman in history. Everyone knows her legend – or a variation of it. And that legend has only grown and expanded down the years; like the game of Chinese whispers, the story has been added to and enhanced with every retelling. It was probably her reputation for generosity that gave rise to the legend for which she is famous today. The story of Godiva's naked ride through Coventry appears to have been first recounted by Roger of Wendover, who died in 1236:

> The Countess Godiva devoutly anxious to free the city of Coventry from a grievous and base thralldom often besought the Count, her husband, that he would for the love of the Holy Trinity and the sacred Mother of God liberate it from such servitude. But he rebuked her for vainly demanding a thing so injurious to himself and forbade her to move further therein. Yet she, out of womanly pertinacity, continued to press the matter in so much that she obtained this answer from him: 'Ascend,' he said, 'thy horse naked and pass thus through the city from one end to the other in sight of the people and on thy return thou shalt obtain thy request.' Upon which she returned: 'And should I be willing to do this, wilt thou give me leave?' 'I will,' he responded. Then the Countess Godiva, beloved of God, ascended her horse, naked, loosing her long hair which clothed her entire body except her snow white legs, and having performed the journey, seen by none, returned with joy to her husband who, regarding it as a miracle, thereupon granted Coventry a Charter, confirming it with his seal.[18]

This legend has grown and expanded over time, providing inspiration for ballads, poetry, paintings and sculptures throughout the centuries. The legend arose from a story that Earl Leofric had introduced a toll on Coventry that the people could not afford to pay. Godiva went to her husband, begging that he rescind the taxes. He proved reluctant to offer the slightest reduction and is said to have told Godiva that he would only rescind the taxes if she rode naked through Coventry. In the earliest accounts Godiva rode through the market place, accompanied by two of Leofric's soldiers, with her long, golden hair let loose to protect her modesty. In the early versions, the religious element of the story is highlighted, with Leofric hailing the fact no one had seen her nakedness as a miracle.

The miraculous elements continued into the fourteenth century, when the tale claimed that Godiva had become invisible during the ride, in order to preserve her modesty. Every generation has told its own version of the legend, adding detail and embellishments. In Elizabethan times, the influence of the Reformation and the rise in Protestantism led to the highlighting of Godiva's 'womanhed' and of her 'modestie' and 'wisdom'. Coventry has transformed into a city, rather than the small village it was in Godiva's time:

But Gaufride sayth that this gentle and good lady did not onely for the freeing of the said Citie and satisfying of her husband's pleasure, graunt unto her sayde Husband to ride as aforesayde: But also called in secret manner (by such as she put special trust in) all those that then were Magistrates and rulers of the said Citie of Coventrie, and uttered unto them what good will she bare unto the sayde Citie, and how she had moved the Erle her husband to make the same free, the which upon such condition as is afore mencioned, the sayde Erle graunted unto her, which the sayde Lady was well contented to doe, requiring of them for the reverence of womanhed, that at that day and tyme that she should ride (which was made certaine unto them) that straight commaundement should be geuen throughout all the City, that everie person should shut in their houses and Wyndowes, and none so hardy to looke out into the streetes, nor remayne in the stretes, upon a very great paine, so that when the tyme came of her out ryding none sawe her, but her husbande and such as were present with him, and she and her Gentlewoman to wayte upon her galloped through the Towne, where the people might here the treading of their Horsse, but they saw her not, and so she returned to her Husbande from the place from whence she came, her honestie saved, her purpose obteyned, her wisdom much commended, and her husbands imagination utterly disappointed. And shortly after her returne, when she had arrayed and appareled herselfe in most comely and seemly manner, then she shewed herselfe openly to the people of the Citie of Coventry to the great joy and marvelous reioysing of all the Citizens and inhabitants of the same, who by her had received so great a benefite.[19]

This Elizabethan legend added the variation that Godiva had ordered the citizens of Coventry to remain in their houses, with doors and windows shuttered so that they would not witness her nakedness, rather than this being achieved through miraculous intervention. The story of Peeping Tom was a twist that was added to the legend in the eighteenth century, where he had disobeyed Godiva's command not to look, and was struck blind on witnessing the countess's naked ride. Whether the blinding is by divine intervention or by the furious people of Coventry depends on the storyteller. In 1820 the Rev'd John Moultrie introduced the divine retribution:

> The steed grew quiet, and a piercing cry
> Burst on Godiva's ear; – she started, and
> Beheld a man, who, in a window high,
> Shaded his dim eyes with his trembling hand.
> He had been led by curiosity
> To see her pass, and there had ta'en his stand;
> And as he gazed ('tis thus the story's read),
> His eye-balls sunk and shrivell'd in his head.[20]

The most famous version of the legend, and the one we would recognise today, was the poem written by Alfred, Lord Tennyson, in 1840 and published in 1842. Again highlighting the morals and priorities of its own time, rather than of Godiva's day, the poem is infused with Victorian romanticism at its best:

> Not only we, the latest seed of Time,
> New men, that in the flying of a wheel
> Cry down the past, not only we, that prate
> Of rights and wrongs, have loved the people well,
> And loathed to see them overtax'd; but she
> Did more, and underwent, and overcame,
> The woman of a thousand summers back,
> Godiva, wife to that grim Earl, who ruled

In Coventry: for when he laid a tax
Upon his town, and all the mothers brought
Their children, clamouring, 'If we pay, we starve!'
She sought her lord, and found him, where he strode
About the hall, among his dogs, alone,
His beard a foot before him, and his hair
A yard behind. She told him of their tears,
And pray'd him, 'If they pay this tax, they starve.'
Whereat he stared, replying, half-amazed,
'You would not let your little finger ache
For such as – these?' – 'But I would die,' said she.
He laugh'd, and swore by Peter and by Paul;
Then fillip'd at the diamond in her ear;
'O ay, ay, ay, you talk!'–'Alas!' she said,
'But prove me what it is I would not do.'
And from a heart as rough as Esau's hand,
He answer'd, 'Ride you naked thro' the town,
And I repeal it'; and nodding as in scorn,
He parted, with great strides among his dogs.
So left alone, the passions of her mind,
As winds from all the compass shift and blow,
Made war upon each other for an hour,
Till pity won. She sent a herald forth,
And bad him cry, with sound of trumpet, all
The hard condition; but that she would loose
The people: therefore, as they loved her well,
From then till noon no foot should pace the street,
No eye look down, she passing; but that all
Should keep within, door shut, and window barr'd.
Then fled she to her inmost bower, and there
Unclasp'd the wedded eagles of her belt,
The grim Earl's gift; but ever at a breath
She linger'd, looking like a summer moon
Half-dipt in cloud: anon she shook her head,
And shower'd the rippled ringlets to her knee;
Unclad herself in haste; adown the stair
Stole on; and, like a creeping sunbeam, slid
From pillar unto pillar, until she reach'd

The gateway; there she found her palfrey trapt
In purple blazon'd with armorial gold.
Then she rode forth, clothed on with chastity:
The deep air listen'd round her as she rode,
And all the low wind hardly breathed for fear.
The little wide-mouth'd heads upon the spout
Had cunning eyes to see: the barking cur
Made her cheek flame: her palfrey's footfall shot
Light horrors thro' her pulses: the blind walls
Were full of chinks and holes; and overhead
Fantastic gables, crowding, stared: but she
Not less thro' all bore up, till, last, she saw
The white-flower'd elder-thicket from the field
Gleam thro' the Gothic archways in the wall.
Then she rode back cloth'd on with chastity:
And one low churl, compact of thankless earth,
The fatal byword of all years to come,
Boring a little auger-hole in fear,
Peep'd – but his eyes, before they had their will,
Were shrivell'd into darkness in his head,
And dropt before him. So the Powers, who wait
On noble deeds, cancell'd a sense misused;
And she, that knew not, pass'd: and all at once,
With twelve great shocks of sound, the shameless noon
Was clash'd and hammer'd from a hundred towers,
One after one: but even then she gain'd
Her bower; whence reissuing, robed and crown'd,
To meet her lord, she took the tax away,
And built herself an everlasting name.[21]

The story has not just been kept to the written word, but also appears in numerous pieces of artwork and statuary, including the famous statue by Sir William Reid Dick, which is situated in Broadgate, in Coventry itself. Since 1678 the story has been re-enacted during the city's summer fair. The legend of Godiva has inspired such diverse projects and products as programs for social welfare and some delicious Belgian chocolates. Each century and generation has retold the story as a reflection of its own morals and influences. However, much as we would like the story of Godiva's selfless act to be true, there are many indications that the event never happened, at least not in the way it has been retold over the centuries. Eleventh-century Coventry was no 'city' but, at best, a small market town – and most likely little more than a village with less than a hundred houses. The fact that Coventry's Benedictine monastery was only founded in 1043 would bear this out, the town would only grow in importance once the monastery was established. Given that Leofric died in 1057, the monastery had been established for no more than fourteen years when Godiva is said to have made her memorable ride.

Another argument against the ride happening as Roger of Wendover, and all later chroniclers, told it is the social status of Godiva and her husband, Earl Leofric. It is hard to imagine that the Earl of Mercia, one of the most powerful men in the kingdom after the king himself, would demean himself and his family by allowing his wife to appear naked in front of his people, the people who owed him loyalty and service. Such an act by his wife would be more likely to make him a laughing stock and be an embarrassment, as opposed to enhancing his reputation and status – and the same could be said of Lady Godiva. The story of Godiva cannot be ignored, however, and many such legends are born out of a kernel of truth. That Godiva rode through Coventry naked is a little too fanciful to be true for my liking, but that she pleaded with her husband, Leofric, for a reprieve from crippling taxes for Coventry's townspeople is not unfeasible. Many kings and noblemen were known to have shown mercy after the intercession of their wives. The most famous example comes from the time of Edward III when his queen, Philippa of Hainault, pleaded with him for the lives of the six burghers of Calais, chosen to die so that their town would be saved from total destruction. Such instances were staged so that a king or lord could back down without showing weakness or indecision on his part, instead he was answering the pleas of a concerned wife. It was part of a noblewoman's role in the Middle Ages, to be the visible conscience and instrument of mercy for her husband.

One highly plausible explanation for the origin of the Lady Godiva story is pilgrimage. Godiva was known for her deep piety and patronage of religious houses. And pilgrimage was a well-established tradition at the time. If Godiva had performed a pilgrimage through Coventry, to the shrine of Saint Osburh of Coventry, a local saint, such an act may well be the origin of the later story. Pilgrims were expected to approach shrines barefoot and devoid of jewels and finery, and therefore any outward signs of status and wealth. If Godiva had performed such a pilgrimage in basic clothing, or in her undergarments, she would, effectively, have appeared 'as naked' of her status and wealth to a general, admiring populace. That the story was then embellished, exaggerated and altered to the one we know today could simply be the consequence of misheard rumours and half-truths, until we get the naked ride through Coventry.

However it originated, we can be certain that the story has been altered and reinvented across almost one thousand years. Short of the discovery of a contemporary chronicle recounting the story, we will never know the extent of the veracity of the story, but it does not stop us speculating. What we do know is that Godiva – or Godgifu – was real. A pious, generous and noble countess who was wife, mother and grandmother of earls – and grandmother of a queen of England. According to William of Malmesbury, she and Leofric were 'generous in their deeds towards God, built many monasteries, such as Coventry, St Mary's at Stow, Wenlock, Leon, and some others; to Coventry he consigned his body, with a very large donation of gold and silver.'[22] Godiva played a part in England's story before the Conquest and her grandchildren were significant actors in the events of 1066. In whatever way she is remembered, one thing is certain; that she does indeed deserve to be remembered.

4

Gytha of Wessex

Gytha of Wessex completes the triumvirate of remarkable women in the first half of the eleventh century in England, whose families were at the centre of events before, during and after 1066. A woman of impeccable pedigree, Gytha was the mother of a large brood of children that included several earls and the queen of Edward the Confessor.

Raised in Denmark, Gytha was the daughter of Thorgils Sprakaleg, a Danish magnate who was said to have been the grandson of a bear and a Swedish maiden.[1] Although obviously not true, such a legend serves to weave a sense of mystery into a family. Gytha was probably either born in the last decade of the tenth century or the first decade of the eleventh, and she had at least two brothers. One brother, Earl Ulf, was married to King Cnut's sister, Estrith, and was the father of Swein Estrithson, King of Denmark, from 1047 to 1076. Ulf had two other children, Beorn Estrithson and Asbjørn. Beorn spent time with his aunt's family and appears later in Gytha's story. Ulf acted as Regent of Denmark for King Cnut before he was killed, apparently on the orders of Cnut himself. The other of Gytha's known brothers is Eilaf, who was Earl of Gloucestershire under King Cnut.

It was in about 1022 that Gytha was married to Godwin. According to *The Life of King Edward*, commissioned by Gytha's daughter, Queen Edith, it was early in his reign that King Cnut took Godwin with him to Denmark, where the king 'tested more closely his wisdom', and 'admitted [him] to his council and gave him his sister [*sic*] as wife'.[2] Although Gytha was not, in fact, Cnut's sister, she was a part of the extended Danish royal family and giving her to Godwin as a wife was a substantial reward and a sign of Cnut's trust in him. What Gytha thought of being given in marriage to a man below her station, no matter how much a favourite of Cnut's he was, we can only surmise. We can assume that she probably had little say in the matter; once Cnut had decided on the marriage, who could refuse such a powerful king?

It is likely that Godwin was the son of Wulfnoth Cild, a Sussex thegn who fell foul of the politics and political machinations of the reign of Æthelred II the Unready. The appellation 'Cild' denotes a young man or warrior and is usually applied to those of rank in Anglo-Saxon England. In 1009 Wulfnoth had been accused of treason by Brihtric, the brother of the powerful and wily Eadric Streona. What treason he had committed is unclear, and there is a suggestion that the charges were unfounded. The accusations came during the muster of the magnificent new fleet, built on the orders of Æthelred II to counter the incursions of the Scandinavians. Wulfnoth fled in the face of these allegations, taking twenty of the new ships with him. According to the *Anglo-Saxon Chronicle,* Brihtric went in pursuit of him with eighty ships, but his force was run aground in a heavy storm and then attacked by Wulfnoth, who set fire to Brihtric's ships. The destruction of the greater part of the fleet put an end to any hope of campaigning off the English coast and Æthelred gave up on the project and went home, despite the fact the fleet had been a year in the building and had cost a considerable sum.[3]

In 1014 Godwin was left an estate at Compton in Sussex by the ætheling, Æthelstan, son and heir of Æthelred. The estate had originally belonged to Godwin's father Wulfnoth and was supposedly returned to Wulfnoth's line when Æthelstan left it to Godwin in his will. Although we cannot be certain that the Godwin mentioned in Æthelstan's will and Gytha's husband are one and the same, Gytha's Godwin was later, in fact, in possession of an estate at Compton in Sussex, suggesting this is the case. There is a possibility that Godwin was married to Thyra before he married Gytha. Thyra was, according to William of Malmesbury, Cnut's sister, and is said to have had a son who, while out riding a horse 'was carried into the Thames, and perished in the stream: his mother, too, paid the penalty of her cruelty; being killed by a stroke of lightning. For it is reported, that she was in the habit of purchasing companies of slaves in England, and sending them into Denmark; more especially girls, whose beauty and age rendered them more valuable, that she might accumulate money by this horrid traffic.'[4] Although this first marriage seems to have been an impressive one for the son of a discredited thegn, as Wulfnoth's reputation was dubious to the English, the Danes may not have felt the same.

According to *The Life of King Edward*, Cnut was impressed with Godwin, thinking him a man 'the most cautious in counsel and the most active in war'.[5] Although *The Life of King Edward* claims Cnut made Godwin an earl on their return to England, he was in fact attesting as such from 1018. However, he would have only held the eastern part of Wessex at that time as Æthelweard was ealdorman of the western shires until 1020, when he was banished. The timeline appears confused, but it does seem more likely that the visit to Denmark happened in 1022–3 when Cnut and his regent in the country, Thurkill the Tall, Earl of East Anglia, had a falling out. Thurkill disappears from the historical records in 1023 and it was from then on that Godwin appears as the foremost earl on Cnut's charters. It is also from that time that Godwin appears as the Earl of all Wessex, the first time one man had held the entire region since the Wessex kingdom of Alfred the Great and his son Edward the Elder. Control of Wessex was all the more significant because of the make-up of Cnut's Anglo-Danish empire. The earl who controlled the ports on the south coast controlled the access, from England, to Denmark and the rest of the empire. It was surely a sign of Cnut's trust in Godwin that he was given such power and influence.

Godwin appears to have accumulated considerable lands during the reign of Cnut. Although only one charter survives from the period, in which Cnut granted him Polhampton in Hampshire, Godwin also possessed manors in Kent, Sussex and Hampshire, some of which had previously belonged to the royal estates in the reign of Æthelred II. Although we don't hear of Gytha at this time – the chronicles rarely mention the women – we can assume that she enjoyed and benefitted from the favour her husband received from King Cnut. It is likely that she spent most of her time in the 1020s and 1030s giving birth to, and raising, her large brood of children. Gytha and Godwin had a large family of at least ten – possibly eleven – children.

Their daughter Edith was probably born within a year of the marriage and would become Queen of England as the wife of King Edward the Confessor. Although we cannot be certain of the order of births, the eldest son seems likely to have been Swein, who was born in about 1023, with Harold – the future King Harold II – probably arriving the year after. Five more sons followed; Tostig, Gyrth, Leofwine, Wulfnoth and possibly Alfgar. Tostig, Gyrth and Leofwine all became earls under Edward the Confessor and were deeply involved in the events of 1066, although not all on the same side. While still only a child, Wulfnoth was taken to Normandy as a hostage in about 1052, with his nephew, Hakon (the son of Wulfnoth's older brother, Swein). Wulfnoth died sometime after 1087, but whether in England or Normandy is unclear. It seems likely that young Hakon died whilst still a hostage in Normandy, although there is also a possibility he was released into Harold's custody in 1064. Little is known of Alfgar; if he existed, he may have been a monk at Reims in France. As well as Edith, Gytha and Godwin are thought to have had two or three more daughters. Little is known of Eadgiva (or Eadgifu), but for her name and that she held the comital estate of Crewkerne in Somerset; she is also on a list of women in confraternity with the New Minster at Winchester but may have been dead by 1066.[6] A younger daughter, Gunhilda, is believed to have become a nun after the Conquest, either at St Omer in France or Bruges in Flanders. Gunhilda died at Bruges on 24 August 1087 and is buried in Bruges Cathedral.[7]

Another daughter, Ælfgifu or Elgiva, was thought to have died around 1066. However, it seems likely that this daughter is spurious and has been mistakenly added to the Godwinson brood. It has been proposed that she is the lady Ælfgiva, who is represented in the Bayeux Tapestry, suggesting that she was offered as a bride to one of Duke William of Normandy's sons by her brother King Harold, then Earl of Wessex. The confusion comes about from the fact that Ælfgifu is mentioned in the Buckinghamshire folios of Domesday Book as 'Ælfgifu, sister of Earl Harold'.[8] According to Ann Williams, this Ælfgifu's inclusion in the Godwinson family has arisen from the mistaken identity of her brother. Although Harold

Godwinson was the famed Earl of Wessex before the Norman Conquest, Ælfgifu was in fact the sister of a thegn called Harold, not the earl. Ann Williams argues that the confusion arose from the habit of the Domesday scribes to include the pre-Conquest titles of landholders in their entries. As Earl Harold of Wessex was one of the largest landholders before the Conquest, the scribe made the mistake of ascribing the land titles to him, rather than the thegn of the same name, accidentally adding the title *comitis* (earl) to the name *Heraldi* (Harold) in the entry for Waldridge, and thus assigning another daughter to Gytha.[9]

The extent of Godwin's power and influence was clearly demonstrated after King Cnut's death in 1035, when two of Cnut's sons, Harthacnut and Harold Harefoot, emerged as rival claimants for the English throne. Although it has been suggested that the succession had been left to Harthacnut, Cnut's son by Emma of Normandy, this is by no means certain. Harthacnut was in Denmark when his father died, defending the country against a Norwegian invasion. Harold Harefoot, who was Cnut's son by Ælfgifu of Northampton, was in England, however, and mounted a challenge for the throne. During an assembly at Oxford, Harold was supported by Leofric, Earl of Mercia, the fleet in London, and the thegns of Mercia and the north. It is a sign of Godwin's power that his support of Harthacnut, whose interests were championed by his mother, Queen Emma, led the two sides to seek a compromise. In the end, it was agreed that Harold Harefoot would act as governor, or regent, of England for himself and Harthacnut. It was agreed that the kingdom would be divided, with Harold ruling in the north and Harthacnut ruling in the south.[10] Emma was allowed to settle in Wessex and hold that part of the country for Harthacnut. According to the *Anglo-Saxon Chronicle* Earl Godwin was her 'most loyal man'.[11]

Despite this accolade, in 1036 Earl Godwin was implicated in a crime that would cause him a great deal of trouble during the reign of Edward the Confessor. It was the year that Emma's sons by Æthelred II, who had been exiled, both mounted expeditions to England. Edward's attempt is only mentioned by Norman chroniclers; he landed at Southampton but was opposed by a large English army. According to William of Jumièges, Edward won the ensuing battle, but decided that further success would elude him without a larger army. He therefore 'turned the fleet about and, richly laden with booty, sailed back to Normandy'.[12] However, Alfred's return to England is covered in detail in chronicles from both sides of the English Channel, although the extent of Godwin's involvement in events differs with each chronicler. Alfred landed in Kent in the autumn of 1036, ostensibly intending to visit his mother, who resided on her estate at Winchester. Although the chronicles differ on some of the details, all agree that shortly after Alfred's arrival on English shores, he was met by Earl Godwin. The *Anglo-Saxon Chronicle* claims that the men of power, including Godwin, were not happy at Alfred's arrival and unjustly favoured Harold as their ruler. Added to the fact that the æthelings' father's failings were still vivid in the memories of the nobles, they would have worried that a contest for the throne threatened to destabilise the country and would have wanted to avoid civil war at any cost. The level of Godwin's involvement in Alfred's tragic demise is still debated. Strangely, the *Anglo-Saxon Chronicle* recounts the events in rhyme:

> Him did Godwin let, and in prison set.
> His friends, who did not fly, they slew promiscuously.
> And those they did not sell, like slaughter'd cattle fell!
> Whilst some they spared to bind, only to wander blind!
> Some ham-strung, helpless stood, whilst others they pursued.
> A deed more dreary none in this our land was done,
> since Englishmen gave place to hordes of Danish race.
> But repose we must in God our trust,
> that blithe as day with Christ live they,
> who guiltless died – their country's pride!
> The prince with courage met each cruel evil yet;
> till 'twas decreed, they should him lead,
> all bound as he was then, to Ely-bury fen.
> But soon their royal prize bereft they of his eyes!
> Then to the monks they brought their captive; where he sought
> a refuge from his foes till life's sad evening close.
> His body ordered then these good and holy men, according to
> his worth,

low in the sacred earth, to the steeple full-nigh,
in the south aisle to lie of the transept west –
his soul with Christ doth rest.[13]

It can be argued that, having initially sided with Harthacnut and Emma, the arrival of Alfred offered Godwin the opportunity to switch his allegiance to Harold Harefoot, and prove his loyalty to his new master, all at once. Godwin took Alfred to Guildford, diverting the young prince from his aim of reaching London or his mother. Alfred and his men having feasted and drunk their fill, were seized in the darkness of night. Alfred was taken to Harold, who ordered his blinding and imprisonment, while many of the ætheling's companions were slain. While there seems to be little doubt that Godwin was complicit in these events, the level of his involvement is open to question. The least biased source on the events, William of Jumièges, claims that it was Godwin's men who killed Alfred's companions, while the ætheling was spared in order to be handed over to Harold, while the *Encomium Emma Reginae* lays the blame squarely at Harold's door, claiming it was his men who launched the attack on Guildford in the dead of night and were responsible for the killings.[14]

Gytha would not have been involved in these events and may not have even known of the extent of her husband's involvement. However, they were to have a profound effect on her life and that of her family in later years, during the reign of Edward the Confessor, who could not easily forget his brother's death, nor the manner of it. Nevertheless, the immediate result of the 'single worst atrocity in England since the Danish conquest', was that Godwin was now in favour with Harold Harefoot.[15] Given that there was still no sign of Harthacnut's return to England to claim the throne, Godwin's support now meant that in 1037 Harold was chosen as 'king over all' and Emma of Normandy was driven from England, seeking refuge in Bruges in Flanders.[16]

The events of Harold's reign, and by extension Godwin's involvement in them, have gone unrecorded. In the years immediately following the murder of Alfred, the *Anglo-Saxon Chronicle* talks of little but the deaths of bishops and abbots, and a great gale. There is mention of the brother of Earl Leofric of Mercia being killed by the Welsh; but regarding Godwin and his family the chronicles are silent. However, on 17 March 1040, King Harold died at Oxford and was buried in London. The fact there is no mention of cause of death in the chronicles suggests it was a natural event, rather than anything more sinister – murder would surely have been commented upon. The *Anglo-Saxon Chronicle* records, 'he ruled England four years and sixteen weeks; and in his day as sixteen ships were retained in pay, at the rate of eight marks for each rower, in like manner as had been before done in the days of King Cnut.'[17]

Harold's death forestalled Harthacnut's impending invasion. The younger man had rejoined his mother in Flanders in 1039 and had spent the subsequent winter planning his invasion of England. In 1041 the English sent for him 'supposing they did well'.[18] According to John of Worcester, Harthacnut arrived before midsummer and was 'received with universal joy and shortly afterwards crowned'.[19] One of Harthacnut's very first acts was to have his half-brother's body exhumed from his grave, beheaded and flung into the Thames Marshes. John of Worcester has Earl Godwin supervising this irreverent act. Harthacnut taxed his people heavily and soon turned everyone against him, 'and he became thoroughly detested by those who at first were most anxious for his coming.'[20]

As for Godwin, with the protection of King Harold removed, Harthacnut blamed him for the death of his half-brother, Alfred. While accusations had been left unsaid during Harold's reign, Ælfric, the Archbishop of York, now openly accused Godwin and Lyfing, Bishop of Worcester, of the murder. Godwin, 'to obtain the king's favour, presented him with a galley of admirable workmanship, with a gilded figurehead, rigged with the best materials, and manned with eighty chosen soldiers splendidly armed.'[21] He also made an oath to the king, with almost all the chief men and greater thegns in England as witness, that it was not by his counsel, or at his instance, that his brother's eyes were put out, but that he had only obeyed the commands of his lord, King Harold.'[22]

In 1040 Harthacnut also recalled his half-brother, Edward, from Normandy to join him as co-ruler, perhaps with an eye to the succession, given that there is no evidence that Harthacnut ever married and therefore had no legitimate children. Harthacnut's rule proved to be an unhappy one for the people of England. Although he taxed for the maintenance of the fleet at the same level as his predecessors, Harold and Cnut, at a rate of eight marks for each rower, the two previous kings had only kept a fleet of sixteen ships, while Harthacnut had a fleet of sixty-two, almost quadrupling the amount of tax that needed to be raised. Despite the fact he reduced his fleet to thirty-two ships in 1041, this would still mean the tax was twice the size it had been in the previous reigns. In May 1041, this level of high taxation resulted in the murder of two of Harthacnut's housecarls, called Feader and Thurstan, according to John of Worcester, who had been sent to Worcester to oversee the tax collection. The king responded by sending an army against Worcester, ordering them to 'put to death all the inhabitants they could find, to plunder and burn the city, and lay waste the whole province'.[23] Earl Godwin was one of the earls put in command of the army, alongside Leofric, Earl of Mercia and Siward, Earl of Northumbria. The war host arrived in Worcester in November and proceeded to ravage the town for four days, but with little loss of life as the citizens had been aware of their impending arrival. A large number of the citizens established themselves on a small island, Beverege, which they had fortified. From there, they resisted Harthacnut's army so well that the earls offered them terms, in which they were allowed to return to their homes. On the fifth day, with the city burned, the army marched away, loaded with plunder.

Therefore, when Harthacnut died unexpectedly in 1042, it was not a sad event. It happened while he was celebrating at the wedding feast of Githa, daughter of Osgod Clapa, at Lambeth, when 'as he stood drinking: he fell suddenly to the earth with a tremendous struggle ... and he spoke not a word afterwards, but expired on the sixth day before the ides of June.'[24] He died on 8 June 1042 and was buried beside his father in Winchester's Old Minster, mourned by none but his mother, Queen Emma.

Despite the fact he had spent more than half his life in exile, Edward, son of Æthelred II and Emma of Normandy and a half-brother of Harthacnut, was the natural and obvious successor. He had spent the last few months living at Harthacnut's court as his brother's co-king, and was chosen as Harthacnut's replacement before his predecessor had even been buried. He was crowned at Winchester on Easter Day 1043 amid much pomp. In the same year,

Edward rode from Gloucester to Winchester, with the Earls Godwin, Siward and Leofric by his side, to relieve his mother of the royal treasury. According to the *Anglo-Saxon Chronicle* this was 'because she was formerly very hard upon the king her son, and did less for him than he wished before he was king.'[25] This was the new king's way of cutting his mother down to size and showing that he was firmly in command. Mother and son were reconciled within a year, although Emma was never to enjoy the same relationship with Edward as she had done with Harthacnut, nor was held in the same esteem as queen as she had been previously.

During the early years of the reign of Edward the Confessor, Godwin's power continued to grow. Edward had spent most of his life in Norman exile and had few friends and supporters in England; in fact, he was a virtual unknown. The support of the powerful Earl Godwin was essential to the success of his accession to the throne. Godwin's influence was demonstrated in 1044 when he secured the appointment of Siward, Abbott of Abingdon, as assistant bishop to the increasingly infirm Archbishop Eadsige of Canterbury. The new bishop was consecrated 'with the permission and advice of the king and Earl Godwin'.[26] Godwin, it seems, was given episcopal manors of Richborough, Sundridge, Saltwood, and Langport and the lands of the secular minster at Folkestone, in return for his support. Among the lands acquired by Godwin during the 1040s was Woodchester in Gloucestershire, which he bought for Gytha.[27] The manor was intended to support her when she stayed at Berkeley, for 'she was unwilling to use up anything from that manor because of the destruction of the abbey.'[28]

As Godwin's star continued to rise; so too did that of his family. In 1043 an earldom, centred on Hereford, had been created for his eldest son, Swein, and in 1044 Harold, the next oldest, was made Earl of East Anglia. Gytha must have been proud to see her husband and sons rise so high, and surely was overjoyed as she became the mother of a queen when her eldest daughter, Edith, married King Edward on 23 January 1045. The family must have appeared unassailable to their fellow and rival nobles. Their extended family was also benefitting from the patronage of King Edward, as Gytha's nephew, Beorn Estrithson, was given an earldom later in 1045. It is highly likely that it was in the 1040s that the family received from the king the royal and comital lands that were listed in Domesday Book as belonging to Godwin and Gytha, including Bosham in Sussex.

For Gytha, it was mostly a time for pride in her children, although one of her sons would disappoint and humiliate her. Swein Godwinson was, by most accounts, an unpleasant man. Although a notable fighter, he was ruthless and determined. In 1046 he had campaigned successfully in South Wales alongside Gruffudd ap Llywelyn of Gwynedd. However, it was on his return from this campaign that he 'commanded the abbess of Leominster to be fetched to him, and kept her as long as it suited him, and afterwards let her travel home.'[29] It is possible that Swein had intended to marry the abbess, named as Eadgiva by John of Worcester, in order to gain control of the vast Leominster estates.[30] The king, however, and probably rightly so, refused to give his permission for the marriage and Eadgiva was returned to her abbey. Eadgiva may well have been the mother of Swein's one known child, a son named Hakon, who would be held as a hostage in Normandy for many years.

Having been refused permission to marry Eadgiva, Swein left England soon after, seeking refuge for the winter of 1047/8 with Count Baldwin in Flanders. Count Baldwin was not on the best of terms with Edward the Confessor and was renowned for harbouring the enemies of England's king. Swein then made his way to Denmark where his cousin, Swein Estrithson, was battling to establish himself as King of Denmark. Swein Godwinson, it is said, 'there ruined himself with the Danes'.[31] He returned to England in 1049, hoping to obtain a pardon from the king. Although few were happy to see him, his cousin, Beorn, agreed to accompany him to King Edward and aid him in his attempts to recover his lands. At the same time, Osgod Clapa, who had himself been outlawed in 1046, had gathered a fleet at Wulpe and King Edward ordered the fleet to assemble under Earl Godwin and Beorn, to protect the country against invasion. The English fleet was at Pevensey, while Swein's ships lay at Bosham. Having persuaded his cousin to accompany him to the king at Sandwich, the treacherous Swein had Beorn dragged aboard one of his ships at Bosham and killed, before burying him in a shallow grave.

It seems likely that this was an act of revenge on Swein's part, for Beorn's presence at the Witan which had declared him *nithing* (wretch, coward) and outlawed him. For this heinous murder of his own kinsman, Swein was again outlawed, many of his own men deserted him and he fled to Bruges with just two ships (he had arrived with eight).[32] Beorn's body was later recovered and buried in Winchester, close to his uncle, King Cnut.

It is not difficult to imagine that Gytha was doing some behind-the-scenes pleading with her husband to try to get her son back into the king's good books. On the other hand, it is also possible that she had had more than enough of Swein's deadly antics. One source suggests that Swein had, at some point, impugned his mother's reputation, claiming that he was not the son of Godwin but of the former king Cnut. The claim was indignantly refuted by Gytha, who gathered together the noble ladies of Wessex to witness her oath that Godwin was Swein's father.[33] It is not impossible to imagine what must have gone through Gytha's mind when Swein made this claim. To be so blatantly accused of infidelity by her eldest son, someone who should have had a care for his mother's reputation, must have been heartbreaking. Whether it was a political move – to pursue a claim to the throne as Cnut's heir – or not, Swein effectively rejected Godwin as his father and called his mother an unfaithful wife. Poor Gytha.

Swein's behaviour, first with his abduction of Eadgiva and then his murder of Beorn, did not help his father to maintain his pre-eminence at King Edward's court. Godwin's position had appeared unassailable at the start of Edward's reign, with his sons and daughter benefitting from Edward's gratitude for Godwin's support. As Marc Morris states, without the support of Godwin, Edward 'would probably have found himself out of a job'.[34] However, as his reign progressed, Edward found himself more able to withstand Godwin, gaining allies among the elite, who chafed under Godwin's control. For example, when Swein Estrithson asked for support in his attempts to claim the Danish throne, while Godwin was in favour of sending aid to his nephew, suggesting England could afford to dispatch fifty ships, Edward refused. The king was supported by Earl Leofric of Mercia, although whether this was a deliberate cultivation on Edward's part, or Leofric wanting to curb Godwin's power, is unclear. However, Godwin's strength was such that he was capable of overcoming these setbacks. Despite the crimes of his son Swein, he was able to negotiate the errant earl's return within months of his second banishment. Through the mediation of Godwin's friend, Ealdred, Bishop of Worcester, Swein was given a royal pardon and allowed to come back to England.

Nevertheless, the king and his foremost earl were now on a collision course, which was to come to a head in 1051. Following the death of Eadsige, Archbishop of Canterbury, in October 1050, the monks of Canterbury, who had the right to choose his successor, selected Æthelric and asked Earl Godwin to obtain the king's approval of their choice. Given that Æthelric was his own kinsman, Godwin readily agreed. However, possibly with a view to curbing Godwin's power, and certainly with a desire not to see his power enhanced any further, Edward refused to support the appointment. The king had his own candidate in mind and seeing as he had the final say in the appointment of abbots and bishops, it was Edward's candidate who was installed as the new Archbishop of Canterbury. This candidate was Robert of Jumièges, Bishop of London, and former abbot of Jumièges in Normandy, who had accompanied Edward to England in 1041 and was 'the most powerful confidential adviser of the king'.[35] His appointment as Archbishop of Canterbury would act as a balance to Godwin's power, and demonstrate that it was Edward who was in charge.

It may have been at this time that Edward informed the Witan that he was naming William, Duke of Normandy, as his heir. The king had been married to Edith, Godwin's daughter, for six years and there has always been the assumption that Edward had taken a vow of celibacy, or that Edward refused to consummate the marriage because Edith was the daughter of Godwin. Whatever the reason, the marriage was childless, and Edward needed to look to the succession. The fact that Edward named William is only mentioned in the Norman Chronicles – the English chronicles are silent on the matter – and it is possible this claim was inserted after the Conquest, but it remains a possibility. If it happened, it would have surely angered Godwin, who had hoped that his grandson would one day rule.

With these events in the background, a confrontation was bound to arise. The spark was a visit by King Edward's brother-in-law, Eustace, Count of Boulogne. The purpose of the visit has remained a mystery, the *Anglo-Saxon Chronicle* merely stating he 'turned to the king and spoke with him about what he wanted, and then turned homeward.'[36] It was during this homeward journey that Eustace's men, whilst looking for lodgings in Dover, tried to force themselves on one householder, who was killed for refusing to accommodate them. A fracas ensued in which a number of men on both sides were slain. Eustace quickly returned to his brother-in-law at Gloucester to give his account of the events, no doubt playing down the role of his own men and squarely laying the blame at the feet of the citizens of Dover. Edward was incensed and ordered the harrying of the town as punishment, much as Harthacnut had done at Worcester, delegating the duty to its earl, Godwin. The earl, however, was 'loth to destroy his own people'.[37]

Angry at this refusal to obey him, the king called a council to be convened at Gloucester. Godwin, incensed that his own people (in Dover) had been attacked, began to gather his forces from throughout his earldom. His sons, Swein and Harold, did likewise in their lands. They mustered at Beverstone, 15 miles south of Gloucester. Finally determined to confront his father-in-law, Edward summoned the earls Leofric and Siward and their men. With the two armies about to face each other, and the country on the brink of civil war, some sought to prevent the confrontation 'because it was very unwise that they should come together; for in the two armies was there almost all that was noblest in England.'[38]

The two sides came back from the brink, with Godwin agreeing to go to London in two weeks' time to stand trial. Hostages were exchanged as surety for the earl's attendance. When Earl Godwin and King Edward finally faced each other, Edward demanded the impossible, while at the same time, making his feelings for Godwin clear. The king offered to take the earl back into his peace 'when he gave him back his brother alive.'[39] Earl Godwin's involvement in the death of Edward's brother, Alfred, had come back to haunt him. Godwin would have known, at that moment, that there was no chance of reconciliation. The earl rode away from London, returning to Bosham. John of Worcester takes up the story:

... but his army gradually dwindling away and deserting him, he did not venture to abide the judgment of the king's court, but fled, under cover of night. When, therefore, the morning came, the king, in his witan, with the unanimous consent of the whole army, made a decree that Godwin and his five sons should be banished. Thereupon he and his wife Gytha, and Tostig and his wife Judith, the daughter of Baldwin, count of Flanders, and two of his other sons, namely, Sweyn and Gyrth, went, without loss of time, to Thorney, where a ship had been got ready for them. They quickly laded her with as much gold, silver, and other valuable articles as she could hold, and, embarking in great haste, directed her course towards Flanders and Baldwin the count.[40]

Godwin and Gytha's two other sons, Harold and Leofwine, were heading west; arriving at Bristol, they took Swein's ship, which had already been prepared and provisioned for him, and sailed to exile in Ireland. The couple's youngest son, Wulfstan, and Swein's son, Hakon, may already have been in the custody of King Edward as hostages. Queen Edith, therefore, was the only Godwin who remained at liberty in England, although not for long. She was banished to the nunnery at Wherwell, where Edward's half-sister was abbess; her land, jewels and possessions were taken from her and Edward may have started divorce proceedings, though they were never completed. Of Godwin's dramatic downfall, the *Anglo-Saxon Chronicle* declared: 'Wonderful would it have been thought by every man that was then in England, if any person had said that it would end thus! For he was before raised to such a height, that he ruled the king and all England; his sons were earls, and the king's darlings; and his daughter wedded and united to the king.'[41]

Godwin and Gytha, along with Swein, Tostig and the family's retainers, spent the winter in Bruges from where Swein, looking to the salvation of his soul, set out on pilgrimage to Jerusalem. According to John of Worcester, Swein walked the whole way, barefoot, but caught a cold on the way home and died at Lycia; however, the *Anglo-Saxon Chronicle* places his death at Constantinople. Wherever the event, the outcome was the same; Swein, the troubled – and troublesome – eldest son was dead, and Harold was now his father's heir. Swein died on 29 September

1052, the news reaching England just before the end of the year. Gytha's grief at the death Swein would have been somewhat diminished by the fact that he died whilst on pilgrimage; an act that would have gone a long way to guaranteeing the salvation of his soul, which had been somewhat blackened by his kidnapping of the abbess Eadgiva and the murder of his own cousin, Beorn.

In the spring of 1052, the family set about orchestrating their return to England. Their fleet sailed at midsummer, slipping past Sandwich and landing farther up the Kent coast. However, a storm forced Godwin to return to Flanders, but the inactivity of the English fleet afforded Godwin a new opportunity. He again set sail for England, attacked the Isle of Wight and was reunited with his sons, Harold and Leofwine, newly arrived from Ireland. They proceeded along the Sussex and Kent coasts, acquiring such provisions and men that, as they reached Sandwich, they had an 'overwhelming host'.[42] They proceeded to London unopposed and anchored on the south bank of the Thames, opposite the forces of the king and his earls who were waiting on the north bank with fifty ships.

Godwin sent to the king, requesting the restoration of his lands and the lands of his sons, but Edward flatly refused. However, public opinion had turned against the king; his strong support for his Norman advisers, and the visit of William of Normandy soon after the Godwin's exile, had soured public opinion, which turned to favour Godwin and his family. Godwin's ships weighed anchor and sailed over to the north bank. Negotiations followed, accompanied by another exchange of hostages, but the two sides were at an impasse, unwilling to give ground. However, the Norman contingent of Edward's administration must have seen the way events were turning, and that Godwin would be welcomed back into the fold. They mounted their horses and fled London, some going north, some west, while Robert of Jumièges forced his way through the east gate, killing any who stood in his way. He made his way to the Essex coast, where he boarded a ship that was barely seaworthy and made it, eventually, to Normandy; presumably with Godwin and Gytha's son, Wulfstan, and their grandson, Hakon, as his hostages.

The following morning Godwin met the king in a council outside London. The Earl begged forgiveness of the king, declaring that he and his sons were innocent of the charges laid against them. Despite his underlying fury, Edward had no choice but to grant Godwin a pardon and restore the lands and titles of the whole family. According to the *Anglo-Saxon Chronicle*, Gytha is even mentioned in the agreement, whereby the council 'gave Godwin fairly his earldom, so full and so free as he at first possessed it, and his sons also all that they formerly had; and his wife and his daughter so full and so free as they formerly had.'[43] Soon after, their daughter, Edith, was fetched from her incarceration in the nunnery and reinstated as queen. Robert of Jumièges and a number of Edward's French advisers were declared outlaws 'because they chiefly made the discord between Earl Godwin and the king.'[44]

For Gytha, being back home, and once in again in the king's good graces, must have been tempered by the fact her youngest son, Wulfstan, and her grandson, Hakon, were now beyond her reach. Despite the fact she was surrounded by her grown children it is not difficult to imagine the fears she must have harboured for her youngest, her baby, and his young nephew. Wulfstan was probably ten years old, or maybe a little older; but Hakon, especially if he was the son of the abducted Abbess Eadgiva, may have been as young as five or six. The *Anglo-Saxon Chronicle* also mentions that Godwin fell sick shortly after the conclusion of negotiations with Edward.[45] Given that the earl died at Easter 1053, we can imagine that Gytha spent the winter nursing her ailing husband.

On Easter Sunday (12 April), Godwin was dining with his sons, Harold and Tostig, and King Edward, at Winchester, when 'he suddenly sank towards the foot-stool, deprived of speech and of all his strength; he was carried to the king's chamber, and it was thought it would pass over, but it was not so; but he continued like this unspeaking and helpless, through until the Thursday and then gave up his life. And he lies there in the Old Minster; and his son Harold succeeded to his earldom.'[46] John of Worcester records Godwin's death in similar vein: '... earl Godwin came to his end while he was sitting at table with the king, according to his usual custom; for, being suddenly seized with a violent illness, he fell speechless from his seat. His sons, earl Harold, Tostig, and Gyrth, perceiving it, carried him into the king's chamber, hoping that he would presently recover; but his strength failing, he died in great suffering on the fifth day afterwards [15th April] and was buried in the Old Minster.'[47] Writing later, with a flair for the dramatic, William of Malmesbury had Godwin's last words to Edward before he collapsed as: 'May God not permit me to swallow if I have done anything to endanger Alfred or to hurt you.'[48] Contemporary chronicles do not mention such a declaration, so while it makes Godwin's death appear as divine justice, it is more than likely untrue.

The ensuing years saw the rise of Gytha's sons. Harold had succeeded to his father's earldom of Wessex and in 1055 Tostig was given the earldom of Northumbria; Earl Siward had died at York, leaving only a young son, Waltheof, to succeed him. It was thought too dangerous to leave a county which bordered Scotland in the hands of a child, and so the earldom was awarded to Tostig. When Ælfgar succeeded to his father Leofric's earldom of Mercia in 1057, he had to relinquish the earldom of East Anglia, which was given to Gyrth, one of Gytha's younger sons. Another son, Leofwine, appears to have succeeded to part of the earldom of Ralph, Earl of Hereford, on his death in 1057, gaining lands in the south Midlands, including in Hertfordshire, Middlesex and Buckinghamshire.[49]

Gytha's movements over the years after Godwin's death have gone unrecorded. The widow of the great earl probably spent most of her time in retirement on her estates, possibly visiting her family on occasion and spending time at King Edward's court with her daughter, Queen Edith. However, her family was threatened yet again in 1065, when the Northumbrians revolted against her son Tostig's harsh rule. The rebellion was sparked by the murder of Gospatric, a scion of the house of Bamburgh and a son of Earl Uhtred the Bold, who was betrayed and murdered with the connivance of King Cnut in 1016. Given his heritage, Gospatric may well have believed that he had a greater right to the earldom of Northumbria than Tostig; the two men were regularly at loggerheads. The bad blood between Gospatric and Earl Tostig had resulted in the ambush and murder of two representatives of Gospatric while attending talks at York. Gospatric, it seems, took his grievances to the king; he was present at Edward's Christmas court in 1064. However, Gospatric was murdered on the fourth night of Christmas, supposedly on the orders of Queen Edith, Tostig's sister, in an attempt to help her brother.

If Queen Edith and Tostig hoped to quash any further dissent through Gospatric's death, they were soon proved mistaken. Unrest in Northumbria continued to grow. Tostig was rarely in the earldom, preferring to spend his time at court, with the king and his sister, and leaving the day-to-day governance of Northumbria to his representatives in the region. It was these representatives, therefore, who bore the brunt of the disaffection with Tostig's rule. According to John of Worcester, a force of 200 armed men, loyal to Gospatric, marched on York, killing about 200 of the earl's retainers, seizing his weapons and treasury, which were stored in the city.[50] The rebels then invited Morcar, the brother of Earl Edwin of Mercia, to become their earl. Morcar was the son of Earl Ælfgar of Mercia, who had died in about 1062, and therefore a grandson of Earl Leofric and Lady Godiva.

The rebellion gathered pace when Earl Edwin joined his own forces with those of Morcar, and the brothers were, in turn, joined by their Welsh allies. The king sent Earl Harold, who had become indispensable to Edward in recent years, to meet with the rebel army at Northampton; Harold's message to the rebels was to withdraw their army and take their grievances to the king. The rebels, however, demanded that Tostig should not only be removed from Northumbria, but banished from England altogether. When Harold returned to the king with the Northumbrians' demands, Tostig accused him of collusion with the rebels, though Harold swore it was not so. Harold, however, was unwilling to go into battle to restore his brother to his earldom. In fact, no one was prepared to restore Tostig by force; the king's own attempts to raise an army proved fruitless, possibly because no one wanted to see civil war in the country. Having run out of options, Edward acquiesced to the rebels' demands, this acceptance conveyed by Harold himself to the rebels, who were now at Oxford. Morcar was confirmed as Earl of Northumbria and the rights they had enjoyed in the past, called the 'Laws of Cnut' by the *Anglo-Saxon Chronicle*, were restored to the Northumbrians.

It must have caused Gytha great distress to see her son, Tostig, with his wife, young children and household, cross the English Channel to Flanders, on 1 November 1065. It was probably the last time she saw her son, as within eleven months he would be dead on the battlefield of Stamford Bridge. Her daughter, Queen Edith, too, was most distressed to see her favourite brother depart England's shores. Nevertheless, Tostig's departure was merely the start of a year of grief for both Gytha and her daughter, although it may not have felt that way during the start of the new year of 1066. On 5 January, Edward the Confessor breathed his last, leaving the kingdom to his brother-in-law, Earl Harold. Gytha must have seen Harold's hasty coronation on 6 January, in the newly rebuilt Westminster Abbey, as the crowning glory for the Godwinson clan, and a sign of new beginnings for all her children. However, if Harold expected a honeymoon period as king, he was to be sorely disappointed. By Easter, England was living in fear of invasion from Duke William of Normandy. These fears were further stoked when 'a sign such as men never saw before was seen in the heavens.'[51] The appearance of the great comet, later to be known as Halley's Comet, was seen as a portent for change in the kingdom.

The comet was visible every night for the whole of the last week of April, and no sooner had it disappeared than news arrived of a hostile fleet attacking England's shores. The threat did not come from Normandy, but from Gytha's exiled son, Tostig. How devastated she must have been, to see one son attacking another. It is possible that Tostig was looking to replace Harold as king but it seems more likely that he intended to recover his lost lands. However, Harold proved implacable and set out for Sandwich to confront Tostig. Tostig withdrew before his brother's arrival and sailed up the coast towards Northumbria, sailing into the River Humber, but he was seen off by the earls Morcar and Edwin and continued north, to seek refuge with King Malcolm of Scotland.

Having seen off his brother, Harold now prepared to face the greater threat of Duke William of Normandy. He stationed levies at points all along the south coast, watching and waiting for the arrival of William's ships. The fear and anticipation that gripped the country cannot have failed to affect Gytha, knowing that her sons were at the heart of events. Leofwine and Gyrth were stalwart in the support of Harold, whilst Tostig was brooding and planning in the court of the Scots king. Throughout the summer, everyone would have been on edge, watching, waiting, preparing. The months of anticipation must have been hard on them all, but in

September, Harold was forced to stand down his army, provisions had run out and 'no man could keep them there any longer. They therefore had leave to go home; and the king rode up, and the ships were driven to London; but many perished ere they came thither.'[52]

As the summer drew to a close, Harold received news that his brother, Tostig, had landed in the north with Harald Hardrada, King of Norway, and 300 ships. They defeated a force of Northumbrians, led by the Mercian brothers, earls Morcar and Edwin, at the Battle of Fulford on 20 September 1066. Tostig and Harald Hardrada then marched into the City of York, which surrendered to them, and from there they returned to their ships with their plunder. They offered peace to Northumbria, if the county supported Harald's bid for the throne. Having received news of the defeat at Fulford, King Harold force-marched his army the 190 miles from London to York in just four days, so that he was able to face the Scandinavians at Stamford Bridge, on the outskirts of the city, on 25 September. He was accompanied by two of his younger brothers, Gyrth and Leofwine. Some chronicles suggest that negotiations before the battle offered the return of Tostig's earldom. When Tostig asked what Harald Hardrada would get, King Harold responded, 'Six feet of ground or as much more as he needs, as he is taller than most men.'[53] The Northumbrian troops had suffered such heavy losses at Fulford that they were unable to join the battle at Stamford Bridge. However, King Harold's troops prevailed without their assistance and despite their near exhausted state after such a march. Harald Hardrada and Tostig were both killed in the battle, which saw about 11,000 of the estimated 20,000 combatants dead at the end of the day.

Harold had no time to savour his victory, nor mourn the loss of his brother, for three days after the battle Duke William of Normandy landed at Pevensey on the south coast. As soon as he received the news, Harold turned his army south and marched to face this new enemy. It may well be that he sent a messenger to his mother while en route, informing her of Tostig's death and of his own success. William of Jumièges states that Gytha tried to persuade Harold against facing Duke William. In the same, tense family conference, Harold's brother Gyrth offered to fight the Duke, 'since he had sworn no oath and owed nothing to him'.[54] Harold was enraged by the suggestion, he 'taunted Gyrth and even insolently kicked his mother Gytha who was trying to hold him back.'[55] By 14 October Harold had arrived at Senlac Hill, 7 miles north of Hastings, where he arrayed his army to face the opposing Normans. Stories have Gytha awaiting the outcome of the battle behind the lines, with Harold's handfast wife, Edith Swanneck. John of Worcester tells the story of the battle: 'The English being crowded in a confined position, many of them left their ranks, and few stood by him [Harold] with resolute hearts; nevertheless he made a stout resistance from the third hour of the day until nightfall, and defended himself with such courage and obstinacy, that the enemy almost despaired of taking his life. When, however, numbers had fallen on both sides, he, alas! fell at twilight.'[56] By the end of the day, three of Gytha's sons lay among the dead; Harold, Gyrth and Leofwine. It is also possible her grandson Hakon died on the field of battle; he was said to have returned to England with Harold in 1064, after being held hostage in Normandy since 1052. Although nothing definite is heard of the young man after his return, it seems likely that he joined the rest of the Godwinson clan to help defend his uncle's crown. According to William of Poitiers, 'Far and wide the earth was covered with the flower of the English nobility and youth, drenched in blood.'[57]

In the aftermath of the battle there is a heartrending story that Gytha and Edith walked the battlefield, searching for Harold's body, which was said to be recognisable by marks that only Edith, his lover of twenty years, would know (probably tattoos). It was reported that Gytha offered Duke William the weight of Harold's body in gold, if she could be allowed to take him for burial. William refused, with an angry retort, saying it would be unfair to bury him, given that so many remained unburied on the field on his account. However, most sources suggest that William then ordered that Harold be buried in an unmarked grave, on a cliff overlooking England's shores. Other stories have Harold's remains being claimed by Edith and taken for burial at Harold's own foundation of Waltham Abbey. Whether it was Gytha or Edith who identified Harold, whether he was buried in Waltham Abbey or an unmarked grave close to the sea, the tragedy for Gytha and Edith was that Harold was dead and William was now England's ruler.

As William consolidated his hold on England and as she was grieving the loss of four sons within a space of three weeks, Gytha probably retreated to her estates in Wessex. Her one surviving son, Wulfnoth, was still a hostage in Normandy and so nothing more is heard of her until 1068. Gytha appears to have settled in the west of Wessex, for she and her family were implicated in a conspiracy in Exeter, from where messages were being sent to other cities urging rebellion. It appears that Gytha planned a Godwinson revival with the sons of Harold and Edith Swanneck. In their late teens or early twenties, the boys fled to Ireland after the death of their father and were now plotting to return with an invasion fleet. Edith and Harold had at least three – possibly four – sons; Godwine, Edmund, Magnus and possibly Ulf (although he may have been Harold's son by his queen, Ealdgyth). The plot, according to Orderic Vitalis, was 'supported by the Danes and other barbarous peoples'.[58] King William had just returned from Normandy when the conspiracy arose.

Exeter was to be the base from which the rebellion could gather and spread throughout the country. When the king demanded Exeter give the king its fealty, the city refused. As William arrived at the city with his army, they played for time, saying they would open their gates, while at the same time preparing to resist. The resulting siege was hard-fought on both sides, with the Conqueror's attempts to storm the city, and mine underneath it, seen off by the determined inhabitants. After eighteen days of siege, the city surrendered. The Norman chroniclers suggest that the inhabitants were worn down by William the Conqueror's relentless assaults, or that the city wall partially collapsed; while the English Chroniclers argue that the surrender came about after the Godwin clan deserted the cause. According to John of Worcester, 'the countess Gytha, mother of Harold, king of England, and sister of Sweyn, king of Denmark, escaped from the city, with many others, and retired to Flanders; and the citizens submitted to the king, and paid him fealty.'[59] Gytha took a boat into the Bristol Channel and landed on the island of Flat Holm, possibly to await the arrival of her grandsons from Ireland. And with Gytha and her supporters gone, the city was able to surrender and agree terms with the king.

Following the failure of the conspiracy, Gytha's lands in England were declared forfeit and distributed among the victorious Normans, as had previously happened to those who had fought at Hastings in 1066. She remained on Flat Holm for some time; her grandsons,

Godwine, Edmund and Magnus, arrived from Ireland later in the year, possibly making a brief stop on Flat Holm to visit her before landing in Somerset and making for Bristol. Although the campaign failed to take the city, they returned to Ireland with considerable plunder after raiding along the Somerset coast. Within a year, two of Harold's sons were back again (although John of Worcester does not specify which two); they sailed from Ireland in the summer of 1069, landing in Devon, near Barnstaple, with a force of sixty-four ships. The local lord, Brian, Count of Brittany, 'came unawares against them with a large army and fought with them, and slew there all the best men that were in the fleet; and the others, being small forces, escaped to the ships: and Harold's sons went back to Ireland again.'[60]

It was probably after this second failed invasion that Gytha left the island of Flat Holm and England, taking with her 'a great store of treasure'.[61] She was accompanied by several surviving members of her family, including her daughter, Gunhilda, and her granddaughter and namesake Gytha (Harold's daughter by Edith Swanneck). After a short stay in Flanders, Gytha may have made her way to Denmark, where her nephew Swein Estrithson was king. Gytha's exile seems to have spurred Swein Estrithson into finally making his own claims to the English throne, saying that he had also been promised the crown by Edward the Confessor. The Danish invasion fleet, commanded by Swein's brother Asbjørn, sailed up the east coast of England and was joined at the mouth of the River Humber by the English rebels, led by Edgar Ætheling. Although the Danes caused an immense amount of trouble with their constant raiding, they avoided a pitched battle with the Normans. King William was eventually able to buy off the raiders, 'he despatched messengers to the Danish earl, Asbjorrn, and promised to pay him secretly a large sum of money, and grant permission for his army to forage freely along the sea coast, on condition that he would depart without fighting when the winter was over; and he, in his extreme greediness for lucre, and to his utter disgrace, consented to the proposal.'[62]

Gytha's daughter, Gunhilda, joined the convent at St Omer, staying there for several years before moving to Bruges. Apart from one visit to Denmark, she then spent the remainder of her years in Bruges, dying there on 24 August 1087. A memorial plaque, discovered in 1786, describes her as a child of noble parents, that her father Godwin 'ruled over the greater part of England' and her mother Gytha 'sprung from a noble family of Danes'.[63] According to Ann Williams, Gunhilda had lived her life as a vowess, taking a vow of perpetual virginity when still a girl. In Bruges she may have been attached to the Church of St Donatien as a vowess, as she donated a collection of relics to the church.[64]

Gytha's granddaughter, Gytha, the daughter of King Harold by Edith Swanneck, was married to Vladimir II Monomakh, prince of Smolensk and (later) Kiev, sometime after her arrival on the Continent. She was the mother of Mstislav the Great, Grand Prince of Kiev, who was born in 1076; he was the last ruler of a united Kievan Rus. Gytha died in 1107. It was through her and her son Mstislav that the Godwinson blood eventually made it back into the English royal family, with Mstislav's direct descendant Philippa of Hainault, wife and queen of Edward III.

Unfortunately for us, once she reaches the Continent, Gytha, the wife of Godwin, disappears from history. Where she lived, and for how much longer, has gone unrecorded, shrouding her last days or years in mystery. It may be that she settled in Denmark with her nephew, Swein Estrithson, and his family, or that she stayed close to her daughter Gunhilda. Whatever her final days, she had been a remarkable woman, a matriarch of, arguably, the most powerful family in England in the eleventh century. She was the mother of a king and a queen, all her sons became earls. She was a landholder in her own right, as testified in the Domesday Survey of 1086, owning land in Gloucestershire, Oxfordshire, Hampshire and elsewhere.[65]

Gytha's life was an extraordinary story of privilege and power, war and loss. She was a wife whose husband decided the fate of kings, and a mother who lost four sons in battle within three weeks in 1066, three in the same battle. It is impossible to imagine the agony of waiting at Hastings, and hearing of the death of her son the king. It speaks for her determination and tenacity that she did not just curl up and give in after such losses. She continued her resistance to William the Conqueror for as long as she could, before going into exile on the Continent, disappearing from the pages of history.

Judith of Flanders

The story of 1066 usually focuses on the ambitions of Harold Godwinson and Duke William. However, there was another army fighting for the prize of England in that year, and that was the Danish army of Harald Hardrada and Tostig Godwinson. Tostig, a younger brother of Harold, had been raised in a family whose ambition hardly overreached their actual power. His father, Godwin, Earl of Wessex, was a powerful man under King Cnut and was able to influence the succession after Cnut's death; he who had the support of Godwin would be king. As we have seen, Godwin's wife, Gytha, was the mother of a large brood, of which Tostig was one of at least six sons. Tostig's marriage to Judith of Flanders was a demonstration of the impressive influence of the Godwinson family.

Although ruled by a mere count, Flanders in the eleventh century was an influential 'county' owing to its strategic position on the northern European coast. It was situated in the far north-eastern corner of France, with Normandy to its west and the rest of France to the south. Its eastern provinces bordered the Duchy of Lorraine, part of the Holy Roman Empire.[1] Judith of Flanders was born sometime in the early 1030s. Her father was Baldwin IV, Count of Flanders; he died in 1035, when Judith was, at most, five years old and possibly still only a baby.

Baldwin had been count since the age of seven, from 987, when his own father had died. His mother, Rozala of Lombardy, acted as regent for her young son until he attained his majority. She died in 1003, by which time Baldwin was old enough to rule alone. The count married twice. His first wife was Orgive of Luxembourg, daughter of Frederick of Luxembourg and niece of Queen Cunigunde of Germany. Orgive was the mother of Baldwin's son and heir, Baldwin V, who was born in 1012. She died in 1030 and was buried at St Peter's Abbey in Ghent. Her son, Baldwin V, married Adele of France, the second daughter of Robert II (the Pious), King of France, and they had at least three children together, including Baldwin VI, Count of Flanders, and Matilda of Flanders, Duchess of Normandy and Queen of England as the wife of William the Conqueror.

After Orgive's death, Baldwin IV married again. In about 1031 he wed Eleanor of Normandy, the daughter of Baldwin's neighbour, Richard II, Duke of Normandy, and his wife, Judith of Brittany. Eleanor's aunt was Emma of Normandy, twice Queen of England as the wife of both Æthelred II and King Cnut. Eleanor's brother was Robert I, Duke of Normandy, the father of William the Conqueror, who became Duke of Normandy and King of England. Eleanor's daughter and only child, Judith, therefore was a first cousin of the future King of England. When her father died in 1035, her older brother, who was about twenty years older than Judith, succeeded as Count Baldwin V and it would be he who decided on Judith's future when the time came for her to marry.

We know nothing of Judith's childhood or level of education. As the daughter of a count, expected to make a good marriage into another ruling or noble family, she would have been taught how to run a large household, embroidery and possibly some languages at a basic level, such as Latin. It is unlikely, however, that she was taught to read and write, skills usually reserved for members of the Church. In the autumn of 1051, Judith was married to Tostig, a son of the powerful Earl Godwin of Wessex and his wife, Gytha. It seems likely that Tostig and Judith were married before the exile from England of Earl Godwin and his family, at the end of 1051, as *The Chronicle of John of Worcester* suggests the couple were already married when the family fled to Flanders, as Judith accompanied them into exile. As we have noted earlier in the chapter on Gytha of Wessex:

When, therefore, the morning came, the king, in his witan, with the unanimous consent of the whole army, made a decree that

Godwin and his five sons should be banished. Thereupon he and his wife Gytha, and Tostig and his wife Judith, the daughter of Baldwin, count of Flanders, and two of his other sons, namely, Sweyn and Gyrth, went, without loss of time, to Thorney, where a ship had been got ready for them. They quickly laded her with as much gold, silver, and other valuable articles as she could hold, and, embarking in great haste, directed her course towards Flanders and Baldwin the count.[2]

Although the *Abingdon (C)* and *Peterborough (E)* manuscripts of the *Anglo-Saxon Chronicle* only mention Earl Godwin and his sons – and his wife, Gytha, in the *Abingdon Manuscript (C)* – the *Worcester (D)* manuscript does mention Judith as accompanying the exiles:

Then he [Godwin] went away by night, and the following morning the king had a council-meeting and with all the raiding-army declared him outlaw – him and all his sons. And he turned south to Thorney, and his wife and Swein his son, and Tostig and his wife, a relative of Baldwin at Bruges, and his son Gyrth ... and Godwine and those who were with him turned from Thorney to Bruges, to Baldwin's land, in one ship with as much treasure as they could stow away for each man.[3]

Although it could be argued that the family fled to Bruges because of their familial links to Count Baldwin through his sister, Flanders already had a reputation as a safe haven for disaffected members of the English nobility. Indeed, Godwin's son, Swein, had already enjoyed two stays in Flanders; the first when he was exiled for the kidnapping and probable rape of Abbess Eadgiva, Abbess of Leominster, in the winter of 1047/48, and the second following his treacherous killing of his own cousin, Beorn, in 1049.

Tostig was probably the third son of Godwin and Gytha of Wessex, with Swein and Harold being his older brothers. He was close to his sister, Edith of Wessex, who was also older than him and had married King Edward the Confessor in January 1045. Born around 1029, Tostig would have been in his early twenties at the time of his marriage and the family's subsequent exile. Judith was no more than six years younger than him, which would suggest she was at least fifteen years old at the time of her marriage. Although Tostig's two older brothers had both been made earls several years before the family's flight to Bruges, it is unclear whether Tostig was also an earl. The only source that credits Tostig with the title at this time is *The Life of King Edward*, but there is nothing else to substantiate the claim. If Tostig was not yet a landed earl at the time of his wedding, then the marriage was a considerable coup for the Godwin clan, as Tostig married above his station. Judith's family pedigree was prestigious, to say the least: the daughter and sister of counts, the autonomous rulers of Flanders, and the granddaughter, niece and cousin of dukes of Normandy. Tostig's own pedigree came primarily from his mother because while Godwin was an earl, his own father, Wulfnoth, had been a mere thegn, a landed lord; whereas Gytha was from a prominent Danish family, her brother, Ulf, was married to King Cnut's sister, and her nephew, Swein Estrithson, had become King of Denmark in 1047.

Judith would have returned to her new 'homeland' of England when Tostig and his family forced their return from exile in 1052. After some vigorous negotiations in London, an uneasy peace was restored between Earl Godwin and the king. King Edward's Norman advisers were banished and his wife – Earl Godwin's daughter, Queen Edith – was released from her convent prison and restored to her lands and titles. Judith and Tostig would have finally been able to settle down to married life, following months of uncertainty and upheaval. Although it is impossible to say for certain, they were probably given one of Godwin's many comital estates, somewhere in Wessex, in which to set up their household. Their marriage appears to have been a successful one, with no rumours of infidelity recorded by the various chroniclers of the time. They are thought to have had two sons together, Skuli Tostisson Kongsfostre and Ketil Tostisson, born in 1052 and 1054, respectively.

Tostig was with his father and the king on Easter Sunday in 1053, at Winchester, when Godwin was taken ill. They were all dining with the king when Godwin collapsed; his sons, Harold, Tostig and Gyrth, carried him into the king's private chamber, where he lingered speechless and helpless for several days, before dying on the Thursday. He was buried in the Old Minster at Winchester; Harold succeeded to his father's earldom of Wessex, but if Tostig hoped this meant he would be given his brother's earldom of East Anglia, he was to be disappointed. This went to Ælfgar, son and heir of Earl Leofric of Mercia. Knowing how ambitious the Godwin family were, this must have upset Tostig, who may well have expected to take over his brother's earldom.

His disappointment was only to last a year or so, however, as a greater opportunity arose in 1055 with the death of Siward, Earl of Northumbria. Earl Siward had marched into Scotland in 1054 'and put to flight King Macbeth, and slew all who were the chief men in the land, and led thence much booty, such as no man before had obtained.'[4] Unfortunately, Siward's oldest son, Osborn, and nephew, Siward, were killed, leaving the earl's youngest son, Waltheof, who was then still a child, as the heir to the earldom of Northumbria. When Siward died at York in 1055, it was decided that five-year-old Waltheof was much too young to take on the responsibility of the vast earldom, which protected England's northern border and was frequently in a state of warfare against the Scots. It was decided by King Edward, possibly after some persuasion from his wife Edith, that the earldom should go to his brother-in-law, Tostig. It is said that Tostig was Edith's favourite brother.

In *The Life of King Edward* Tostig is said to have been held in special affection by the king; he is described as a man of great courage, wisdom and shrewdness, handsome, graceful and strong. He is the model eleventh-century noble, able to show restraint but implacable against the king's enemies. He and his brother Harold are held up as the two stalwarts upon whom the peace of the kingdom rested.[5] Tostig's appointment as earl may have upset Ælfgar, Earl of East Anglia, who is thought to have wanted the northern earldom for himself, further adding to the enmity between the two most powerful noble families of England, the Godwinsons and the family of Leofric of Mercia. According to the *Anglo-Saxon Chronicle* it was shortly after Tostig's accession to Northumbria that Ælfgar first rebelled, he 'sought Gruffudd's territory in North-Wales; whence he went to Ireland, and there gave him a fleet of eighteen ships, besides his own; and then returned to Wales to King Gruffudd with the armament, who received him on terms of amity.'[6] The joint force of Welsh and Irish then marched on Hereford, putting Earl Ralph's forces to flight. Ælfgar's army killed more than 400 of Hereford's citizens and plundered the cathedral, stealing its relics, before burning it to the ground. When an English army led by Earl Harold and gathered from the four corners of the kingdom, stood firm before the marauding Welsh at Gloucester, peace was finally achieved. Ælfgar's sentence of outlawry was reversed and his earldom restored, perhaps suggesting that the original sentence had been rather harsh, the allegations of treason unfounded.

Tostig's appointment as its earl also caused consternation in Northumbria. In the past, Northumbria had always been treated with a light touch from the central English government and was, for the main part, left to its own devices. Since the turn of the century it had been ruled alternately by the ancient house of Bamburgh or Danes appointed by King Cnut and his successors. Tostig was very much a southerner, an unwanted interloper who was unaccustomed to the politics and customs of England's northern provinces. Tostig faced many challenges in Northumbria, the region was notoriously independent, the people were used to lower taxation than the rest of the country and paid about one-sixth of the revenue paid by other regions. The earldom had a reputation for lawlessness, which was further exacerbated by frequent raiding from over the Scottish border (and vice versa, of course). In his overzealous attempts to raise revenue and deliver justice to the region, Tostig ruffled many Northumbrian feathers, which would eventually lead to rebellion and his own deposition.

The early years of his tenure as Earl were made easier by internal unrest in Scotland, meaning that Tostig did not have to deal with any major incursions from the north. King Malcolm III was locked in a power struggle with King Macbeth, which would eventually lead to Macbeth's death at the Battle of Lumphanan in August 1057. Although Macbeth was briefly succeeded by his stepson, Lulach, it was Malcolm who was eventually victorious, with Lulach himself being defeated and killed in March 1058. However, his victory over his internal enemies meant that Malcolm could then turn his sights south, on Northumbria.

From 1058, Malcolm III launched a series of raids into Northumbria, testing the strength of its new earl, but Tostig overcame the Sottish king 'as much by cunning schemes as by martial courage and military campaigns'.[7] Tostig's scheming culminated in a personal meeting between the Scottish and English kings, Malcolm and Edward, an interview for which Edward expressly made the journey north. As a consequence, a peace was agreed and, following the northern custom, with the usual exchange of hostages, Malcolm and Tostig declared themselves 'sworn brothers'.[8] The peace may have lasted had Tostig remained in his earldom. However, in 1061 Tostig and Judith left Northumbria to go on pilgrimage to Rome, accompanied by several English bishops:

> Tostig with fruitful purpose, crossed the Channel with his fortunate wife and his younger brother, Gyrth, and travelled to Rome through Saxony and the upper reaches of the Rhine. And what tongue or what words could properly tell with what devotion and generosity he worshipped on the outward and return journey each saint's shrine? At Rome he was received with fitting honour by Pope Nicholas, and at his command sat in the very synod of Rome immediately next to him. There had come, however, in his party Ealdred, bishop of Worcester, who had just then been presented with the archbishopric of York by the most holy king Edward, so that at Rome he could both plead the business which the king had entrusted him and also obtain the use of the pallium.[9]

The journey to Rome was an embassy, accompanying Ealdred, the archbishop-elect of York, who was travelling there to receive his pallium from the pope, Nicholas II (r. 1059–61). On the outward and return journeys, Tostig and his entourage stopped at every shrine along their route, visibly demonstrating their religious fervour. They reached Rome in the spring of 1061, where they were received honourably by Pope Nicholas; Tostig given the honour of attending a synod, possibly that held on 15 April at Easter 1061, at which Tostig is said to have sat next to the pope.[10] The embassy to Rome is mentioned in the *Anglo-Saxon Chronicle*, which alludes to problems with their return journey: 'This year went Bishop Aldred

[Ealdred] to Rome after his pall; which he received at the hands of Pope Nicholas. Earl Tosty [Tostig] and his wife also went to Rome; and the bishop and the earl met with great difficulty as they returned home.'[10] Shortly after departing Rome, Tostig's party were caught up in a local dispute between the papacy and the Tuscan nobility; they were attacked while travelling along the Via Cassia by Gerard, Count of Galeria. Tostig was able to escape by the ruse of one of his own thegns, a man named Gospatric, who pretended to be the earl. It is by no means clear if this Gospatric is the same nobleman who was killed on Queen Edith's orders at the Christmas court of 1064, nor if he was the future Earl of Northumbria after the Conquest. Indeed, Gospatric was a common name in Northumbria and could have been a third, unfamiliar thegn sharing a name with his more famous contemporaries. After their escape, Tostig's party returned to Rome, where they were treated sympathetically by the pope, who gave them gifts from the treasury of St Peter and an apostolic benediction before they set out again for home. For his part in the ambush, Gerard of Galeria was excommunicated. Judith and a large portion of the party had gone on ahead and were unaware for some time of what had befallen Tostig. Judith must have been relieved to hear of the failure of the attack when Tostig eventually caught up with her.

While Tostig was on his pilgrimage, Malcolm took the opportunity to raid deep into Northumbria, not even sparing the Holy Island of Lindisfarne from his depredations. However, despite the reputation for 'martial courage and military campaigns' ascribed to him by the *Life of King Edward*, on his return Tostig again sought to negotiate a peace with Malcolm, rather than pursue a punitive military campaign against his Scottish neighbour.[11]

Tostig and Judith's relationship with the Church at Durham was particularly cordial, although some stories have come down to us of disagreements between Earl and Church. From Symeon of Durham we learn the story of Judith's attempts to break the rules of the community of St Cuthbert. Despite there being a specific injunction forbidding women to enter the precincts of the church in which lay the shrine of St Cuthbert, Judith was determined to get around this. She sent one of her own maidservants to attempt entry, but the poor girl fell ill as soon as she crossed the boundary and died shortly afterwards, demonstrating the power of St Cuthbert's will. Symeon of Durham also mentions several gifts given by Tostig and Judith, including a crucifix, church ornaments and images of the Virgin Mary and St John the Evangelist, decorated in gold and silver. The gifts were offered to make amends for Judith's attempts to break the rules and gain access to the shrine. Another story that shows the relationship with the Church was not always amicable was the legend of the thief named Aldan-hamal. He had been imprisoned by Earl Tostig for robbery and invoked the help of St Cuthbert to escape. Having orchestrated his freedom, the thief sought sanctuary with the cathedral and when one of Tostig's officers, Barcwith, sought to recapture him by breaching sanctuary, Barcwith was struck down by St Cuthbert for his violation of God's house.[12]

Despite these transgressions by the Earl and Countess, the relationship between them and the Church at Durham was generally cordial and mutually appreciated. The couple were notable for almsgiving in Northumbria, and for having close links to the community of St Cuthbert in Durham, to which they gave several relics. Moreover, this close relationship with the Church in Durham was mutual; Æthelwine, Bishop of Durham, was generous enough to give Judith a relic containing some of St Oswine's hair and Tostig and Judith are both commemorated in the Durham *Liber Vitae*.[13]

Within weeks of his return from Rome, Tostig was travelling again, this time to join his brother, Harold, on a campaign against Wales. Tostig invaded the north of Wales from Chester, as Harold invaded the south from Bristol. The campaign proved so successful that the Welsh themselves betrayed their king, Gruffudd ap Llywelyn; they murdered him and presented his head to Harold and Tostig. Despite this success, Tostig's position in his own earldom was coming under greater threat. He appears to have been one of King Edward's most trusted ministers and was very close to the king and his wife, Tostig's own sister, Edith. In 1065 Tostig was staying at court, possibly hunting with the king, when revolt broke out in Northumbria. Tostig was rarely in the earldom, preferring to spend his time at court with the king and his sister, and leaving the day-to-day governance of Northumbria to his representatives in the region, such as his trusted lieutenant, Copsi.

The revolt was sparked by the murder of Gospatric, a scion of the house of Bamburgh, and a son of Earl Uhtred the Bold, who himself was betrayed and murdered with the connivance of King Cnut in 1016. Tostig and Gospatric had clashed several times. An ambush planned by Tostig had resulted in the murder of two of Gospatric's representatives who were attending talks at York. Gospatric, it seems, took his grievances to the king; he was present at Edward's Christmas court in 1064 to do just that. Tostig was accused of robbing churches and depriving men of their lands and lives out of greed, rather than a desire for justice. Edward promised to restore the laws of Cnut to the north of England, suggesting, perhaps, that Tostig had been trying to impose West Saxon law on the lawless north. However, Gospatric was murdered on the fourth night of Christmas, with rumours implicating Queen Edith, Tostig's sister, in the treacherous deed. It may be that Queen Edith and Tostig hoped to quash any further dissent with Gospatric's death. They were soon to be disappointed. The *Anglo-Saxon Chronicle* relates what happened next:

> Soon after this all the thanes in Yorkshire and Northumberland gathered themselves together at York, and outlawed their Earl Tosty [Tostig]; slaying all the men of his clan that they could reach, both Danish and English; and took all his weapons in York, with gold and silver, and all his money that they could anywhere there find. They then sent after Morkar [Morcar], son of Earl Elgar [Ælfgar], and chose him for their earl. He went south with all the shire, and with Nottinghamshire and Derbyshire and Lincolnshire, till he came to Northampton; where his brother Edwin came to meet him with the men that were in his earldom.[14]

Morcar and Edwin were the sons of Earl Ælfgar of Mercia, who had died in 1062, and grandsons of Earl Leofric and the legendary Lady Godiva. The eldest, Edwin, was now Earl of Mercia. The two brothers had a longstanding rivalry with the sons of Earl Godwin and saw an opportunity to gain from Tostig's problems by taking the lead in the rebellion. Indeed, it is entirely possible that the rebellion had arisen as a result of unrest fuelled by the machinations of the Mercian brothers.

With the Northumbrians marching south, joined by their Mercian and Welsh allies, England looked set for conflict, a civil war that no one wanted. King Edward sent his most powerful adviser, Tostig's brother Harold, to negotiate with the rebels. Messages travelled back and forth, between the Northumbrian camp, and King Edward, with Harold as the go-between. Tostig accused his brother of collusion with the rebels, though Harold publicly swore an oath to prove his innocence. In fact, no one was prepared to restore Tostig by force, the king's own attempts to raise an army proved fruitless; possibly because no one wanted to see civil war in the country. Anxious to avoid all-out war, and with none of his senior earls and thegns eager for conflict, including Harold, Edward acquiesced to the rebels' demands that Morcar replace Tostig as their earl. Morcar was confirmed as Earl of Northumbria and the rights they had enjoyed in the past, called the 'Laws of Cnut' by the *Anglo-Saxon Chronicle*, were restored to the Northumbrians.

Tostig was banished from England; he and Judith, their children and their entire household crossed the English Channel on 1 November 1065. They made their way to Flanders to seek refuge with Judith's brother, Count Baldwin. According to the *Life of King Edward* the family was warmly welcomed on arrival in Flanders, just before Christmas:

> When Edward could not save his earl, he graciously heaped on him many gifts and then let him depart, profoundly distressed at the powerlessness that had come upon hm. And a short time after, Tostig took leave of his sorrowful mother and some of his friends, and with his wife and infant children and a goodly company of his thegns crossed the Channel and came to that old friend of the English people, Count Baldwin. He received the husband of his sister honourably and graciously, as was his wont, and bade him dwell and rest from his labours in a town of St Omer, because it was there that his solemn court met on special days and it was the first place met by those who have crossed the British ocean. Thus he gave him there both a house and an estate, and put in his hands the revenues of the town for his maintenance; and he ordered all the knights who were attached to that place to be at the service of Tostig, his deputy commander. This happened a few days before Christmas.[15]

In England, King Edward died on 5 January 1066 and the next day, Tostig's brother, Harold, was crowned king, in Westminster Abbey. With no sign of his exile being rescinded and the rift with his brother still an open wound, Tostig began scheming to return to England. Orderic Vitalis, writing just fifty years or so after events, claimed that Tostig had visited Duke William in Normandy, hoping to arrange an alliance against Harold. The Duke proved unreceptive, however, and it seems that Tostig then made overtures to Harald Hardrada, King of Norway. According to *King Harald's Saga*, written by Snorri Sturluson in the late twelfth century, Tostig travelled first to Denmark and then to Norway to try to persuade both kings Swein Estrithson and Harald to invade England. Orderic Vitalis also mentions Tostig's visit to King Harald in Norway, and the king's enthusiastic reception of the idea of an invasion, stating: 'At once he ordered an army to be gathered together, weapons of war prepared, and the royal fleet fitted out.'[16] In the spring of 1066, Tostig started raiding English shores. He may have taken Judith and his sons, in the hope of recovering his earldom and returning his family to England. His two sons would have been aged twelve and fourteen by this point, old enough to get their first taste of warfare. Tostig arrived on the Isle of Wight 'with as large a fleet as he could get; and he was there supplied with money and provisions. Thence he proceeded, and committed outrages everywhere by the sea coast where he could land, until he came to Sandwich.'[17] On hearing of his brother's attacks, and with rumours of Duke William of Normandy preparing an invasion, Harold, now king of England, 'gathered so large a force, naval and military, as no king before collected in this land.'[18]

On hearing that his brother was on his way to confront him, Tostig, after pressing several boatmen from Sandwich into his service, took to the sea again and sailed north, into the Humber. With a force of sixty ships, Tostig plundered Lindsey, the county to the south of the Humber and east of the River Trent, killing many; however, he was confronted by the Earls Morcar and Edwin, and forced back to sea. His reduced force (according to the *Anglo-Saxon Chronicle* he now had only twelve 'smacks') eventually arrived in Scotland, where he was welcomed by King Malcolm III Canmore, who entertained him and provisioned his ships.

Tostig was in Scotland for most of the summer and was joined there by King Harald Hardrada of Norway, with his force of at least 200 ships; if each ship held forty men, then Harald probably had a fighting force of about 8,000 men. Harald's arrival adds weight to the argument that Tostig had courted the Norwegian king at his court in Norway sometime during his Flanders exile. Tostig now swore fealty to King Harald, and at the end of the summer, their combined fleet made its way south along the east coast, raiding as they went. King Harold must have received news of Harald and Tostig's incursions into the north within days of having disbanded the army that had stood ready to repel invasion the whole summer.

As King Harold of England reassembled his forces and prepared to march north, the earls of Mercia and Northumbria also began to gather their army; Harald Hardrada and Tostig set up camp at Riccall, plundering the neighbouring countryside for provisions. However, they held off attacking York. Before King Harold arrived, the joint forces of Northumbria and Mercia faced Tostig and Harald's combined force at Fulford:

> ... then gathered Edwin the earl and Morcar the earl from their earldom as great a force as they could get together; and they fought against the army and made great slaughter: and there was much of the English people slain, and drowned, and driven away in flight; and the Northmen had possession of the place of carnage... And then, after the fight, went Harald, King of Norway, and Tosty [Tostig] the earl, into York, with as much people as seemed meet to them.[19]

Harald won the support of the city of York, which agreed to give up hostages and provisions for the Norwegian fleet, concluding a lasting peace 'provided that they all marched south with him to conquer the country.'[20] Harald and Tostig then took their men back to their camp and ships at Riccall to await the delivery of hostages from throughout the county, before they marched south. In the meantime, Harold of England had marched his men 200 miles in just four days. By 24 September, he had reached Tadcaster on the outskirts of York, expecting Harald and Tostig to be holding the city, but they were not within the city walls. The next day Harold marched his force through York and surprised the Norwegian army at Stamford Bridge, where they were awaiting the delivery of the promised hostages, armed but not dressed for battle, having on only their helmets but no mail. As the *Anglo-Saxon Chronicle* tells the story: 'Then came Harold, King of the English, against them, unawares, beyond the bridge, and they there joined battle, and very strenuously, for a long time of the day, continued fighting: and there was Harald, King of Norway, and Tosty [Tostig] the earl slain, and numberless of the people with them, as well of the Northmen as of the English: and the Northmen fled from the English.'[21] Magnanimous in his victory, King Harold 'allowed Harold's son Olaf, and Paul, earl of Orkney, who had been left with part of the army to guard the ships, to return to their own country, with twenty ships and the relics [bodies] of the [defeated] army; having first received from them hostages and their oaths.'[22]

Tostig's body was recovered from the battlefield. According to William of Malmesbury, he had been recognised by a wart between his shoulder blades, suggesting his more familiar features had been disfigured in the fighting.[23] Tostig Godwinson was taken to York and given honourable burial, possibly attended by his brother Harold who, it is believed, went into the city to ensure the loyalty of its citizens to the English king.

Judith's whereabouts during Tostig's invasion are not mentioned. It is possible that she stayed safe in Flanders with her family and two young sons, the oldest of whom was about fourteen by 1066, but she may have travelled with her husband; there is a suggestion that at least one of her sons fought at Stamford Bridge and travelled to Norway with the survivors.[24] Following Tostig's defeat at Stamford Bridge, and Harold's subsequent death at the Battle of Hastings, Judith's two sons by Tostig eventually sought refuge with King Olaf 'the Peaceable' of Norway, Harald Hardrada's son who had been allowed to return to Norway following his father's defeat and death at Stamford Bridge.[25] Little is known of their movements after that, other than that the oldest, Skuli Tostisson Kongsfostre, must have married and had children as he was the great-great-grandfather of King Inge II of Norway.

For a time, Judith remained in Flanders from where her older, half-brother, Count Baldwin V, arranged a second marriage for her in about 1070, to Welf IV, the newly created Duke of Bavaria. The couple were to have two sons and a daughter; Welf, who succeeded his father as Duke of Bavaria and died in 1119, Henry and Kunizza, who married Count Frederick of Diessen and died in 1120. Henry succeeded his brother as Duke of Bavaria and died in 1126; he had at least seven children by his wife, Wulfhilde of Saxony [26]

We do not know the extent to which Judith was a landholder in England, she is not recorded in Domesday Book as having held land before 1066. However, this could be due to any land she held being in Northumbria, north of the River Tees, which was not part of the Domesday Survey of 1086. As Countess of Northumbria, from just a few years after her marriage to her husband's deposition in 1065, it was with this region that she is mostly associated. She was a major supporter of the northern saints, giving generously to St Cuthbert's at Durham and promoting the veneration of St Oswald, whose head was buried at Durham, and St Oswine. A patron of the arts, she is renowned for the commissioning of four gospel books, luxurious creations produced in England, probably at Winchester. When Judith left England, she took these gospels, with other manuscripts and relics in her private collection, with her to Flanders. After she remarried, they accompanied her to southern Germany.

On 12 March 1094, with the approval of her husband and sons, Judith drew up a list of bequests. She bequeathed the four gospels and other treasures, to the monastery at Weingarten, a foundation of her husband's family, thus helping to disseminate Anglo-Saxon art throughout southern Europe.[27] Among the bequests was also a relic of Christ's blood, given to her by her father.[28] It may well be that Judith was already ill when she drew up her list of bequests as she died a year later, on 5 March 1095. She was buried at the Abbey of Weingarten, where her second husband would also be buried, following his death at Paphos, Cyprus, while returning from Crusade in 1101. Judith is remembered at Weingarten as a widowed queen of England, perhaps a testimony to how close her first husband got to the English throne.

PART TWO

THE NORMAN
INVASION

6

1066

'King Edward the Pacific, the pride of the English, son of king Ethelred, died at London on Thursday, the eve of the Epiphany.'[1] In England, 1066 opened with the death of the old regime. The ageing king, Edward the Confessor, had fallen ill towards the end of 1065 and breathed his last on the eve of the Feast of the Epiphany, 5 January 1066. At the end, he had named Harold Godwinson, his brother-in-law and Earl of Wessex, as his successor. Within hours of the old king's death, Harold's nomination was confirmed by the *Witan*, the Great Council of England. Edward 'was buried the next day with royal pomp, amidst the tears and lamentations of the crowds who flocked to his funeral.'[2] The old king's burial in the unfinished Westminster Abbey was followed almost immediately by Harold's coronation. In a little over twenty-four hours, the smooth transition of power from old to new regime was completed, and a new dynasty was founded, supposedly guaranteeing the stability of England for years to come.

However, the speed of events itself tells the story that this was a worrying time for England; a coronation was not usually arranged so quickly. Indeed, Edward the Confessor was crowned at Easter 1043, some ten months after his accession on the death of his predecessor, Harthacnut. Thus 1066 would be one of the most tumultuous years in English history; it was a watershed, the year when the old Saxon line of rulers died out, Edward the Confessor being the last king from the ancient line of Cerdic. He was the last descendant of Alfred the Great, through the direct male line, to wear the crown; although every monarch, from Henry II onwards, could also claim descent from Alfred the Great but through the female line of St Margaret, Queen of Scotland, daughter of King Edward's nephew, Edward the Exile, and mother of Henry I's wife, Matilda of Scotland. The very new royal House of Godwin, under Harold II, would have looked like a good choice. King Harold was politically and militarily experienced and had a number of teenage sons who could succeed him.

Throughout the last half-century, a number of events and characters had led England to this definitive moment. The Danish and Anglo-Saxon dynasties had fought over England since the time of Æthelred II; three generations of Danes had held the throne, alternating with Æthelred and his sons, Edmund II Ironside and Edward the Confessor himself. Edward the Confessor's long reign of almost twenty-three years had brought some much-wanted relative peace and stability to the country, providing England with the security and prosperity it sorely needed. However, events of 1064 had almost guaranteed the showdown that King Harold would face on the battlefield of Hastings. The Bayeux Tapestry, that most famous visual narrative of the Norman Conquest, begins its story in 1064, and with good reason. By that year it was certain that the ageing King Edward and his queen, Edith of Wessex, would never produce an heir to the English throne and the king needed to start thinking about who would follow him on the throne. There has been a suggestion that Duke William visited England in 1051 and was promised the crown by Edward at that time. However, the fact that in 1057 Edward went to extraordinary lengths to bring his nephew, Edward the Exile, the son of Edmund II Ironside, from Eastern Europe suggests that the king had other ideas for the succession. The king's plans were scuppered when the younger Edward died suddenly within days of his arrival at the English court; whether his death was by natural causes, or more nefarious acts, is still debated. Edward the Exile left a son, Edgar the Ætheling, who would still be little more than a child in 1066; he was adopted by Queen Edith and probably raised at court to be prepared for his future life as king, a life that never materialized for him.

So why, you might ask, is 1064 seen as the year that started the inexorable build-up to the Norman Conquest? It was in that year that Earl Harold of Wessex departed England's shores for Normandy. No one is certain what Harold's actual mission was supposed to be, it is possible he was intending to go to Normandy to try to obtain the release of his younger brother, Wulfnoth and his nephew, Hakon. The boys had been taken to Normandy as hostages by Robert of Jumièges, the erstwhile Archbishop of Canterbury who was banished from England in 1052 after the return from exile of Earl Godwin and his family. Norman sources suggest that Harold had been sent by Edward the Confessor to assure the duke that he had been named as the king's heir and, possibly, that Harold would support his accession when the time came. After having been either attacked mid-Channel, or driven ashore by a storm, Harold's ships were forced to beach in the county of Ponthieu and Harold and his entourage were taken captive by the Count, Guy of Ponthieu. Count Guy was a vassal of Duke William of Normandy and on hearing of Harold's plight, William ordered his release and welcomed the earl to his own court.

Once at the court of the Duke of Normandy as his guest, Harold was expected, as was the feudal custom, to accept William's hospitality and stay for forty days. He joined the duke on a military expedition into Brittany, where he saved the lives of two Norman soldiers who had fallen into quicksand; it was Harold who dragged them free. The English earl further distinguished himself during the campaign, demonstrating great personal courage and was rewarded for his bravery by being knighted by the duke.[3] While it was a great honour, the knighthood also created a problem for Harold; it meant that he owed deference to the man who had knighted him, putting Harold in an inferior position to Duke William.[4]

If Harold's mission to Normandy was to recover his brother and nephew, he was to be only partially successful. Harold was initially allowed to see his brother, Wulfnoth, and nephew, Hakon, although only from a distance it seems. Although Hakon was allowed to return home with Harold, Wulfnoth remained a hostage.[5]

The most controversial scene in the Bayeux Tapestry, on which William's claim to the English throne and his claim of perjury by Harold rests, is where Harold is seen swearing an oath on holy relics. According to Norman chroniclers, the oath was Harold's pledge of loyalty to the duke and his promise to support William's right to the English throne, when the time came. The controversy arises in that the Normans claim that Harold gave the oath freely, whereas English arguments are that Harold was forced to make the oath in order to achieve his freedom; an oath under duress is not binding. He was only released from William's court once he had promised to support William's claim to the throne. While William no doubt saw this as one step closer to his goal – the English throne – Harold must have thought that little weight could be given to his oaths. After all, the king's successor was decided by the *Witan*, the Great Council of England, and it was only with their approval that a king could rule.

Moreover, while the succession rules were not based on primogeniture, as they are now, there were several established stipulations for who could become king. At the dawn of the eleventh century, hereditary principles were on their way to being established within the Anglo-Saxon royal house and primogeniture may well have decided the day, had the uninterrupted rule of the House of Wessex continued with the succession of Athelstan the Ætheling following Æthelred's death in 1016. However, the Danish incursions meant Æthelstan died before his father and Sweyn Forkbeard took the throne from Æthelred II in 1014, only for the Saxon king to be restored on Sweyn's death a few short weeks later. Æthelred was succeeded by his more able son, Edmund II Ironside, who fought valiantly against the incursions of the Danes, led by Cnut. However, Edmund's untimely death saw Cnut then seizing the crown, his claim 'owed only to conquest by his father and nothing else'.[6]

Historian Marc Morris argues that there were three key elements to the line of precedence to the throne in the eleventh century.[7] The first element was a blood link to the previous king, or any earlier king; this is demonstrated by the attempts to sully the claim of Harold I Harefoot by suggesting that he was not a son of Cnut and therefore had no right to the crown. The *Anglo-Saxon Chronicle* even reported; 'Some men said of Harold, that he was the son of King Cnut and of Ælfgifu the daughter of Ealdorman Ælfhelm; but it was thought very incredible [unbelievable] by many men.'[8] The second requirement for a king was that he had in some way been designated as successor by the previous monarch, just as Harthacnut had acknowledged

Edward as his heir by bringing him back from exile and giving him a place at court; and Edward the Confessor, in turn, is said to have named Harold as his successor on his deathbed. The primary requirement for all kings of England, however, was their election by the leading magnates of the kingdom. Election by the majority of England's nobles at the *Witan* (*Witanagemot*) guaranteed that the king had the support needed to govern well. Such essential support was demonstrated in the accessions of both Harold Harefoot and Edward the Confessor; Harold was only able to secure the throne for himself, as opposed to being co-regent with his brother, when Earls Leofric and Godwin backed him against the supporters of Harthacnut. With Edward the Confessor, it was the support of Earl Godwin, again, which guaranteed Edward's succession, despite the fact he was a virtual unknown in the country, who had spent most of his life as an exile in Normandy.

It is possible that Harold's journey to Normandy, which is so colourfully depicted in the Bayeux Tapestry, never actually happened. The Tapestry and Norman chroniclers emphasise the visit as a demonstration of Harold's perfidy, suggesting that when the time came he deliberately ignored his oath to William in order to take the throne for himself. However, the English chroniclers are remarkably silent; neither the various editions of the *Anglo-Saxon Chronicle* nor John of Worcester deign to mention Harold's month-long stay in Normandy. And it is not that Harold goes unmentioned in 1064; indeed, his campaign in Wales, which culminated in the assassination of Gruffydd ap Llywelyn by his own people in August 1064, with the Welsh king's head being sent to Harold, is well documented and told in some detail.[9] It seems likely that if he did go to Normandy, it was in the spring of 1064, before the Welsh campaign.

Later English chroniclers, writing post-Conquest, do mention the journey, though they may have been writing to appease their new masters. It may also be that the *Anglo-Saxon Chronicle* and others were silent because they saw the outcome of the visit, and Harold's oath to William, as a shameful action. While there are still many mysteries as to the detail, most historians agree that Harold probably did journey to Normandy in 1064 and repudiated any oath he may have made immediately he was safely back on England's shores.

Events in England were moving rather rapidly in the years 1064 and 1065. Following the campaign in Wales, trouble was brewing in Northumbria. Gospatric, of the noble house of Bamburgh, once the undisputed rulers of Northumbria, complained of the misrule of Tostig and journeyed to see the king, at his Christmas court, to have his grievances heard. Unfortunately, it seems, Tostig's sister, Queen Edith, hoped to solve the problem by getting rid of Gospatric, who was murdered, apparently on the queen's orders, four days after Christmas. Rather than getting rid of the problem, Gospatric's murder was the catalyst to outright revolt in Northumbria. The Northumbrians marched on York, taking control of Tostig's armoury and treasury and killing any of his officials they came across. They then deposed Tostig as their earl and asked Morcar, the brother of Earl Edwin of Mercia, to take control of the earldom. The speed with which Morcar and Edwin took advantage of the unrest suggests that they may have had a hand in fanning the flames, though there is no conclusive evidence of their involvement. Nevertheless, they were quick to take advantage of the situation and Morcar marched his Northumbrians south, joining up with Earl Edwin's Mercians and their Welsh allies along the way. As they reached Northampton, Harold, as the king's representative, met with them to ascertain their demands, which were, essentially, the removal of Tostig and a return to their old laws.

Tostig and King Edward were eager to crush the rebels, with all-out war if necessary. However, when Edward attempted to raise an army, it became clear that no one was prepared to fight a civil war in order to restore Tostig to his earldom, including Tostig's own brother. Tostig accused Harold of betraying him, an accusation he vehemently denied with a public oath in front of the king and his advisers. With the evident reluctance of his barons to resort to armed conflict, King Edward was forced to acquiesce to the rebels' demands. He confirmed Morcar as Earl of Northumbria and agreed to the restoration of the 'Laws of Cnut'.[10] Tostig and his family were banished from England, leaving for exile in Flanders on 1 November 1065.

It is possible that King Edward agreed so readily to the demands of the rebels as he was already fatally ill. However, whether his decline was before or after the departure of Tostig, of whom he was particularly fond, we cannot say for certain. His health does appear to have declined rapidly towards the end of 1065, and although he survived until after Christmas, the king was too ill to attend the dedication of his refoundation of Westminster Abbey on 28 December 1065; Queen Edith attended the dedication in the king's place.

At Edward's death, Harold was not the only choice for king; there were candidates from within the king's own family. As we have seen, young Edgar Ætheling, still only a teenager, was passed over due to his youth and inexperience. Although England had had youthful kings in the past – indeed Æthelred II was only ten years old when he came to the throne – it seems the country wanted an experienced warrior and politician to face the challenges ahead. Another candidate would have been Ralph of Mantes, Earl of Hereford, Edward the Confessor's nephew through his sister, Goda. However, Ralph had died in 1057 and his son, Harold, was still a child, being raised in the household of Queen Edith. Edmund, the brother of Edward the Exile, is not mentioned as a candidate, nor was he mentioned when his brother returned from Hungary in 1057, so it seems likely that he had died in his eastern exile in the late 1040s or early 1050s; otherwise it would have been prudent for the king to send for him following Edward the Exile's unfortunate demise in 1057.

Harold's reign may have started with a sense of optimism, as many new reigns do, although Harold seems to have been aware that his position was, in some ways, precarious and he would be in need of allies. If Tostig thought that Harold's succession would mean his immediate recall and the restoration of his earldom of Northumbria, he was to be sorely disappointed. Instead, Harold sought to make allies of Earls Edwin and Morcar, and so would need to keep Morcar happy by allowing him to retain Northumbria. An early entry for 1066 in the *Anglo-Saxon Chronicle* refers to a trip to York, Northumbria's capital, by Harold, although it is sparse on the details, simply stating, 'This year came Harold from York to Westminster, in the Easter succeeding the midwinter when the king [Edward] died.'[11] Easter that year was 16 April, by which time Harold had already made the return journey of 400 miles to York from London. Although we do not know the exact purpose of Harold's visit, it must have had something to do with Harold courting the support of the Mercian brothers. It may even have been at this time that Harold married the sister of Edwin and Morcar, Ealdgyth, thus creating a familial alliance with the Mercian brothers.

'Then throughout all England, a sign such as men never saw before was see in the heavens. Some men declared that it was the star *comet*, which some men call the haired star; and it appeared first on the eve of the *Greater Litany*, *24 April*, and shone thus all week.'[12] The appearance of what would later become known as Halley's Comet would have been a sign of great portent for all in the eleventh century, one that meant great upheaval was coming. The fact that only a week or so later Tostig landed on the Isle of Wight with 'as large a fleet as he could get', would have appeared to confirm the fears instilled by the comet's arrival.[13] King Harold hastily gathered together his own force to face his brother, with both ship-based and land-based fighting men. On the Isle of Wight, Tostig was given supplies and money. He then proceeded along the south coast, raiding and pillaging. As he reached Sandwich, he was told that Harold was marching to stop him, but decided not to face his brother, leaving port and taking with him boatmen from Sandwich who had been pressed into his service. The *Anglo-Saxon Chronicle* breaks up its reports of these events with the news, 'it was credibly reported that Earl William from Normandy, King Edward's cousin, would come hither and gain this land; just as it afterwards happened.'[14] Harold's great army, initially raised to face Tostig, may have grown so large due to this new intelligence and the threat of invasion that England now faced.

As described previously, Tostig sailed north into the Humber and raided Lindsey, until he was chased away by the Earls Edwin and Morcar. He eventually landed in Scotland, with a much-reduced force; of the sixty ships reported sailing into the Humber, Tostig arrived in Scotland with only twelve remaining. As Tostig spent his summer in Scotland, Harold spent his on the Isle of Wight, awaiting an invasion from Normandy that didn't, at that time, materialise. On 8 September, with supplies running short and the men desperate to go home, Harold disbanded his army. Within days of sending his men home, he would have received news that Tostig, with his new ally, Harald Hardrada, had landed in Northumbria. When Harald Hardrada had arrived in Scotland at the end of the summer, Tostig submitted to him and gave his oath of fealty to the Norwegian king. King Harald had already travelled to Orkney, where he recruited more men and left some of his family to await the outcome of his expedition against England. It seems likely, though by no means certain, that the two men had arranged this during Tostig's exile in Flanders, and that they were now putting their plan into action. King Harald sailed into the Tyne; he ravaged the coast of Northumberland and sacked Scarborough, 'with a very great sea-force – no small one; that might be, with three hundred ships or more; and Earl Tosty [Tostig] came to him with all those that he had got; just as they had before said: and they both went up with all the fleet along the Ouse toward York.'[15] England's king was preparing to march north to face them, but not knowing when he would arrive, Earls Edwin and Morcar placed their army between Harald's army and York. They made their stand on the side of the River Ouse at Gate Fulford:

> Edwin and Morcar, at the head of a large army, fought a battle with the Norwegians on the northern bank of the river Ouse, near York, on the eve of the feast of St. Matthew the Apostle [20th September], being Wednesday; and their first onset was so furious that numbers of the enemy fell before it. But, after a long struggle, the English, unable to withstand the attack of the Norwegians, fled with great loss, and many more of them were drowned in the river than slain in the fight. The Norwegians remained in possession of the field of death; and, having taken one hundred and fifty hostages from York, and leaving there one hundred and fifty hostages of their own, returned to their ships.[16]

Victorious, Harald and Tostig immediately began negotiations with York for the city's surrender. York agreed to surrender hostages and the Norwegian army entered the city without opposition, perhaps due to the presence of their former earl, Tostig. They eventually withdrew to their ships at Riccall to await the delivery of further hostages from the surrounding regions. Meanwhile, King Harold was marching north as fast as he could. He covered the distance of 200 miles in about four days and by 24 September, he and his men had arrived at Tadcaster, on the outskirts of York. On 25 September Harald Hardrada and his men made their way to Stamford Bridge, the rendezvous point for the collection of the hostages from all over Northumberland. Instead of the hostages, they came face-to-face with King Harold's army, which had marched through York at dawn in search of the enemy. The ensuing battle was a hard, fierce fight on both sides. The *Saga* writer, Snorri Sturluson, claims that although they had their weapons and helmets, the Norwegians were not dressed for battle and that having been caught by surprise, they were without their mail.[17] One story of the battle, added to the C manuscript of the *Anglo-Saxon Chronicle* in the twelfth century, relates: 'There was one of the Norwegians who withstood the English people so that they could not cross the bridge nor gain victory. Then one Englishman shot with an arrow but it was to no avail, and then another came under the bridge and stabbed him through under the mail-coat. Then Harold came over the bridge, and his army along with him, and there made a great slaughter of both Norwegians and Flemings.'[18]

At the end of the battle, Harald Hardrada lay dead, as did King Harold's own brother, Tostig. The surviving Norwegians, along with Harald Hardrada's son, Olaf, who had remained with the ships during the battle, were allowed to sail home. It is possible, though not certain, that Tostig's son, Skuli, was among the survivors who sailed for Norway; the entire complement of survivors fitting into just twenty-four ships. With the battle over, Harold rode into the city of York, where Tostig's body was laid to rest, probably in his brother's presence. Harold spent a few days in York, possibly upbraiding them for their support of the Norwegians. However, within days of the Battle of Stamford Bridge, William, Duke of Normandy, landed on the South coast. With 270 miles between York and Pevensey, it would have taken several days for a messenger to reach Harold with the news; he set off south immediately. Marc Morris argues that Harold would not have been able to move quickly with his foot soldiers and may have dismissed them in Yorkshire, riding south with his mounted housecarls to meet the new threat, and hoping to recruit men along the way.[19] The troops of Edwin and Morcar had played no part in the battle at Stamford Bridge, and did not accompany Harold south. It seems likely that their army had been so badly hurt at Gate Fulford that they needed to recruit more men before following Harold south. They would reach London about the same time as the king was fighting at Hastings.

According to Orderic Vitalis, Harold spent six days in London on his way south, possibly waiting for his army to assemble from throughout the southern shires. Duke William would have been waiting on the southern shores around Pevensey and Hastings, anxious for news, not only of Harold's army but of who his opponents may be. It seems likely that he knew of Harald Hardrada's expedition, but he would not have yet known of the outcome of the subsequent battles. William of Poitiers wrote that the duke eventually heard the news from Robert fitz Wimarc, a Norman living in England, who advised Duke William to stay behind his fortifications as Harold was heading south to confront him after having defeated and killed both Tostig and Hardrada and destroyed their huge armies.

Messages were exchanged between the two leaders, setting out their opposing claims to the throne, with William claiming Edward the Confessor made him his heir, with oaths sworn and hostages exchanged, and reminding Harold of his own promise to uphold the duke's claim during his stay in Normandy. Harold in turn responded with Edward the Confessor's deathbed nomination of him as his heir. Each, in turn, offered terms to avoid conflict, with William offering that Harold could retain his earldom of Wessex if he were to accept the duke as king.[20] Harold, rather disingenuously, suggested that William could return to Normandy unmolested if he paid compensation for the substantial damage to the area his army had already caused; the Bayeux Tapestry does actually show Norman soldiers setting a house alight, with a woman and child fleeing the flames.

Before his army was fully mustered, Harold marched his troops to meet the Norman threat. According to William of Poitiers, 'the furious king was hastening his march all the more because he had heard that the lands near to the Norman camp were being laid waste.'[21] Although Harold had hoped to take William by surprise, the duke had received news of the arrival of Harold's army and had his men stand ready throughout the night of 13 October, in anticipation of a night-time raid that never happened. The next morning, he marched to confront Harold, who was drawn up 7 miles to the north-west of Hastings at a place that had no obvious name, the *Anglo-Saxon Chronicle* merely states the English were at 'the grey apple tree'. [22] Instead of Harold achieving surprise, the *Chronicle* goes on to say that 'William came upon him [Harold] unexpectedly, before his army was set in order.'[23]

On the morning of 14 October, 1066, before the two armies joined battle, William addressed his troops. 'What I have to say to you, ye Normans, the toughest of nations, does not spring from any doubt of your valour or uncertainty of victory, which never by any chance or obstacle escaped your efforts. If, indeed, once only you had failed of conquering, it might be necessary to inflame your courage by exhortation. But how little does the inherent spirit of your race require to be roused!'[24] The long harangue, as told by Henry of Huntingdon, has William relating much of the story of Normandy. It closes with:

Is it not shameful, then, that a people accustomed to be conquered, a people ignorant of the art of war, a people not even in possession of arrows, should make a show of being arrayed in order of battle against you, most valiant? Is it not a shame that this King Harold, perjured as he was in your presence, should dare to show his face to you? It is a wonder to me that you have been allowed to see those who by a horrible crime beheaded your relations and Alfred my kinsman, and that their own accursed heads are still on their shoulders. Raise, then, your standards, my brave men, and set no bounds to your merited rage. Let the lightning of your glory flash, and the thunders of your onset be heard from east to west, and be the avengers of the noble blood which has been spilled.[25]

When battle commenced, the English were arrayed on foot, on the hilltop, Harold taking his place at the centre of the line. The Normans were at the base of the hill, the men arrayed in three lines;

the first line was made up of archers, the second of men-at-arms, probably carrying swords, and the third of cavalry. The English had no cavalry, they traditionally fought on foot. For hours the Normans tried to break through the English lines, the effectiveness of their cavalry neutralised by the fact they were fighting uphill. The turning point came when a rumour ran through the Norman army that William had been killed. The Normans began to flee, the English in pursuit, and the invaders were only steadied by William standing in front of his army, taking off his helmet and showing himself to his men. The Normans then turned themselves about and attacked the English with renewed vigour. The *Anglo-Saxon Chronicle* tells how the battle ended:

> The English being crowded in a confined position, many of them left their ranks, and few stood by him with resolute hearts; nevertheless he made a stout resistance from the third hour of the day until nightfall, and defended himself with such courage and obstinacy, that the enemy almost despaired of taking his life. When, however, numbers had fallen on both sides, he, alas! fell at twilight. There fell, also, his brothers, the earls Gyrth and Leofwine, and almost all the English nobles.[26]

Edith of Wessex

Edith of Wessex often gets overlooked in the story of eleventh-century England. She is frequently sidelined as a pawn used in her father's aspirations for power and control of the king. At first glance, Edith appears to be one of those many medieval women who have been ignored by historians, discounted as being of no significance. However, Edith was from one of the most powerful families in England and Queen of England for more than twenty years; and she was anything but insignificant. As queen, she played an important role in English politics and in commissioning the *Vita Edwardi regis*, she made herself the custodian of Edward the Confessor's saintly memory and legacy.

Edith of Wessex was one of the oldest children of Godwin, Earl of Wessex, and his wife, Gytha. Through her mother, she was related to the Danish royal family; Gytha's brother, Ulf, was married to King Cnut's sister, Estrith, and their son, Swein Estrithson, was to become King of Denmark in 1047. Edith's father and grandfather had both been prominent nobles in the South Saxon lands during the reign of Æthelred II. Godwin also served in the household of Æthelstan, the ætheling and oldest son of Æthelred II the Unready; Godwin was left land in the young prince's will, an estate at Compton in Sussex, when Æthelstan died in June 1014. On Æthelstan's death, it is likely that Godwin transferred his allegiance to the ætheling's younger brother Edmund, who formed the main opposition to Eadric Streona, one of Æthelred II's leading counsellors. Eadric Streona's brother,

Brihtric, had accused Godwin's father, Wulfnoth, of treachery in 1009. Wulfnoth had fled the accusations, taking with him several ships from the newly constructed Saxon fleet. Subsequently the rest of the fleet, which had set off in pursuit of him, was destroyed when it was run aground by a storm.[1] Following the deaths of Æthelred II and Edmund II Ironside in 1016, England's new king was the Dane, Cnut. Godwin rose high under the three consecutive Danish Kings, Cnut, Harold Harefoot and Harthacnut. Of all his English supporters, Cnut found Godwin 'the most cautious in counsel and the most active in war.'[2] After Cnut's expedition to Denmark, in 1022–3, in which he was accompanied by Godwin, the king 'admitted [him] to his council and gave him his sister [*sic*] as wife.'[3] Godwin had been attesting as earl since 1018, probably as earl of western Wessex; however, on his return from Denmark he was created Earl of all Wessex, in other words; 'earl and *baiulus* [steward or administrator] of almost all the kingdom.'[4]

The marriage of Edith's parents was arranged by King Cnut and took place sometime between 1018 and 1023, although most likely in the latter part of the period, with Edith's year of birth being no later than 1027 and most likely around 1025. She may have been her parent's oldest child, or second oldest; the order of birth is unclear, but it may be that her brother, Swein, was older by a year. Most historians accept the order of birth with Swein as the oldest, then Edith, followed by Harold, Tostig, Gyrth, Leofwine and Wulfnoth. Edith had at least two sisters, Edgiva and Gunhilda, but their place in the order of birth is difficult to ascertain. The children's names were a combination of English and Danish names, testament to their mixed heritage through their parents. The youngest boy, Wulfnoth, was named after his grandfather, the Saxon thegn who was, probably falsely, accused of treachery by Brihtric, the brother of Eadric Streona. Edith was probably named after her mother, Gytha, as one variation of her name is Eadgyth; the more familiar spelling of Edith could well have been used to anglicise her name when she became queen.

As a child, Edith was sent to be raised and educated at the convent at Wilton, an established abbey famed for its education of noble and royal women. She must have been well treated there, for she kept a fondness for the nunnery for the rest of her life, making donations to it and financing repair and expansion projects. In later years, she paid for the rebuilding of the abbey in stone, to protect it from the ravages of fire to which other abbeys had succumbed. She also sent other noble and royal girls to Wilton to be educated, including Margaret and Christina, the daughters of Edward the Exile, who returned to England in 1057. At Wilton, Edith would have been taught everything she would need to know for her future as the wife of a nobleman; she would have undergone instruction in religion, spinning and embroidery, household management and possibly music and dancing. She was known to be skilled in verse and prose and, according to William of Malmesbury, she was 'a woman whose bosom was the school of every liberal art, though little skilled in earthly matters'.[5] As the daughter of a Saxon father and Danish mother, she was fluent in both languages, in addition to Latin, French and Irish, a useful skill in a multicultural country like England.

As we have seen, Godwin's success continued under Cnut's successors, Harold I Harefoot and Harthacnut. The earl was implicated in the death of Alfred the Ætheling, brother of the future king, Edward the Confessor, and son of King Æthelred II and Queen Emma. In 1036, a year after King Cnut's death, Alfred was enjoying Godwin's hospitality at Guildford, after landing in Kent, ostensibly on a visit to his mother, Queen Emma, at Winchester, although he may well have arrived with the hope of wresting the throne from the Danish line. Alfred's men were attacked by the men of Harold Harefoot; many were killed or maimed while the ætheling was seized, taken to imprisonment at Ely and blinded. Although it is still not clear whether or not Godwin had a hand in Harold's actions, or was merely caught in the middle, Alfred's death at Ely in 1037, probably as a result of his wounds, would later come back to haunt Godwin; King Edward the Confessor would use the earl's involvement as an excuse to rid himself of the influence of the Godwin family in 1051, even if only temporarily. Conflicting reports from the time make it impossible to know for certain whether Godwin was involved in Alfred's death, or if he was an innocent bystander caught up in King Harold's actions. Writing a century later, Henry of Huntingdon claims Godwin was already planning to make his daughter queen and that Alfred, 'by reason of his primogeniture and his superior ability would disdain such a marriage.[6] And so, Godwin set his sights on Edward, persuading the English nobles that 'it was not safe to allow a bold and crafty race [Alfred's Norman supporters] to take root among them.'[7] It is hard to think of the wily Earl Godwin as being wholly innocent, but it seems fanciful to think that he plotted Alfred's murder during the reign of King Harold I in order to put his daughter on the throne as the wife of Edward, at a time when it appeared highly unlikely that Edward would ever attain the crown. Although we may never know the level of Godwin's involvement in the murder, it seems that King Edward, despite the fact he had to work with Godwin to maintain his kingship, was far from convinced of the earl's innocence.

After King Harold I Harefoot's death, Earl Godwin was prominent in assisting in the transition of power to King Harthacnut, son of Emma and Cnut. Harthacnut had been in Denmark when his father died and, although a power-sharing agreement with Harold Harefoot, Cnut's son by Ælfgifu of Northampton, had been in place, Harthacnut had lost out on the kingship of England when he failed to return to the country to claim the crown. His mother, Queen Emma, with the support of Earl Godwin, had held Wessex for him for a time. However, when it became apparent that Harthacnut was in no hurry to return to England, King Harold I Harefoot seized the initiative, and the crown, and sent Emma into exile in Bruges, Flanders. Harthacnut was on the verge of invading England when he heard of Harold I Harefoot's death, in March 1040. As a result, Harthacnut returned peacefully and was universally accepted as king. His half-brother, King Harold, had been buried in Westminster and Harthacnut's first act was to order that his body be dug up and thrown into the Thames marshes. Neither Harold I nor Harthacnut were popular kings of England; both brothers had remained unmarried and failed to produce a legitimate heir. As a result, on Harthacnut's death, the throne passed back to the descendants of King Alfred the Great in the person of Edward, later known as Edward the Confessor, the youngest son of Æthelred II the Unready.

By the time Edward came to the throne in 1042, Godwin's prominent position appeared unassailable and it was mainly due to his influence that Edward's accession, as an unknown prince who had spent most of his life in foreign exile, was achieved without opposition. Indeed, according to John of Worcester, 'Edward was proclaimed king at London, chiefly by the exertions of earl Godwin, and Lyfing, bishop of Worcester.'[8]

Edith first appears in the *Anglo-Saxon Chronicle* in the entry for 1045: 'In this year King Edward took to wife Edgitha [Edith], the daughter of Earl Godwin, ten nights before Candlemas.'[9] Such a short statement belies the importance of this event, which took place on 23 January 1045, for all involved. For Edith, it was the start of her life as a wife and queen. For Godwin it was the triumph of his career; his daughter was marrying the King of England. It was an event which, at once, both demonstrated and guaranteed the pre-eminence of himself and his family at King Edward's court. For Edward, it was the cementing of the friendship between himself and his foremost earl. Edward was about forty years of age, while Edith was probably twenty or a little younger, at least half his age. The wedding was probably followed immediately by Edith's anointing and coronation, as she is consistently styled 'queen' in the chronicles of the time, rather than 'lady'. We have few descriptions of Queen Edith; the relevant pages describing Edith, her wedding day and her relationship with Edward are missing from the *Vita Edwardi regis*. According to William of Malmesbury, writing a century later, 'on seeing her, if you were amazed at her erudition, you must absolutely languish for the purity of her mind, and the beauty of her person.'[10]

It is frequently argued that Edward was backed into a corner by Earl Godwin and the marriage to Edith was forced upon him. However, Edward would have known that one of his primary duties as king was to marry and produce an heir. Writing after Edward's death, Osbert de Clare claimed that a search was made for 'a wife worthy of such a husband … from among the daughters of the princes'.[11] Edith was, in fact, an ideal choice of bride for the king; the eldest daughter of Earl Godwin, she was 'recommended by the distinction of her family'.[12] Moreover, she was no child, so the king would not have to wait to consummate the marriage. Her mother had produced a large brood of children and so it would have been believed that Edith would do the same. Also, there was little alternative choice for a bride of suitable rank within England; neither of the two other prominent earls, Leofric of Mercia and Siward of Northumbria, had girls in their families of marriageable age. Edward could have looked for a bride on the Continent, but this would have been time-consuming to arrange, sending out envoys in search of suitable brides, making formal approaches to overseas kings and negotiating the international treaty such a marriage would require. At his age, the king did not have the time to waste on such complex negotiations when there was a suitable bride much closer to home. All in all, the choice of bride was a good one, it made sound political sense for both the king and the earl. In 1045 England, Edward and the Godwin family would have been looking forward to the arrival of a prince and heir. Earl Godwin and Countess Gytha must have been happily anticipating the birth of a grandson who would one day sit on the throne of England. Unfortunately, this was not to be, and, in more than twenty years of marriage Edward and Edith failed to produce a single living child.

Edith's role as queen was an important part of the government of the kingdom. It was her responsibility to run the palaces in which the king and court resided. The court was wherever the king was, and it was not only home for him and his family, but also the centre of royal administration. It was an important symbol of royal dignity. Edith was assisted in this by numerous royal and household officials, but the ultimate responsibility was hers. She gave the instructions for the ordering of the palaces and possibly had control of the treasury, as Queen Emma had done before her. Queen Edith took especial care of King Edward's image, ensuring his royal dignity and that of his household was preserved at all times. She was aware that her husband's public image was as important to his kingship as his work with his nobles, in council. With the preservation and enhancement of Edward's royal image in mind, Edith made sure that the royal apartments were richly decorated and furnished with tapestries, which could serve as bedclothes or wall hangings. She safeguarded the king's public image by taking care to ensure that Edward always appeared regally dressed, using luxury fabrics, silks and royal purple, and the richest furs, such as marten skins, accompanied with jewels, gold and ivory. Edith commissioned a jewel-encrusted staff for Edward to carry, a visual reminder to others of his royal dignity. The king and queen were generous in their bequests to churches and abbeys, donating, among other things, vestments, copes, illustrated books and altar cloths.[13]

Her commissioning of the *Vita Edwardi regis*, written shortly after the Norman Conquest, is testimony to her desire to control and preserve King Edward's image, even after his death. That it also painted the Godwinson family in a favourable light is understandable; it was probably her family loyalties that brought her into conflict with the French members of her husband's household, the privy counsellors and royal administrators who resented her being 'in all the royal counsels ... strongly preferring the king's interests to power and riches'.[14] Edith's presence as one of the king's counsellors is also attested to in the many charters on which she is witness, and on which she is acknowledged as the king's *'conlaterana'*, or 'she who is at the king's side.'[15]

As the decade came to a close, however, it was apparent that Edith had failed in her primary duty as queen; to produce an heir. She was a staunch supporter of her family and it was in her care for them that her enemies may have seen the means to her downfall, to putting her aside and finding Edward a new queen. Earl Godwin's power had continued to grow unabated during the 1040s. Two of his sons, Harold and Swein, were given earldoms of their own, as was Countess Gytha's nephew, Beorn Estrithson. With so many earls, and Edith as queen, the family, in general, was seen as the power behind the throne. The dark deeds of her eldest brother, Swein, did not help matters; his two exiles, first for the kidnapping and rape of Eadgiva, abbess of Leominster, and the second for the murder of his own cousin, Beorn Estrithson, were more than sufficient proof to many that the Godwinsons saw themselves as above the law. Disaffection was growing in the late 1040s, with Edward attempting to stamp his authority on Earl Godwin and his family. A number of Edward's French affinity were allowed to establish castles within the Godwinson earldoms, such as that established by Robert fitz Wimarc at Clavering in Essex, part of Harold's earldom of East Anglia. Godwin's power would have risen higher if his kinsman, Ælric's, election as Archbishop of

Canterbury had been endorsed by King Edward in 1050. The king, however, quashed the election and put forward his own candidate, Robert of Jumièges, who had been Bishop of London since 1044 and was a member of Edward's Norman affinity.[16]

The growing disaffection with the Godwin clan came to the fore in 1051, following a visit by Count Eustace of Boulogne, widower of the king's sister, Goda. On his journey home, the Count of Boulogne's men were refused lodgings at a house in Dover and killed the homeowner in retaliation. This sparked an armed conflict with the town, which left many dead on both sides. Eustace returned to the king to explain his actions, claiming the townsmen had attacked his men first.

As Dover was part of his earldom, King Edward ordered Godwin 'to carry war into Kent toward Dover'.[17] Godwin refused. In the stand-off that ensued, both Earl Godwin and King Edward called their armed retainers to them. The king was in Gloucester and sent for support from Earl Siward from Northumbria and Earl Leofric from Mercia, and their troops. Earl Godwin gathered together his men, and those of Harold and Swein, at Beverstone, just a few miles outside Gloucester. Tensions ran high, but the fact that neither side wanted a civil war meant that conflict, for the moment, was avoided. The two sides exchanged hostages and Earl Godwin and his sons were summoned to a council in London to answer the charges laid against them. As the earl reached London, however, his men, and those of his sons, began to fade away. Swein was declared outlaw and Godwin and Harold ordered to attend the king's council, the *witan*, with no more than twelve men. When Godwin's request for hostages, as surety of his safety, was refused, he was allowed a truce of five days to leave the country. With his wife, and sons Swein, Tostig and Gyrth, and Tostig's wife, Judith, with as many of their possessions as they could carry, Earl Godwin returned to Bosham and took ship to Flanders. Harold and his brother Leofwine made their way to Bristol, from where they took to the sea in one of Swein's ships, making for Ireland.

As for Edith, the *Anglo-Saxon Chronicle* records 'the king dismissed the lady who had been consecrated his queen, and ordered to be taken from her all that she had in land, and in gold, and in silver, and in all things; and committed her to the care of his sister at Wherwell.'[18] John of Worcester records Edith's banishment as harsh treatment, stating, 'The king repudiated the queen Edgitha [Edith], on account of his wrath against her father Godwin, and sent her in disgrace, with only a single handmaid, to Wherwell, where she was committed to the custody of the abbess.'[19] The *Vita Edwardi regis,* however, suggests that Edith was sent to the royal abbey of Wilton, 'with royal honours and an imperial retinue'.[20] It must be remembered that the *Vita Edwardi regis* was written to honour the memory of King Edward, and so may have tempered Edith's treatment so as to make the king appear more generous towards his wife than he actually was at the time. It must have been a worrying and lonely time for Edith, secluded in a nunnery and all her family across the seas, not knowing when she would see them again, nor what the future held. To make matters worse, Archbishop Robert of Jumièges was counselling Edward to have his marriage annulled and to marry again, in the hope of producing an heir. It is testimony to the relationship that Edward and Edith had, despite the problems with her family, that Edward refused to countenance the Archbishop's suggestion.

In the spring of 1052, with a show of force, Earl Godwin and his family successfully returned from their short exile; the Norman contingent of the King's household, including Archbishop Robert of Jumièges, fled in the face of Earl Godwin's return. The archbishop was declared outlaw and sailed for Normandy. Before the king and his council, Earl Godwin swore that he was 'guiltless of that which was laid against him, and against Harold his son and all his children'.[21] The king had no choice but to forgive Godwin 'and Godwin was clean granted his earldom as fully and completely as he ever owned it, and his sons all just what they earlier owned, and his wife and his daughter as fully and as completely as they earlier owned; and they affirmed complete friendship between them.'[22] Queen Edith was released from the nunnery, whether it was at Wilton or Wherwell, and Edward 'restored her to her former dignity'.[23]

The uneasy peace had been restored for a time, but at the Easter celebrations of 1053, any remaining problems with Godwin came to an abrupt end. While he was feasting with the king at Winchester, the earl was taken ill and died several days later. None of the chronicles mention Edith as being present, only her brothers, but its seems likely that she would have accompanied her husband on a visit to her own family, even if she wasn't present at the actual feast. The earl was buried in the Old Minster at Winchester, where he would be lying for eternity close to his old kings, Cnut and Harthacnut, and Queen Emma, who had passed away the previous year. Edith's oldest surviving brother, Harold, was now Earl of Wessex. Godwin was the first of the old guard of powerful earls to die, but in 1055 Earl Siward of Northumbria died and in 1057 Earl Leofric of Mercia followed them to the grave. Earl Leofric was succeeded by his son, Ælfgar, but Earl Siward's son, Waltheof, was still a child considered too young to shoulder the responsibilities of such a powerful earldom on the northern border. It seems likely that Earl Harold and Queen Edith both used their influence with the king in order to get their brother, Tostig, chosen as the new Earl of Northumbria in 1055.

After more than ten years of marriage, Edith and Edward remained childless and it was decided that contingencies were needed to secure the succession. Edward the Exile, the son of Edmund II Ironside and nephew of Edward the Confessor, was sent for, from his forty-year exile in Hungary. He returned to England in 1057 but died within days of reaching his homeland and before he even had the chance to meet his uncle. He had been accompanied by his wife, Agatha, and three children, Margaret, Christina and Edgar. With his father's death, young Edgar, who was still only a child, possibly as young as five or six, was now the ætheling (meaning throne-worthy). He was adopted by Edith, who raised him and took charge of his education, along with several other noble boys, including Harold, the son of Ralph, Earl of Hereford, who also died in 1057. Edgar's sisters, Margaret and Christina, were sent to the convent at Wilton to complete their education. Christina would later take holy orders, becoming the abbess of Romsey Abbey and overseeing the education of her nieces, Edith and Mary, the daughters of her sister, Margaret, Queen of Scotland.

Edith's influence was seen at various times throughout Edward's reign. In 1060 when Cynesige, Archbishop of York, died at York on 22 December, he was replaced by Aldred, Bishop of Worcester and the see of Hereford, 'which had been entrusted to his administration on account of his great diligence, was given to Walter, a Lorrainer, and chaplain to queen Edgitha [Edith].'[24] Walter was a Lotharingian and one of Edith's two known chaplains; the other was Ælfgar, a tenant of Peterborough Abbey. Giso, Bishop of Wells, had also acknowledged Edith's help in securing the endowments of his see and 1065 saw the completion of the rebuilding, in stone, of the abbey at Wilton, financed by Queen Edith. It was rededicated by Hermann, Bishop of Ramsbury. Bishop Hermann was also Bishop of Sherborne, thanks again to Edith's influence, who was holding the episcopal manor there in 1066. She also gave land in Sussex to St John's Church at Lewes, and endowed Abingdon Abbey with Lewknor in Oxfordshire. As with many notable ladies, however, some foundations see her differently. The monks at Evesham accused her of ordering the collection of relics at Gloucester, so that she might choose some for herself. They claimed that their own relics of St Ordulf were saved by the intervention of the saint himself.[25] Edith is also said to have been reprimanded by the king when she offended a visiting churchman, Gervin, the Abbot of Saint-Riquier in Ponthieu, by refusing a kiss of greeting from him. Edith made amends for the offence by presenting the abbot with a richly embroidered cope.[26]

The years before the Norman Conquest were years of upset and upheaval for Edith and her Godwinson family. Tostig's rule in Northumbria was far from peaceful and would erupt into open revolt in 1065; the earl himself appears to have spent more and more time away from his earldom, frequently staying at court, hunting with the king and going on pilgrimage to Rome. The catalyst was the death of Gospatric, a Northumbrian thegn who was a member of the noble house of Bamburgh, who took his complaints against Tostig, of heavy-handedness and excessive taxation, to the king at his Christmas court. Edith, it seems, took matters into her own hands in order to help her favourite brother. John of Worcester alleges that Gospatric was 'treacherously killed by order of queen Edgitha [Edith] at the king's court on the fourth night of Christmas, for the sake of her brother Tosti [Tostig]'.[27] Unfortunately – or rather, predictably – Gospatric's murder only served to exacerbate things and within months the Northumbrians had risen, marched on York and seized Tostig's armoury and treasury, killing 200 of the earl's supporters. Moreover, the Northumbrians invited Morcar, the brother of Earl Edwin of Mercia, to become their new earl and lead them in the march south to seek justice. Despite his inclination towards a military solution, in order to appease the Northumbrians and avoid civil war, Edward was persuaded to accept the new arrangement, confirming Morcar in his new earldom and agreeing to reinstate the 'Laws of Cnut' within Northumbria.[28]

Tostig was sent into exile with his wife, two sons and the rest of his household. When she had to say goodbye to her favourite brother as he left England's shores on 1 November 1065, Edith is said to have 'wept inconsolably ... for when misfortunes had attacked them in the past, she had always stood as a defence, and had both repelled all the hostile forces with her powerful counsels and also cheered the king and his retinue.'[29] However, the declining health of her husband, King Edward the Confessor, must have begun to take all her attention shortly afterwards. By December the king was failing rapidly, he was unable to attend the consecration of Westminster Abbey on Holy Innocents' Day, 28 December 1065, and Edith had to take his place. The abbey was Edward's crowning glory and, perhaps, greatest achievement and had taken more than fifteen years to complete. The king died on the Eve of Epiphany, 5 January 1066. On the Bayeux Tapestry, Edward's deathbed scene depicts Edith sitting at the foot of the king's bed as he passes away. The king was buried in his newly consecrated abbey at Westminster the following day.

Edith and Edward had been married just eighteen days shy of twenty-one years. Apart from Edith's brief banishment to a nunnery, when the Godwin clan were exiled in disgrace in 1051, they appear to have been a couple who were content with each other. Indeed, when Edward was given the opportunity to repudiate Edith, he refused. Edith's commissioning of the *Vita Edwardi regis* is testament to her high regard for her husband and king. One shadow hung over the whole marriage, however, and that was the lack of an heir. There have been thousands and thousands of words written, over the centuries, on why Edward and Edith never produced children. And yet, we cannot say for certain that Edith was never pregnant, nor that she didn't give birth to one or more short-lived or stillborn children.

Throughout the centuries, chronicles have been circumspect when it comes to royal children and they often go unrecorded, at least until they have passed the tender years when infant mortality was high. The evidence for this, of course, is in the fact that we frequently do not know their specific dates of birth, nor even the year in which they were born, in the eleventh century and many others.

With Edward the Confessor, however, there is another possible explanation for the lack of children. Much has been made of Edward the Confessor's saintliness and the idea that he was celibate. Indeed, Osbert de Clare, the Westminster monk who was making an argument for Edward's canonisation, claimed that the king remained a virgin his entire life, although how he knew this we do not know. De Clare claimed Edward 'lived in true innocence' and 'preserved the purity of his flesh'.[30] Another chronicler, William of Jumièges, repeated the gossip he had heard, saying, 'as they say, the pair preserved perpetual virginity.'[31] The *Vitae Edwardi regis*, the Life of King Edward, commissioned by Queen Edith, is ambiguous on the subject. It states that Edward 'preserved with holy chastity the dignity of his consecration' and that he lived his life 'in true innocence dedicated to God'.[32] However, it also states that Edith and Edward were 'one person dwelling in a double form', which is what one might expect of a husband and wife.[33] Moreover, we do know that, on her wedding night, Edith was 'delivered to the bridal apartments with ceremonial rejoicing', suggesting that no one expected the marriage to remain unconsummated.[34]

Stories of Edward's virginity survived through the centuries and were believed by succeeding generations. A century later, William of Malmesbury discussed Edward the Confessor's chastity and the reasons behind it:

When she became his wife, the king acted towards her so delicately, that he neither removed her from his bed, nor knew her after the manner of men. I have not been able to discover, whether he acted thus from dislike to her family, which he prudently dissembled from the exigency of the times, or out of pure regard to chastity: yet it is most notoriously affirmed, that he never violated his purity by connection with any woman.[35]

Edward was succeeded on the throne by Edith's brother, King Harold II, who was hastily crowned at Westminster Abbey on the same day as King Edward was laid to rest in the abbey. Edith's relationship with Harold is hard to pin down. It is possible that there was some animosity between the brother and sister, following their brother Tostig's banishment. Tostig is said to have been Edith's favourite brother and the fact that Harold refused to support Tostig's position as Earl of Northumbria by force, may have led to a breach between the two older siblings. The *Vita Edwardi regis* states that Harold 'did not so much divert the king from his desire to march [against the rebels] as wrongfully and against his will desert him.'[36] Tostig himself was so convinced that Harold had acted treacherously against him that Harold was forced to take a public oath, swearing that he was not in league with the rebels.

Edith is not mentioned in the events of 1066; it is possible that she initially retired to her own estates to grieve for her husband. Even if she was not on the best of terms with Harold, it is hard to believe that she would have wanted to see her family destroyed as utterly as they were by the evening of 14 October 1066, with four of her brothers dead on battlefields in the space of three weeks; Tostig in Yorkshire, Harold, Gyrth and Leofwine at Hastings. Her relationship with William the Conqueror, however, was cordial and this has given rise to suggestions of conspiring against her brother; William of Poitiers alleged that Edith worked to secure William's accession, against the interests of her brother. It is more likely, however, that Edith was merely accepting the situation for what it was. William would have treated her kindly and fairly, simply because she was a crowned and anointed queen. The *Carmen Hastingae Proelio* tells how Queen Edith advised the people of Winchester to submit to William on his arrival in the city after the Battle of Hastings.[37] Rather than demonstrating her support for William, however, this was more likely to be a consideration for the lives of the citizens of the capital of her family's Wessex domains.

After the Conquest, Edith was allowed to keep her lands. She mainly resided at Winchester, although she did spend some time at the nunnery at Wilton, from where she attested a sale of land to Bishop Giso of Wells in February 1072. She also visited

Archbishop Stigand, deposed as Archbishop of Canterbury by King William and replaced by the king's own candidate, Lanfranc. At Easter 1071, she attended the consecration of Walcher as the new Bishop of Durham. More or less retired from the national stage, Edward the Confessor's queen played little part in the politics of the reign of William the Conqueror, although she may have been the one to persuade William to be lenient with the citizens of Exeter following her mother Gytha's attempts to raise rebellion there in 1067.

Queen Edith died at Winchester on 18 December 1075, aged about fifty years old, 'and the king caused her to be brought to Westminster with great pomp; and he laid her with King Edward, her lord.'[38] She had been Queen of England for just shy of twenty-one years, and lived nine years into the new, Norman, regime. She had counselled and supported her husband throughout their marriage, save for the few short months she was secluded in the nunnery. Edith was the first English queen to receive the *Aurum Reginae*, the 'Queen-gold', the right of the queen to receive every tenth mark in taxes paid to the king from the city of London.[39] She held property throughout the kingdom and on Edward's death, was probably the richest woman in England. Members of her household are also mentioned as landholders in Domesday Book, including her chamberlain, Ælfweard, Wulfweard White, and his son-in-law, Æthelsige, a steward, whose marriage was arranged by Queen Edith herself. Her steward, Godwine, attested a charter in 1062, while her *cameraria*, or waiting woman, Matilda was married to a Worcestershire thegn, called Ælfweard.[40]

Of Edith, William of Malmesbury said; 'Both in her husband's lifetime, and afterwards, she was not entirely free from suspicions of dishonor; but when dying, in the time of King William, she voluntarily satisfied the by-standers of her unimpaired chastity, by an oath.'[41] Stories of her piety and support of the Church are found far and wide, as are the stories of her avarice at the expense of the Church. She is praised for giving land to Bishop Giso of Wells, to whom she leased Milverton Somerset, and persuaded her husband, the king, to grant Wedmore to the same bishop. However, she is also alleged to have coveted three estates belonging to Peterborough, for which the abbot paid thirty-six gold marks (£216) to redeem; and to have seized the property that was bequeathed to Peterborough by Archbishop Cynesige of York, which included a gospel book and £300's worth of treasure.[42]

The author of the *Vita Edwardi regis* praised Edith for her learning, virtue and chastity, her generosity and piety, an opinion echoed by Goscelin of Bertin.[43] Godfrey of Winchester wrote of Edith:

> The nobility of your forebears magnified you, O Edith,
> And you, a king's bride, magnify your forebears.
> Much beauty and much wisdom were yours
> And also probity together with sobriety.
> You teach the stars, measuring, arithmetic, the art of the lyre,
> The ways of learning and grammar.
> And understanding of rhetoric allowed you to pour out speeches,
> And moral rectitude informs your tongue.
> The sun burned for two days in Capricorn
> When you discarded the weight of your flesh and went away[44]

The Wives of Harald Hardrada

Harald Hardrada, King of Norway, was the wild card in the events of 1066. His claim on the English throne was even more tenuous than the claims of William, Duke of Normandy, and King Harold II himself. Moreover, Harald's interests had previously been mainly focused in Eastern Europe, rather than the west. He was, however, a formidable warrior, the most renowned of his age, and victory in England would have created a new Scandinavian empire. Just as with King Cnut and King Harold II, Harald Hardrada's marital affairs were far from straightforward; he was married to two women simultaneously. Little is known about Harald's wives, and even less of their relationship with the Norwegian king, but we find a little of their stories within Harald's own legend.

Harald Hardrada, who was known at the time as Harald Sigurdsson – Hardrada being a name he acquired after his death – was born in 1015. He was the son of a Norwegian petty king known as Sigurd the Sow. His mother was Ásta Guthbrandsdóttir, who had previously been the wife of Harald Grenski, the great-great-grandson of Harald Fairhair, the first king of Norway. Ásta had an older son with Harald Grenski, Harald Hardrada's older, half-brother, Óláf Haraldsson. Óláf II Haraldsson was twenty years' Harald's senior and declared himself king of Norway in the same year that Harald was born, 1015.

Norway had been ruled by King Sweyn Forkbeard, King of England, Denmark and Norway, until his death in England in February 1014 caused the disintegration of his Scandinavian empire.

Óláf had spent some of his youth raiding England and visiting Normandy, before returning to Norway in 1015 to lay claim to the throne, with the support of the five petty kings of the Norwegian Uplands. A year later, he defeated Earl Sweyn, who had been virtual ruler of Norway after the death of Sweyn Forkbeard, at the Battle of Nesjar, and proceeded to consolidate his hold on the country. Within a few years his control of Norway was greater than any previous king; he had managed to destroy the petty kings of the south and subdue the aristocracy. He was originally betrothed to Princess Ingegerd, the daughter of King Olof Stötkonung of Sweden, without her father's approval. Nothing came of the betrothal and Ingegerd later married Yaroslav I the Wise, Prince of Kiev, and was the mother of Harald Hardrada's wife, Elisiv. In 1019 Óláf married Astrid, the illegitimate daughter of the same King Olof of Sweden, and therefore the half-sister of his ex-fiancée. Óláf and Astrid had one child, a daughter named Wulfhild, who married Ordulf, Duke of Saxony, in 1042. Óláf also had an illegitimate son, Magnus, with a concubine named Alvhild; he would ascend the Norwegian throne and be known as Magnus the Good.[1]

Despite his initial successes as king, however, Óláf alienated many of his people, apparently accusing the wives of many of his nobles of witchcraft, and by 1026 was facing tough opposition. In that year, his forces, combined with those of Sweden, had been defeated by Cnut, King of England and Denmark, at the Battle of Helgeå and in 1028 his nobles sided with Cnut against him. Cnut claimed the Norwegian throne and Óláf fled into exile, first to Sweden and then to Kiev. He returned the following year but was killed at the Battle of Stiklestad, fought between Óláf and his adherents and those disaffected nobles who supported King Cnut. Óláf's death made it into the English chronicles, with John of Worcester saying 'Olaf, king and martyr, son of Harold, king of Norway, was wickedly slain by the Norwegians.'[2] The *Anglo-Saxon Chronicle* records the story more fully, for the year 1030: 'This year returned King Olaf into Norway; but the people gathered together against him, and fought against him; and he was there slain, in Norway, by his own people, and was afterwards canonized.'[3] Óláf was declared a saint in 1164. Óláf's younger half-brother, Harald Hardrada, was only fifteen years of age at the time of the Battle of Stiklestad but fought alongside Óláf and was wounded in the battle. Following Óláf's death, Harald first fled to Sweden before moving on to Kievan Rus, where Óláf's illegitimate son, Magnus, still a child, would also seek shelter. Harald spent three or four years at the court of Yaroslav I the Wise, Prince of Kiev, husband of Óláf's sister-in-law, Ingergerd. At fifteen, Harald's military skills were already impressive and Yaroslav made him a captain in his army; the young Norwegian fought alongside the Kievan prince on his campaigns against the Poles in 1031.

Having gained a reputation that spread throughout eastern Europe, in 1034 or 1035 Harald and his force of 500 men moved on to Constantinople, where he joined the ranks of the Varangian Guard, in the service of the Byzantine emperor, Michael IV (reigned 1034–1041). Snorri Sturluson recounts Harald's first view of Constantinople:

Before the cold sea-curling blast
The cutter from the land flew past,
Her black yards swinging to and fro,
Her shield-hung gunwale dipping low.
The king saw glancing o'er the bow
Constantinople's metal glow
From tower and roof, and painted sails
Gliding past towns and wooded vales.[4]

A formidable warrior and commander, Harald eventually became leader of the whole Varangian guard, seeing action against Arab pirates and the towns of Asia Minor that supported them. Harald's conquests included as many as eighty Arab strongholds and took him as far east as the River Euphrates. Harald also fought around Jerusalem and in 1038 he joined an expedition to Sicily, during which he fought alongside Norman mercenaries. Throughout his adventures in Byzantium, Harald sent his plunder back to Prince Yaroslav in Kiev; treasure which, given the number of towns he had taken, must have been quite considerable. Norse Sagas tell the story of Harald's adventures in the emperor's service, describing battles in Asia, Africa, Sicily and Bulgaria; although the stories have been colourfully embellished, they are based in fact. His contribution to putting down the revolt led by Peter Delyan in Bulgaria earned him the nickname 'Devastator of the Bulgarians'.[5] Harald's own skald (the ancient Scandinavian word for a composer and reciter of poems honouring heroes and their deeds), Tjodolv Arnorsson, said Harald had participated in no less than eighteen great battles during his Byzantine service.[6] Snorri Sturluson agreed with the number:

> Harald the Stern ne'er allowed
> Peace to his foemen, false and proud;
> In eighteen battles, fought and won,
> The valour of the Norseman shone.
> The king, before his home return,
> Oft dyed the bald head of the erne [sea eagle]
> With bloody specks, and o'er the waste
> The sharp-claw'd wolf his footsteps traced.[7]

The death of Emperor Michael IV in December 1041, however, brought a change in circumstances for twenty-five-year-old Harald. Michael IV's death led to a power struggle between Michael's wife, Empress Zoe, and his nephew, Michael V. Michael IV had gained the throne by marrying Zoe, the daughter of Emperor Constantine VIII, as her second husband, the first having been murdered in his bath. Their marriage, however, was full of distrust and Zoe was allowed no power or say in government. When Michael V was crowned, Zoe was banished to a monastery, an act which caused an uprising in Constantinople. Michael V was dethroned after only four months and sixty-four-year-old Zoe was created co-ruler, alongside her sister, Theodora, who had been forced – by Zoe – to take holy vows many years before.

As for Harald, conflicting reasons are given for the fact that he was arrested and imprisoned for a time following Michael IV's death. One story tells of an envious Michael V, suspicious of the amount of treasure the Norwegian had amassed in his service to Emperor Michael IV, accusing Harald of having defrauded the Byzantine treasury. Another, very likely spurious, story suggests that Harald was imprisoned for requesting marriage with a young lady named Maria, supposedly a niece or granddaughter of Empress Zoe.

William of Malmesbury, on the other hand, suggests he was arrested for defiling a noble woman, while another proposes he was accused of murder.[8] Whatever the cause, Harald was the victim of the power struggles between the rival palace factions. Although the exact timing of the arrest and imprisonment is confusing, one possibility is that Harald was imprisoned for wanting to leave his service in the Varangian Guard. Harald and two of his companions, Haldor and Ulf, were lowered into a dungeon, with only one high window for access. Snorri Sturluson claimed that he escaped with the help of his dead half-brother, St Óláf:

> Next night a lady of distinction with two servants came, by the help of ladders, to the top of the tower, let down a rope into the prison and hauled them up. Saint Olaf had formerly cured this lady of a sickness and he had appeared to her in a vision and told her to deliver his brother.[9]

He then led the contingent of Varangian Guards who supported the Empress, his friend, against those Varangians who stayed loyal to the emperor. When Michael V was eventually deposed, blinded and exiled, the Sagas claim that it was Harald himself who carried out the blinding. Following the accession of Empress Zoe, and her marriage to the new emperor, Constantine IX, Harald requested that he be released from his duties and allowed to return home. It is said that the empress refused him permission to leave, but the Norwegian managed to escape Constantinople with two ships and his most loyal supporters. One of the ships was destroyed by the iron chains which blocked the seagoing entrance and exit to Constantinople, but the other made it through by shifting the weight in the ship so that it effectively jumped over the chain. Harald returned to his friend Yaroslav I in Kiev, to whom he had sent the vast amounts of plunder he had amassed from his adventures in Byzantium. In 1044, whilst still at Yaroslav's court, Harald married the Kievan prince's daughter, Elisiv (also known as Elisiff, Elizabeth or Elizaveta).

Elisiv was born around 1025 and would probably have met Harald when he first appeared at her father's court as a fifteen-year-old fugitive from Cnut's conquest of Norway in 1034–5.

Elisiv was probably the oldest daughter of Yaroslav's eleven children with his wife, Ingegerd. Through her mother, Elisiv was the granddaughter of Sweden's king, Olof Stötkonung. Her father, Grand Prince Yaroslav, was responsible for the rise in power and influence of Russia in the eleventh century; his court was considered modern and cultured. Indeed, when Anna of Kiev, Elisiv's sister, married Henry I of France, she was said to miss the culture and sophistication of the court in Kiev. Anna wrote to her father shortly after her marriage in 1051, saying 'What a barbarous country you sent me to – the dwellings are sombre, the churches horrendous and the morals – terrible.'[10] Yaroslav's children were well educated and able to read and write, including the girls; Anna demonstrated her superior level of education when she signed her marriage contract with her full name, in her own hand. King Henry I of France, her new husband, could only manage to write a cross. Although we have no description of Elisiv, we know that Anna was renowned for her 'exquisite beauty, literacy and wisdom' and we can assume that Elisiv, having shared in her sister's upbringing, was no less accomplished.[11]

Elisiv had as many as ten siblings, of whom many made illustrious royal marriages. Of her sisters, Anastasia, married Andrew I, King of Hungary. It is also possible, though far from certain, that another sister was Agatha, the wife of Edward the Exile and mother of Edgar Ætheling and St Margaret, Queen of Scotland. Edward had fled to Kiev as a child, with his brother Edmund, following the death of his father, Edmund II Ironside, King of England. Of Elisiv's brothers, the oldest, Vladimir, reigned as Prince of Novgorog until his death in 1036, Isiaslav married the sister of the King of Poland and would succeed his father as Grand Prince of Kiev; he was succeeded as Prince of Kiev by his brother Sviatoslav, who was in turn succeeded by another brother Vsevolod, who married a daughter of the Byzantine emperor.

It is possible that marriage between Harald and Elisiv had been discussed during the Norwegian's first visit to Kiev in 1030. However, given that she would have only been nine or ten years of age when Harald left for Constantinople, it seems hard to believe the claims that Elisiv had refused him on the grounds that he was not wealthy enough to marry her; her father, on the other hand, may well have done so. This may also explain Harald sending his plunder back to Kiev for safekeeping, as proof of his increasing wealth and eligibility as a husband for Elisiv, even if he still held no princely title and was exiled from his homeland. In 1044, therefore, there was no financial objection to Harald and Elisiv marrying and there is evidence that Harald was genuinely in love with his Russian bride; Harald wrote poetry to his Russian princess:

> Past Sicily's wide plains we flew,
> A dauntless, never-wearied crew;
> Our Viking steed rushed through the sea,
> As Viking-like fast, fast sailed we.
> Never, I think, along this shore
> Did Norsemen ever sail before;
> Yet to the Russian queen, I fear,
> My gold-adorned, I am not dear.[12]

Stuf the Blind echoed the love story:

> Agder's chief now got the queen
> Who long his secret love had been.
> Of gold, no doubt, a mighty store
> The princess to her husband bore.[13]

The last two lines suggest that Elisiv brought a substantial dowry to the marriage, probably jewels and gold rather than land, as her sister Anna had done when she married King Henry of France. With the treasure Harald amassed during his sojourn in Constantinople and Elisiv's dowry, Harald now had the means to return home. He initially made for Sweden, arriving there in 1046. He formed an alliance with Swein Estrithson, who was a nephew of King Cnut through his mother, Estrith, Cnut's sister. Estrith may have been the daughter of Sweyn Forkbeard by Sigrid the Haughty, who was also the mother of Olof Stötkonung, King of Sweden, by her first husband, Erik the Victorious, King of Sweden; making Estrith and Olof half-siblings. This also meant, therefore, that Swein was cousin to Harald's wife, Elisiv, who was herself a granddaughter of

King Olof through her mother, Ingegerd. He was also related to the powerful Godwinson clan in England through his father, who was brother to Countess Gytha, Earl Godwin's wife. A triumvirate was completed when Harald also formed an alliance with Anund Jacob, King of Sweden, who succeeded his father, King Olof, in 1022. As the son of King Olof, Anund was the brother of Ingegerd of Sweden and therefore uncle to Harald's wife, Elisiv.

Much had changed in Scandinavia since Harald's journey into exile fifteen years before. King Cnut, King of England, Denmark and Norway, had died in 1035 and had been succeeded by his sons, Swein in Norway, Harthacnut in Denmark and Harold I Harefoot in England. However, in the same year as his father's death, Swein had been driven out of Norway due to his oppressive rule. He was replaced as king by eleven-year-old Magnus, the illegitimate son of Óláf II Haraldsson, the king who had died fighting at the Battle of Stiklestad in 1030 and who was the half-brother of Harald Hardrada. It was, therefore, Harald's illegitimate nephew who now sat on the Norwegian throne. Magnus was a popular king, who earned himself the epithet, Magnus the Good. In 1042 Magnus had challenged Harthacnut for the throne of Denmark, but agreement had been reached between the two men, whereby whichever king lived longest would be the other's heir. Magnus therefore inherited Denmark on Harthacnut's death in 1042, but not England, which went to Harthacnut's surviving half-brother, Edward the Confessor. This agreement, however, ignored the claims of Swein Estrithson, who had been left in charge of Denmark when Harthacnut went to England. Swein invaded Denmark in 1043 but was defeated by Magnus at the Battle of Lyrskov Heath, near Hedeby. At one stage, the two men came to uneasy terms, whereby Swein was made earl under Magnus, but Swein continued to oppose Magnus, now King of Norway and Denmark.

Although he may have initially only wanted to claim his father's petty kingdom in the north, Harald was soon in opposition to his nephew and launched a bid for the throne. As Harald was contesting Magnus' rule in Norway, and Swein was doing the same in Denmark, it meant that the two men were natural allies. Harald and his allies made several lightning raids into Denmark, in an attempt to show Magnus's inability to retaliate and protect his subjects. Rather than go to war, however, Magnus chose political compromise to appease Harald, by making him co-king of Norway in 1046. Harald would rule over Norway, as King Harald III, and Magnus would rule Denmark, while also being ultimate overlord of the two countries, with Magnus saying:

> I give thee half of the Norwegian power, with all the scat and duties, and all the domains thereunto belonging, with the condition that everywhere thou shalt be as lawful king in Norway as I am myself; but when we are both together in one place, I shall be the first man in seat, service and salutation; and if there be three of us together of equal dignity, that I shall sit in the middle, and shall have the royal tent-ground and the royal landing-place. Thou shalt strengthen and advance our kingdom, in return for making thee that man in Norway whom we never expected any man should be so long as our head was above ground.[14]

The uneasy peace between Magnus and Harald was ended in 1047, with Magnus's death at the young age of twenty-three. Magnus died suddenly on 25 October; he was unmarried and childless but rather than leave Denmark to his uncle, Harald, Magnus had arranged for Harald's erstwhile ally, Swein Estrithson, to succeed him. The two kings had kept separate courts, Harald's court in Norway was presided over by his queen, Elisiv. Within a couple of years of arriving in Norway, the couple had two daughters, Ingegerd and Maria Haraldsdóttir. Ingergerd was probably born in 1046, with Maria arriving a year of two after. According to Snorri, in the winter 'after King Magnus the Good died, King Harald took Thora, daughter of Thorberg Arnason, and they had two sons; the oldest called Magnus, and the other Olaf.'[15] Harald probably went through some form of marriage ceremony, more likely a handfasting than a Christian marriage, with Thora in 1048. The marriage appears to have been a political arrangement, in order to garner the support of the powerful Giskeætten family, the chiefs of which played a significant role in power politics.

Thora was the daughter of Thorberg Arnason and Ragnhild Erlingsdóttir and was probably born about 1025; her brother, Fin Arnason, was a good friend of Harald's and was married to

Bergliot, the daughter of Halfdan, a brother of Harald Hardrada and St Óláf.[16] The marriage also provided the desired son and heir, which his first marriage had failed to do; both of Thora's sons would later become kings of Norway. Of Harald's two sons, Magnus appears to have been as warlike as his father. In 1058, aged no more than ten or eleven, he led a fleet to England in support of Earl Ælfgar of Mercia, after the earl had been outlawed only a year since he had succeeded to his father's earldom. Magnus was little more than a figurehead for the expedition and unlikely to have been expected to make crucial military decisions, but it would have been good experience for the young prince, and a taste of what the future held for him. By the time he was sixteen, Magnus was a successful warrior and is said to have clashed with his father; the two almost coming to blows until the king was restrained by friends.[17]

It has been suggested that the marriage may have come following the death of Elisiv, or that Elisiv never even left Russia, but given that her daughters were born once Harald was back in Scandinavia, this seems improbable. Harald's daughters are not likely to have been the daughters of Thora, as Maria was engaged to Eystein Orre, who would have been her uncle had she been Thora's daughter. Harald having two wives simultaneously seems the most likely explanation. As demonstrated by King Cnut and King Harold II of England, two wives and, therefore, two families, were not uncommon in Scandinavian culture; although in these two cases an earlier wife was put aside for the sake of a more prestigious marriage, whereas Harald Hardrada's first marriage was the more prestigious, while the second was politically expedient.

With Magnus dead, Harald was now sole and undisputed king in Norway. However, he also had his eyes set on Denmark and the desire to unite the two crowns, as they had been under Cnut and Magnus before him. With that in mind, according to the *Anglo-Saxon Chronicle*, in 1048, 'Harold, the uncle of Magnus, went to Norway on the death of Magnus, and the Northmen submitted to him. He sent an embassy of peace to this land [England], as did also Sweyne from Denmark, requesting of King Edward naval assistance to the amount of at least fifty ships; but all the people resisted.'[18] Swein obviously knew that Harald would want Denmark and sent to England for assistance, which was refused. Harald, on the other hand, was intent on making peace with England so that they would stay out of Scandinavia's internal power struggles.

A decade of conflict followed but Harald's campaigns to conquer Denmark did not go as planned. Swein proved reluctant to face Harald in battle unless he was confident of victory, a strategy which wore down the Norwegians. It was only when Harald had to let go of his Norwegian levies that Swein struck, catching Harald off guard. The Norwegian king's army only escaped by floating their plunder and dumping their prisoners in the water in order to slow down their pursuers. Swein compassionately allowed his ships to recover their comrades from the sea before continuing the chase, thus giving the Norwegians the time to escape.

Harald achieved a great victory in 1062 with the sea battle of Nisa but was still unable to completely vanquish the Danes. In another confrontation, Harald captured his old friend Fin Arnason, who was fighting for the Danes. It seems that Harald had brought his wife, Thora, Fin's sister along on the campaign and when Fin refused Harald's offer of quarter (life), Harald made a further offer:

> "Wilt thou accept thy life, then, from thy she-relation Thorer [Thora]?"
> The earl: "Is she here?"
> "She is here," said the king.
> Then Earl Fin broke out with the ugly expressions which since have been preserved, as a proof that he was so mad with rage that he could not govern his tongue: –
> "No wonder thou hast bit so strongly, if the mare was with thee."
> Earl Fin got life and quarter and the king kept him a while about him...[19]

Harald made overtures of peace with Denmark in 1064 and although Swein was reluctant at first to believe that the Norwegian king was genuine, a treaty was finally ratified in 1065, with an exchange of prisoners and both kings undertaking that they would never fight each other again. It could be surmised that Harald concluded the peace with Denmark in view of the proposed invasion of England in 1066. However, no one expected Edward the Confessor to be dead by Twelfth Night in 1066, nor could Harald have foreseen the opportunity to claim the English throne that arose from the English king's death. It seems more than likely that Harald's peace with Swein Estrithson was a genuine need or desire to get on with his Scandinavian neighbours; the happy consequence, for Harald, was that the Norwegian king could grasp the opportunities that arose in England in 1066. It is uncertain what made Harald embroil himself in the challenge for England's crown in 1066, whether he saw himself as the heir of Magnus and therefore inheritor of the promise between Harthacnut and Magnus, that they were each other's heirs and everything would go to the survivor, or whether he just saw an opportunity and the chance to unite the old Anglo-Scandinavian kingdom once more. Snorri Sturluson says that on hearing of his brother's accession to the throne of England, Tostig visited his cousin, Swein Estrithson, in Denmark to ask for his aid in returning to England. When Swein refused to help, Tostig then turned to Harald in Norway. According to Snorri, Tostig told Harald, '... I will bring the matter so far that most of the principal men in England shall be thy friends, and assist thee; for nothing is wanting to place me at the side of my brother Harold but the king's name. All men allow that there never was such a warrior in the northern lands as thou art; and it appears to me extraordinary that thou hast been fighting for fifteen years for Denmark, and wilt not take England that lies open to thee.'[20]

Whatever the reason for his involvement, at the beginning of September Harald sailed his fleet of more than 200 ships to Shetland and then to Orkney, where he gathered reinforcements and left his wife and daughters to await news of events. There is some confusion as to which wife was left on Orkney, some sources say Elisiv, who, as Harald's wife and queen would have expected to become queen of England, had he been successful. Some historians argue that as Thora was a relative of the Earl of Orkney, she would have been more likely to travel with Harald than Elisiv. We know from Thora's joining one of Harald's expeditions to Denmark that he was not averse to taking his wives with him to war. However, given that young Magnus was left behind to rule Norway, aged only sixteen, it seems likely that his mother was also left behind, to advise him. According to Snorri; 'Thora, the daughter of Thorberg, also remained behind; but he took with him Queen Ellisif [Elisiv] and her two daughters, Maria and Ingegerd. Olaf, King Harald's son, also accompanied his father abroad.'[21]

After leaving his queen and daughters on Orkney, Harald joined forces with Tostig, who had spent the summer at the court of King Malcolm III in Scotland. They sailed down the eastern coasts of Scotland and England before landing at Scarborough, where the townspeople opposed them until they set fire to a part of the town. The army then moved into the Humber and arrived at York, where the Earls Morcar and Edwin stood ready to oppose them. The Battle of Fulford saw the annihilation of their English army, the survivors running to York for safety. In the face of the victorious Norwegian army, York sued for peace, offering to deliver the city to Harald, and to provide hostages from among the children of the most illustrious citizens. Harald arranged for more hostages from throughout the surrounding counties to be delivered to him at Stamford Bridge. It was as he was awaiting the arrival of these hostages, on 25 September 1066, with two-thirds of his army armed but not in their armour, that King Harold of England arrived to face him.

It seems that Harald was caught by surprise by the English king. A third of his army had remained with the boats at Riccall, under the command of Harald's son, Olaf. According to Snorri Sturluson, England's King Harold offered to restore Tostig to his earldom if he would change sides, but to Harald Hardrada he only offered, as earlier quoted slightly differently from another source, 'seven feet of English ground, or as much more as he may be taller than other men.'[22] Tostig refused his brother's offer and the ensuing battle was a fierce one, with many killed on both sides. Eventually Harald was killed; 'King Harald Sigurdson was hit by an arrow in the windpipe, and that was his death-wound. He fell, and all who had advanced with him, except those who retired with the banner.'[23] Tostig was also killed in the battle, which saw Harold of England victorious. At the battle's end, Olaf, who had been guarding the fleet, was allowed to take the survivors and his father's body and sail back to Norway, collecting Queen Elisiv and her daughter, Ingegerd, from Orkney along the way.

Harald and Elisiv's daughter, Maria, is said to have died suddenly on 25 September 1066, the same day as the Battle of Stamford

Bridge, on hearing of her father's death. She had been betrothed to Eystein Orre, the brother of Harald's second wife, Thora; Eystein was also among the dead at Stamford Bridge. Maria's sister, Ingegerd, returned to Norway with her mother and half-brother. She was first married to Olaf I, King of Denmark, who died in 1095, with whom she had a daughter, Ulvhild. Following Olaf's death, Ingegerd married Philip, King of Sweden. She was widowed again in 1118 and died around 1120, having been consecutively queen of Denmark and Sweden. Norway was ruled successively by Harald's sons Magnus and Olaf; their mother, Thora, may have remarried, although there is some confusion. According to Adam of Bremen, she married either King Swein of Denmark or an unknown Swedish king.[24] As with much of her life, the year of Thora's death remains unknown.

Of Harald's queen, Elisiv, little is known after King Harald's death, not even the year of her own death. This Russian princess, who captured the heart of one of the greatest Viking warriors of all time, disappears into the mists of history.

Edith Swanneck

The story of Edith Swanneck is one of the greatest love stories of medieval England, though it is alloyed with betrayal and loss. We know very little about Edith; indeed, we are not entirely certain of her identity so she is a shadowy figure in the annals of history, barely making an appearance in the chronicles of her time. Her story is pieced together through that of Harold and of her children. There is, therefore, much conjecture, but very little definite fact surrounding Edith's story.

As with many names in the eleventh century, even the spelling of Edith's name provides an extra smokescreen when it comes to finding the real Edith Swanneck. Edith could also be known as Eadgyth, Eadgifu, Eddeua or Edeva, lending even more mystery to her identity. Unlike with most leading characters of the Norman Conquest era, we know absolutely nothing of her parentage. She was probably born around 1025, somewhere in East Anglia, as that seems to be where she had most of her land. It seems likely that she met Harold at about the same time as he became earl of East Anglia, in 1044. If so, it is possible that Edith the Swanneck and the East Anglian magnate, Eadgifu the Fair, are one and the same. Eadgifu the Fair held more than 270 hides of land and was one of the richest magnates in England before the Norman Conquest; she was also known as Eadgifu the Rich, for that reason. The majority of her estates lay in Cambridgeshire, but she also held land in Buckinghamshire, Hertfordshire, Essex and Suffolk; in Domesday Book, Eadgifu held the manor at Harkstead in Suffolk, which was attached to Harold's manor of Brightlingsea in Essex and some of her Suffolk lands were tributary to Harold's manor of East Bergholt. Such close proximity to Harold's lands would lend weight to the argument that she was Edith Swanneck. Moreover, while it is by no means certain that Eadgifu is Edith Swanneck, several historians – including Ann Williams – make convincing arguments that they were the same person.[1] Their names, Eadgifu and Eadgyth, are so similar that the difference could be merely a matter of spelling or mistranslation; indeed, the abbey of St Benet of Hulme, Norfolk, remembers an Eadgifu Swanneshals among its patrons.[2] While 'Eadgifu' and 'Eadgyth' may have been fairly common names, 'Swanneshals' was not, suggesting St Benet's was referring to Harold's Edith.

Harold Godwinson was probably born between 1022 and 1025. He received the earldom of East Anglia in 1044 and, as the oldest surviving son of Godwin, Earl of Wessex, succeeded to his father's earldom in 1053. Harold's sister, Edith, was the wife of King Edward the Confessor, while three of his surviving brothers, Tostig, Gyrth and Leofwine were all earls. Harold was not only one of the king's foremost earls but also one of his most respected advisors and war leaders. In short, the Godwinsons were the most powerful family in the kingdom, after the king himself. Or possibly even more powerful, as it was the support of Godwin that allowed the smooth accession of Edward following the death of his half-brother, King Harthacnut. The marriage of Edith and Harold was known as a *more Danico*, a marriage in the 'Danish fashion', more commonly known as a 'handfasting'. Such marriages were not uncommon in the early part of the eleventh century, with King Cnut having undergone one such with his first wife, Ælfgifu of Northampton. They had the advantage of recognising any children born of the union as legitimate, while allowing either spouse to marry more advantageously should the opportunity come along; as Cnut did when he married Emma of Normandy following his accession to the English throne.

Harold and Edith had at least five children; including at least three sons, Godwin, Edmund and Magnus, and two daughters, Gytha and Gunhild. Their eldest son was probably Godwin, born in 1049, with Edmund born in 1050 and Magnus born around

1051, Gytha may have been born in 1053 and Gunhild was the youngest, born in 1055.³ Confusion arises with two other possible sons, Harold and Ulf, who would have been the youngest of Edith's brood; however, it is unclear whether they were the children of Harold and Edith, or the posthumous twin sons of Harold and Ealdgyth of Mercia, Harold's queen, who may have given birth to them in December 1066. Unfortunately, there is no definite information either way.

There is no mention of Edith during the family dramas of the 1040s and 1050s, so we have no idea of her level of involvement within the wider sphere of the Godwinson family. It may well be that she stayed on her own, or Harold's, estates when he was away on the country's or family's business. However, the fact that they had at least five children, in the space of six or seven years, means they managed to find time together, despite Harold's duties as earl. As a notable landholder in her own right, Edith may have attended some of the major events of the era, although as a woman, she would have been denied access to others, such as the *witan*. She may have attended court on occasion, such as for the wedding of Harold's sister, also called Edith, to King Edward in January 1045.

Edith merits no mention when Earl Godwin and his family were exiled to Flanders at the end of 1051. As his parents and brothers, Swein and Tostig, all made the journey to Bruges, Harold and his brother Leofwine had taken their brother Swein's ship to Ireland, probably leaving Edith residing quietly on her own estates, away from the suspicious court. Harold returned a few months later, in the spring of 1052, sailing his nine ships into the mouth of the River Severn and raiding into Somerset and Devon. The people of the two counties opposed him and Harold 'put them to flight and slew there more than thirty good thanes, besides others.'⁴ Harold eventually turned his fleet eastward, to join his father, Godwin, who had brought his own fleet out of Bruges. Together they raided along the south coast, from the Isle of Wight to Ness, gathering ships at Pevensey, Romney, Hythe and Folkestone along the way. Earl Godwin had managed to gather loyal supporters to him from throughout the Wessex heartlands of Essex, Sussex, Surrey and Kent, who 'said they would with him live or die'.⁵ However, Edward had a fleet of forty ships at Sandwich, waiting for Godwin to appear; when they were launched against him, the earl's forces managed to escape, and Edward's fleet returned, first to Sandwich and then to London. Godwin returned to the Isle of Wight to replenish his supplies before again sailing eastwards around the Kent coastline. Eventually, they arrived at London, where King Edward and his fifty ships were stationed. Godwin and Harold 'then sent to the king, praying that they might each be possessed of those things which had been unjustly taken from them'.[6] At the *witan*, called after Edward's Norman advisers had fled the city, Godwin 'cleared himself ... before his lord King Edward, and before all the nation.'[7] The king resisted Earl Godwin's overtures, until it was made clear to him that the remaining earls of the kingdom would not support a violent confrontation with Godwin and his sons. Edward eventually, if reluctantly, accepted Godwin, his family and adherents, back into his friendship, returning to them all their confiscated lands and titles.

It is not hard to imagine Harold riding off to reunite with Edith once his lands and titles were returned. In 1052 they were a young family, with at least three children and possibly a fourth child on the way. Edith probably provided comfort for Harold the following year, when his father died after falling ill on Easter Sunday 1053, having suffered some sort of seizure during a meal with the king at Winchester. The event would have changed their life considerably, with Harold inheriting his father's earldom of Wessex and relinquishing that of East Anglia to Ælfgar, the son of Earl Leofric of Mercia. Although Harold would have still held lands in East Anglia, his main responsibilities would now lie south of the River Thames in his vast county of Wessex. This may have put a strain on the relationship but does not seem to have damaged it in any significant way; their last daughter, Gunhild, was born in 1055, two years after Harold took over his father's earldom.

Harold's responsibilities as Earl of Wessex would see him become the king's right-hand man, as adviser and as the general of Edward's armies. It was Harold who led the campaigns against the Welsh, such as that of 1055, when the outlawed Earl Ælfgar sought help from Gruffydd ap Llywelyn, King of Gwynedd. According to the *Anglo-Saxon Chronicle* the sentence of outlawry was without foundation and may have been the result of the political machinations associated with Tostig's accession to the earldom of Northumbria, vacant following the death of Earl Siward, and much coveted by Ælfgar. Ælfgar was soon back in the king's good graces, suggesting that the sentence of outlawry was, indeed, unfounded. However, this was not before he and his Welsh allies marched on Hereford. Earl Ralph, King Edward's nephew, and his men fled on horseback in the face of the advancing army, earning him the name Ralph the Timid. Ælfgar and his allies ravaged Hereford and burnt Bishop Athelstan's newly built minster to the ground. The priests and many others were killed and the Minster's treasures stolen by the marauding army. Four or five hundred people were killed in Hereford. Earl Harold gathered an English army at Gloucester to face Ælfgar, but the two sides managed to come to terms, where 'amity and friendship were established between them'.[8] The sentence of outlawry was reversed and Ælfgar's lands and titles returned to him.

In the following year, Bishop Athelstan died and his successor, Leofgar, who had been Harold's mass priest, joined in the campaign against the Welsh. The bishop 'took to his spear and to his sword, after his bishophood; and so marched to the field against Gruffydd the Welsh king. But he was there slain and his priests with him, and Elnoth the sheriff, and many other good men with them; and the rest fled... Difficult it is to relate all the vexation and the journeying, the marching and the fatigue, the fall of men, and of horses also, which the whole army of the English suffered.'[9] Eventually, Earls Harold and Leofric negotiated a peace with Gruffydd, who swore oaths that he 'would be a firm and faithful viceroy to King Edward'.[10] Poor Bishop Leofgar had held his bishopric for all of eleven weeks and four days; he was succeeded by Bishop Eldred.

With her large brood of children around her, Edith must have been aware of the concerns at court regarding her namesake, the queen, who had failed to produce the much-needed son and heir for King Edward. In 1057 Edith would have joined the rest of England in the short-lived rejoicing over the arrival of Edward the Exile from Hungary. The son of Edmund II Ironside, Edward was to become his uncle's heir, but died within days of arriving at the English court. Edith's own sons may have been introduced to Edward's son, Edgar, the new ætheling, who was of a similar age to them. Following his father's death, Edgar was adopted by Queen Edith and raised in her household. The year 1057 also saw the deaths of two earls: Leofric of Mercia died and was succeeded by his son Ælfgar and Ralph of Hereford – Ralph the Timid – was succeeded by his young son Harold, who was also taken into Queen Edith's household and brought up alongside Edgar the Ætheling.

Earl Harold was campaigning in Wales, again, in 1063 attacking Rhuddlan from the sea while his brother Tostig attacked by land. The two brothers made truces with the Welsh, who handed over hostages, while still campaigning against Gruffydd. Eventually, Gruffydd's own men turned against the Welsh king, killing him and sending his head, as a token, to Harold, who sent it on to King Edward. Edward gave Wales into the care of Gruffydd's two brothers, Bleddyn and Rhiwallon, who swore oaths and gave hostages as proof of their good faith, and promised they 'would pay tribute from the land as was paid long before to other kings'.[11] In1065, Gruffydd's son, Caradoc, would destroy Harold's new hunting lodge, which was in the process of being built in Portskeweth in Wales, and kill all the labourers, probably in revenge for his father's death.

It seems likely that it was in the spring of 1064 that Harold took ship to Normandy, probably in the hope of obtaining the release of his brother, Wulfnoth, and nephew, Hakon, who had been held there as hostages since the Godwinson's return from exile in 1052. Edith may have waved goodbye to him as his ship left England; Harold may have even been accompanied by one or more of his sons, although they do not get a mention, so it is merely conjecture. The eldest boys were now about fourteen and fifteen years old, old enough to learn the duties that may be expected of them in later years. Harold may also have carried messages from King Edward, and it is during this trip that the Normans claim Harold swore an oath to uphold Duke William of Normandy's entitlement to the English throne when Edward died. The embassy to Normandy was only partly successful; Harold's nephew, Hakon, was released and allowed to return to England with his uncle, but his brother Wulfnoth remained as a hostage, possibly as leverage against Harold's promise to promote William's claim to the throne.

The year 1065 saw yet another family crisis, when Tostig's earldom of Northumbria rose in revolt against him. Gospatric, a scion of the House of Bamburgh, had been murdered at King Edward's Christmas court, and tension had been simmering ever since. With Tostig away at court, visiting his sister and hunting with the king, the Northumbrians attacked York, seizing the earl's armoury and treasury, and killing 200 of his supporters. Then the Northumbrians turned to Morcar, brother of Earl Edwin of Mercia, who had succeeded his father, Earl Ælfgar, in 1062, to ask him to become their new earl. Together with Edwin's Mercians, the Northumbrians marched south, reaching Northampton where they were met by Earl Harold, who opened negotiations with the rebels and carried their demands to the king. The Northumbrians demanded that King Edward recognise Morcar as their earl and returned the county to the 'laws of Cnut'. Edward was prepared to oppose these demands with force, but Earl Harold and the other leading men of the land refused to commit to a civil war to return Tostig to his earldom. Tostig accused his brother of treachery, of colluding with Edwin and Morcar, but Harold swore a public oath that he had not. One can imagine Edith being incensed that Harold's own brother could make such an accusation, though whether she was even anywhere near the events is impossible to know. Her oldest sons, however, now in their mid-teens, are likely to have been part of their father's household by this time and may have related the events to their mother. Tostig was eventually exiled – with his wife, children and household – leaving for Flanders on 1 November 1065. Even if he wasn't bothered about his brother's departure, Harold must have had concern for his mother, Gytha, and sister, Edith, who were both devastated by Tostig's exile.[12]

Events moved rapidly following the Northumbrian uprising; King Edward's health fell into a severe decline, probably not helped by the exile of his dear friend, Tostig. By Christmas it was evident that he was near death. His wife had to attend the dedication of his new church at Westminster Abbey in his stead; the abbey had been more than ten years in the building. Within days of Westminster Abbey's consecration, King Edward was dead, and was buried in his new foundation the following day, on

6 January 1066. On the same day, the Abbey probably hosted its first coronation of an English king, as Earl Harold was crowned King of England.

These must have been soul-searching times for Harold and Edith. One wonders if Edith knew that Harold becoming king would cause such a great change in her relationship. Having been his constant companion for twenty years, Edith was suddenly an unacceptable consort as queen of England. How Harold broached the subject with Edith, we do not know, nor do we know if he informed her of his intention to marry another before the event, or if he waited until he could present it as a *fait accompli*. Ealdgyth was the daughter of Ælfgar, Earl of Mercia, and, according to William of Jumièges, very beautiful. She was the widow of Gruffydd ap Llywelyn, King of Gwynedd from 1039 and ruler of all Wales after 1055, with whom she had had at least one child, a daughter, Nest. As we have seen, Gruffydd had been murdered in 1063, following an expedition into Wales, some sources suggest it was by Harold himself, however, according to the *Anglo-Saxon Chronicle* the deed was performed by Gruffydd's own men. Harold's subsequent marriage to Ealdgyth not only secured the support of the earls of Northumbria and Mercia, but also weakened the political ties of the same earls with the new rulers of north Wales.

As Harold's wife, Ealdgyth was, therefore, for a short time, queen of England. However, with Harold having to defend his realm, first against Harold Hardrada and his own brother, Tostig, at Stamford Bridge in September of 1066 and, subsequently, against William of Normandy at Hastings, it is unlikely Ealdgyth had time to enjoy her exalted status. At the time of the Battle of Hastings, 14 October 1066, Ealdgyth was in London, but her brothers took her north to Chester soon after the outcome of the battle was known. Although sources are confused, it is possible that Ealdgyth was heavily pregnant and gave birth to at least one son, Harold Haroldson, within months of the battle.

Notwithstanding his marriage to Ealdgyth, it seems Edith the Swanneck remained close to Harold and it was she who was waiting close to the battlefield when the king faced William of Normandy at Senlac Hill, near Hastings, on October 14, 1066. She is said to have awaited the outcome alongside Harold's mother,

Right: Detail of a miniature of Queen Emma before an altar. (Courtesy of the British Library Catalogue of Illuminated Manuscripts)

Below: *Genealogical Chronicle of the English Kings*: Detail from the roll of Cnut, king of England, Denmark, and Norway, and his sons Harald Harefoot and Harthacnut. (Courtesy of the British Library Catalogue of Illuminated Manuscripts)

Miniature of King Cnut and Emma of Normandy before a large gold cross on an altar. (Courtesy of the British Library Catalogue of Illuminated Manuscripts)

Winchester Cathedral, resting place of Emma, Cnut and Harthacnut. (Courtesy of Peter 2010)

Above: Jewelled binding of one of the four beautiful Gospel books commissioned by Judith of Flanders showing Christ in Majesty and the Crucifixion. The title on the cross is of translucent green enamel. (Courtesy of the Morgan Library, purchased by J. P. Morgan in 1926)

Above right: Statue of Lady Godiva by William Thomas, England, 1862. (Courtesy of Rijks Museum)

Right: Statue of Alfred Lord Tennyson, author of *Lady Godiva*, Lincoln, England (Author's collection)

Above: The memorial plaque commemorating the 1066 Battle of Stamford Bridge. (Author's collection)

Below: The memorial commemorating the 1066 Battle of Stamford Bridge. (Author's collection)

Stow Minster, Lincolnshire, a foundation supported by Lady Godiva and her husband, Earl Leofric. (Author's collection)

Pevensey Beach, Sussex, landing site of the Norman invaders. (Author's collection)

Pevensey Castle, Sussex, one of the first castles built by the Norman invaders. (Author's collection)

The battlefield of Hastings. (Author's collection)

Battle Abbey Gatehouse, Battle, Sussex. (Author's collection)

Statue of King
Harold II,
Waltham Abbey,
Essex. (Author's
collection)

Memorial plaque to King Harold II, Waltham Abbey, Essex. (Author's collection)

Waltham Abbey, Essex, purportedly the final resting place of King Harold II. (Author's collection)

Bamburgh Castle, Northumbria, ancient seat of the Earls of Northumbria. (Author's collection)

Westminster Abbey, burial site of Edward the Confessor and site for the coronations of William the Conqueror and Queen Matilda. (Photo courtesy of Daniel Gleave)

The Tower of London, built on the orders of William the Conqueror. (Photo courtesy of Karen Mercer, Bexlin Photography.)

Lincoln Cathedral, where the great-grandson of Harold II and Edith Swanneck is buried. (Author's collection)

Right: *Genealogical Chronicle of the English Kings*: Rollo, Duke of Normandy, and his descendants, and William the Conqueror. (Courtesy of the British Library Catalogue of Illuminated Manuscripts)

Below: Cliffords Tower, York, one of the many fortresses constructed by William the Conqueror. (Author's collection)

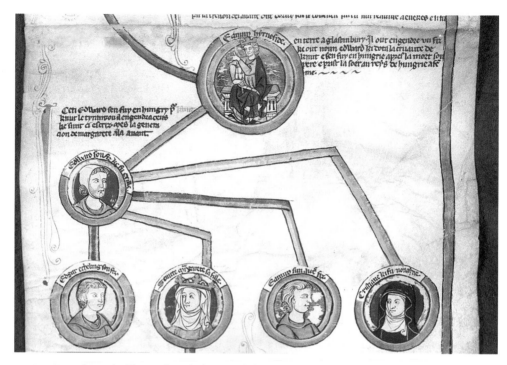

Genealogical Chronicle of the English Kings: Edmund II Ironside and his descendants: Edward Ætheling, Edgar, Margaret, Edmund, and Christine. (Courtesy of the British Library Catalogue of Illuminated Manuscripts)

Edinburgh Castle. (Photo courtesy of Craig Cormack)

Dunfermline Abbey, founded by St Margaret, Queen of Scotland. (Photo courtesy of theerstwhilekate)

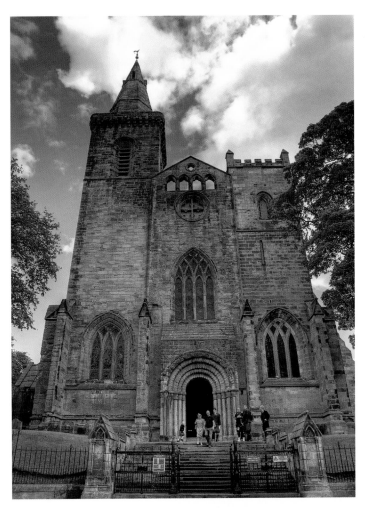

The new Queensferry Bridge, replaces the old Queens Ferry, named after St Margaret, Queen of Scotland. (Photo courtesy of John McSporran)

Lewes Castle, Sussex, built by the de Warenne family, holders of the Rape of Lewes. (Author's collection)

The Priory of St Pancras, Sussex, first Cluniac priory in England and original burial place of Gundrada de Warenne. (Author's collection)

The Church of St John the Baptist, Southover, Sussex, final resting place of Gundrada and William de Warenne. (Author's collection)

Scene from the the Bayeux Tapestry, showing the death of Edward the Confessor, attended by Queen Edith of Wessex. (With the kind permission of Dennis Jarvis)

Scene from the the Bayeux Tapestry depicting a woman and child fleeing a burning house, set alight by the Norman invaders. (With the kind permission of Dennis Jarvis)

Scene from the the Bayeux Tapestry, depicting 'Ælfgyva and a certain cleric'. (With the kind permission of Dennis Jarvis)

Detail of the 'Ælfgyva and a certain cleric' scene from the Bayeux Tapestry. (With the kind permission of Dennis Jarvis)

Gytha, and two monks from Waltham Abbey, sent to witness the battle for their brethren. Having lost a son, Tostig, just three weeks before, fighting alongside the Norwegians and against his brothers at the Battle of Stamford Bridge, Gytha lost three more sons – Harold, Gyrth and Leofwine – in the battle at Hastings. Her grandson, Hakon, may also have died in the battle; he was brought back from Normandy by Harold in 1064, after having been held hostage there since 1052.[13]

It is heart-wrenching, even now, to think of Edith and the elderly Gytha, wandering the blood-soaked field in the aftermath of the battle, in search of the fallen king. Sources say that Gytha was unable to identify her sons amidst the mangled and mutilated bodies. The monks of Waltham Abbey, Osgod Cnoppe and Ethelric Childemeister, accompanied Edith as she searched for Harold on the battlefield. She had to undo the chain mail of the victims in order to recognise certain intimate identifying marks on the king's body – probably tattoos. 'She had at one time been the king's concubine and knew the secret marks of his body better than others, for she had been admitted to a greater intimacy of his person. Thus they would be assured by her knowledge of his secret marks when they could not be sure from his external appearance.'[14] The sources are confusing, however, and some contemporary accounts have Gytha finding the body of Harold and offering William her son's weight in gold to be allowed to take his body for burial. William apparently refused, saying that Harold's body should lay unburied among the countless others who had followed him. According to William of Poitiers:

> The two brothers of the King were found near him and Harold himself, stripped of all badges of honour, could not be identified by his face but only by certain marks on his body. His corpse was brought into the Duke's camp, and William gave it for burial to William, surnamed Malet, and not to Harold's mother, who offered for the body of her beloved son its weight in gold. For the Duke thought it unseemly to receive money for such merchandise, and equally he considered it wrong that Harold should be buried as his mother wished, since so many men lay unburied because of his avarice.[15]

The monks of Waltham Abbey had a tradition of Edith bringing Harold's body to them for burial, soon after the battle. Although other sources suggest Harold was buried close to the battlefield, and without ceremony. The *Carmen Hastingae* and William of Poitiers both claim that the English king was buried on the summit of a nearby cliff, overlooking the English Channel. It is hard not to hope that Edith was able to perform this last service for the man she had loved for twenty years. Any trace of Harold's remains was swept away by Henry VIII's Dissolution of the Monasteries, so the grave of England's last Anglo-Saxon king is lost. However, Waltham Abbey still displays a memorial in the abbey gardens, dedicated to the last Anglo-Saxon king and marking the possible site of his grave.

Harold's mother, Gytha, eventually fled into exile on the Continent, taking Harold and Edith's daughter, another Gytha, with her. The *Saxo Grammaticus*, written at the end of the twelfth century, claimed that two of Harold's sons fled to Denmark immediately after the battle with their sister, Gytha, and that it was King Swein Estrithson who arranged Gytha's marriage to Grand Prince Vladimir of Kiev.[16] It may well have been also with the approval or assistance of Countess Gytha that her granddaughter and namesake was married to Vladimir II Monomakh, prince of Smolensk and (later) Kiev, sometime after her arrival on the Continent. Although no date is given for the marriage, it must have been by 1075, as the younger Gytha was the mother of Mstislav the Great, Grand Prince of Kiev, who was born in 1076; he was the last ruler of a united Kievan Rus. According the *Russian Primary Chronicle*, Edith and Harold's daughter, Gytha, died on 7 May 1107; although her name is not given, she is merely recorded as the first wife of Vladimir II.[17] It was through Gytha and her son Mstislav that the Godwinson blood eventually made it back into the English Royal Family, through Mstislav's direct descendant Philippa of Hainault, wife and queen of King Edward III of England.

Immediately after the Battle of Hastings, other sources claim Edith and Harold's sons fled to Ireland, where they enlisted the help of Diarmit mac Máel and in 1068 Godwine, Edmund and Magnus, returned to England with a force of Dublin Norse mercenaries, possibly making a brief stop on Flat Holm to visit their grandmother, Gytha, before landing in Somerset and making for Bristol. Although the campaign failed to take the city, they returned to Ireland with considerable plunder after raiding along the Somerset coast. Within a year, two of Edith and Harold's sons were back again (although John of Worcester does not specify which two). They sailed from Ireland in the summer of 1069, landing in Devon, near Barnstaple, with a force of sixty-four ships. The local lord, Brian, Count of Brittany, 'came unawares against them with a large army and fought with them, and slew there all the best men that were in the fleet; and the others, being small forces, escaped to the ships: and Harold's sons went back to Ireland again.'[18] Little is heard of the boys after this. It seems likely that they travelled to Denmark and joined the court of their cousin, King Swein Estrithson. All but one of them lived into the 1080s, though the dates of their eventual deaths remain uncertain.

Harold and Edith's youngest daughter, Gunhild, joined the nunnery at Wilton. It is unclear whether she took holy vows as a nun, or her stay in the nunnery was for her protection against forced marriage, or worse, at the hands of the Norman invaders. Gunhild was healed from a malady in her eyes, tumours, by Wulfstan of Worcester, because 'he owed not a little to her father's memory'.[19] This could also have been the reason she stayed at Wilton, possibly in the care of her aunt Queen Edith, rather than fleeing to the Continent with the rest of her family. Sometime in the early 1070s, Gunhild left Wilton to live with Count Alan Rufus (Alan the Red), either as his concubine, or handfast wife. Count Alan, Lord of Richmond in Yorkshire, was one of the twelve sons of Eudo, Count of Brittany. Whether or not Gunhild left the convent willingly, or was kidnapped, seems to be in question, but when Alan died in 1093, instead of returning to the convent Gunhild became the mistress of Alan's brother and heir, Alan Niger (Alan the Black). It appears that Anselm, Archbishop of Canterbury, tried unsuccessfully to get Gunhild to return to the convent. In 1075, Alan Rufus had taken over the forfeited lands of Earl Ralph de Gael, lands that had belonged to Edith the Fair before the Norman Conquest. He now held vast lands in East Anglia – lands that had once belonged to Eadgifu the Fair and, if

Eadgifu was Edith the Swanneck, it is possible that Alan 'married' Gunhild to strengthen his claims to her mother's lands.[20]

Gunhild's daughter, Matilda, married a Norman knight from Lincolnshire, Walter D'Eyncourt. Their son William was fostered at the court of King William II Rufus and died whilst still young. The full inscription of his, now-lost, memorial plaque in Lincoln Cathedral read; 'Here lies William, son of Walter D'Eyncourt, kinsman of Remegius, Bishop of Lincoln who made this church – the said William, scion of the royal stock, died on the 3rd day of November [missing line, probably the year] while being reared in the court of King William, son of the great King William who conquered England.'[21]

Of Edith the Swanneck, there is no trace after Harold is interred at Waltham Abbey. It may be that she went to Ireland with her sons or retired to the convent at Wilton with her daughter, Gunhild, we simply do not know. Edith died as she had lived, away from the centre of events, out of the limelight. Overall, history has treated Edith kindly; empathising with a woman who remained loyal to her man to the end, despite the fact her status, as wife or concubine, was always in question.

Ealdgyth

The love of Harold Godwinson's life was Edith Swanneshals, also known as Edith Swanneck, but she was not his wife according to the Church, and she was not his queen. She and Harold had gone through a handfasting ceremony, otherwise known as a Danish marriage, which meant their children were considered legitimate, though probably not throne-worthy, not æthelings. Edith, moreover, was not seen as a suitable wife for a king, and certainly no queen; although she was, apparently, rich, she could not bring Harold powerful allies to strengthen his hold on the throne. This meant that when Harold came to the English throne in January 1066, he needed to find a more acceptable wife, preferably one with powerful friends.

Harold Godwinson was born around 1022 and did more in the forty-four years he was on this earth than most people could achieve in three lifetimes. He received the earldom of East Anglia in 1044 and, as the son of Godwin, Earl of Wessex, he succeeded to his father's earldom in 1053. His sister was the wife of King Edward the Confessor, and his brother was the Earl of Northumberland (for a time). Harold was not only one of the king's foremost earls but also one of his most respected advisors. In short, the Godwinsons were the most powerful family in the kingdom, after the king himself, with Harold the most able of the clan. At one point, Harold, with his father and brothers, had been exiled from England after quarrelling with the king. He is even said to have sworn an oath to back William of Normandy's claim to the

English throne in the likely event that Edward the Confessor died without an heir; a claim that William used to the full, in order to secure papal approval for his invasion of England. However, when it came to the moment of truth, when Edward the Confessor died, it was Harold who took the throne and prepared to defend England against the rival claimants from Norway and Normandy.

Harold's queen was Ealdgyth, a daughter of the House of Mercia, English earls whose power in England was only overshadowed by the Godwinson family. Mercia was one of the three primary earldoms, and former kingdoms, of England – the others being Wessex and Northumbria. Ealdgyth (also spelt Aldgyth) was the granddaughter of Earl Leofric of Mercia and his wife, the legendary Lady Godiva. Her father was Ælfgar, who may have been an only child or, at least, an only son, as there is no mention of him having any siblings in the chronicles of the time. Ælfgar had married, probably in the late 1020s, a kinswoman of King Cnut's first handfast wife, Ælfgifu of Northampton, who was also called Ælfgifu.[1] Her family held lands in East Anglia and the east Midlands, which may explain why Ælfgar was given the earldom of East Anglia, temporarily when the Godwinsons were exiled in 1051, then permanently when Harold succeeded to the earldom of Wessex in 1053. Ælfgar's earldom of East Anglia, added to Leofric's earldom of Mercia, would have meant that the Mercian family controlled the entirety of the English Midlands. They were therefore responsible for guarding much of the east coast against Danish incursions and, in the west, protecting the Welsh border. The chronicles of the time record many instances of Welsh incursions into Mercia:

In the same year, Gruffydd, king of Wales, ravaged a great part of Herefordshire: the inhabitants of that province, with some Normans from a castle, flew to arms and attacked him; but, having slain a great number of them, he obtained the victory and carried off much plunder. This battle was fought on the same day on which, fourteen years before, the Welsh slew Edwin, earl Leofric's brother, in an ambuscade.[2]

Ælfgar appears to have had a difficult relationship, not only with the Godwinson family, but with the king himself. He was twice declared an outlaw in the 1050s, the first instance being in 1055, shortly after Tostig, the brother of Earl Harold, was given the earldom of Northumbria, a position which Ælfgar may have coveted for himself. The *Anglo-Saxon Chronicle* is contradictory as to Ælfgar's guilt, the Abingdon Manuscript (C) of the *Chronicle* argues that Ælfgar 'was outlawed without any fault', whereas the Peterborough Manuscript (D), states 'Earl Ælfgar was outlawed because it was thrown at him that he was a traitor to the king and all the people of the land. And he admitted this before all the men who were gathered there, although the words shot out against his will.'[3] John of Worcester, however, backs up the (C) Manuscript, stating that he was outlawed 'without any just cause or offence'.[4] Guilty or not, Ælfgar fled to Ireland and then to Wales, where he joined forces with King Gruffydd of Gwynedd.

The two men led their great army into England and as John of Worcester put it, they 'entered Herefordshire, intending to lay waste the English marches.'[5] Hereford's earl, Ralph de Mantes, King Edward's nephew, was waiting for them with an army. Ralph's mounted forces, however, fled in the face of their enemy; Ralph 'with his French and Normans, were the first to flee', earning the earl the nickname 'Ralph the Timid'.[6] The rest of the English army, seeing their leaders run, followed suit, with the Welsh chasing and killing in their wake. About 500 were killed and many others wounded. Having seen off the English army opposing them, Gruffydd and Ælfgar then entered Hereford, from where, 'having slain seven of the canons who defended the doors of the principal church, and burnt the monastery built by bishop Athelstan, that true servant of Christ, with all its ornaments, and the relics of St. Ethelbert, king and martyr, and other saints, and having slain some of the citizens, and made many other captives, they returned laden with spoil.'[7]

Another English army, led by Earl Harold, was mustered to face Ælfgar and his allies and Harold, 'zealously obeying the king's orders, was unwearied in his pursuit of Gruffydd and Ælfgar, and boldly crossing the Welsh border, encamped beyond Straddell [Snowdon]; but they knowing him to be an intrepid and daring warrior, did not venture to wait his attack, but retreated into South Wales. On learning this, he left there the greatest part of his army, with orders to make a stout resistance to the enemy if circumstances should require it; and returning with the remainder of his host to Hereford, he surrounded it with a wide and deep trench, and fortified it with gates and bars'.[8] Meanwhile, an exchange of messages between the opposing leaders led to an agreement between them in which peace was established with the exchange of hostages. Ælfgar was restored to his earldom, perhaps proving the *Anglo-Saxon Chronicle's* assertion that Ælfgar was outlawed unfairly.

In 1057 Ealdgyth's grandfather, Earl Leofric, died and Ælfgar succeeded to the earldom of Mercia. His mother, Lady Godiva, would survive her husband by several years; she would have seen her grandchildren grow into adults and take their places in the world. Although we do not know exactly how many children Earl Ælfgar and his wife, Ælfgifu, had, they did have at least three. Ealdgyth had two brothers, Edwin and Morcar, who were to play leading roles in the years before and after the Norman Conquest. The children's order of birth is not known, although Edwin was probably the eldest son, given that he succeeded his father to the earldom of Mercia, while Morcar would become Earl of Northumbria following the revolt against Tostig in 1065.

As with many women of the era, we know nothing of the childhood and education of Ealdgyth. Her parents were probably married in the late 1020s, which would suggest that Ealdgyth was born sometime in the 1030s, although, given that she was thought a suitable bride for King Harold in 1066, her birth is likely to have been later in the decade, or possibly early in the 1040s, making her in her twenties when she married Harold. If she had been in her thirties, her age would have been a hindrance to the marriage; kings needed young, fertile wives to produce their son and heir, rather than a woman in her thirties, whose fertility may be on the decline. Ealdgyth may have spent a few years enjoying a convent education, like many young girls of her social status in the eleventh century. Given that her grandmother was a renowned patron of religious institutions, this seems a distinct possibility. From Godiva, she may also have inherited her grandmother's strength and reputation as a defender of the people, but we do not know this for certain. Of her personal attributes, we know very little, simply that Ealdgyth was described as 'beautiful' by William of Jumièges.[9] We don't know, either, when Ealdgyth was first married. Given that her first husband was Gruffydd ap Llywelyn, it seems likely that her marriage was arranged at the time of one of her father's alliances with the Welsh king.

The marriage may have been arranged during Ælfgar's first outlawry in 1055, or possibly during the second, which occurred in 1058. It seems likely that Gruffydd would have helped Ælfgar once again because of the family ties that had been forged if Ealdgyth's marriage had occurred during the first exile. The chronicles do not give any details of the reasons for Ælfgar's second exile; indeed, the *Anglo-Saxon Chronicle* is deliberately evasive, saying, 'it is tedious to tell how it all fell out.'[10] No explanation, therefore, is forthcoming. Ælfgar again fled to King Gruffydd's court, perhaps taking Ealdgyth with him. The exile was of short duration, for he 'soon came in again by force'.[11] This time he returned with the support of Gruffydd and a Norwegian army under the command of Harald Hardrada's ten-year-old son Magnus.

Ealdgyth and Gruffydd were married for at least five years, therefore, and more likely eight. She brought a small amount of Mercian land to her marriage as dowry, which amounted to, at least, an estate at Binley, Warwickshire.[12] Gruffydd and Ealdgyth had one child, a daughter named Nest, who would marry a Herefordshire lord, Osbern fitz Richard, and inherited her mother's Binley land. Their daughter, in turn, married another Marcher lord, Bernard de Neufmarché. Of the finer points of Ealdgyth and Gruffydd's relationship, we have no knowledge. She may have found it difficult to be an English woman at the Welsh court, given that Gruffydd was constantly at odds with his English neighbours.

King Gruffydd was king of Deheubarth and Gwynedd from 1039 until his death in 1063. His father, Llywelyn ap Seisyll, had married into the ruling dynasty of Deheubarth; his wife was Angharad, a daughter of Maredudd ab Owain, who had ruled Deheubarth from 986 to 999. Llywelyn was ruler of Gwynedd by 1018 and had established himself as ruler of Deheubarth by 1022, having defeated a rival, Rhain, an Irish adventurer who claimed to be the son of Maredudd ab Owain, at the Battle of Abergwili. When Llywelyn died in 1023, Gruffydd was probably still only a child, and so it was the old ruling line of Gwynedd that achieved the upper hand, until Iago ab Idwal was killed, possibly by Gruffydd ap Llywelyn, and replaced by Gruffydd himself, in 1039. Gruffydd, therefore, was an aggressive and seasoned warrior. In the same year, Gruffydd confirmed his position by fighting against Mercian troops at the Battle of Rhyd-y-Groes, in which Edwine, the brother of Earl Leofric of Mercia (Ealdgyth's grandfather), was killed. It took longer for Gruffydd to establish himself as undisputed ruler of Deheubarth. He had two main rivals in south Wales, Hywel ab Edwin from 1039 to 1044 and Gruffudd ap Rhydderch between 1044 and 1055. In 1041 Gruffydd defeated Hywel, captured his wife and 'took her as his own', but still failed to win the kingdom.[13] Gruffydd himself was captured by Hywel's Scandinavian allies in 1042, but eventually defeated and killed his rival in 1044. However, Gruffudd ap Rhydderch was able to take advantage of Hywel's death before Gruffydd could consolidate his victory and established himself as the new king of Deheubarth.

Gruffydd had to pause hostilities for a time, when his bodyguard was attacked and 140 of them killed by forces from Ystrad Tywi. Although he was able to exact revenge, Gruffydd was left weakened and unable to pursue war in south Wales. When Gruffudd ap Rhydderch died in 1055, Gruffydd was able finally to establish his undisputed rule over Deheubarth. From then on Gruffydd's focus was on England, and he pursued an aggressive policy towards his larger neighbour, allying with the exiled Ælfgar in 1055 and 1058 to take the war into England. The 1055 campaign against Hereford led to a retaliatory strike in 1056 by Leofgar, the new Bishop of Hereford, who led a force into Wales and was defeated and killed, along with a large number of his army, at Glasbury-on-Wye. Leofgar had been a chaplain to Earl Harold, who was now ready to go to war against Gruffydd. Peace was only established with the intercession of Earl Leofric of Mercia, Bishop Eldred of Worcester and King Edward himself. Gruffydd's holdings and territorial acquisitions were recognised in return for his sworn oath that 'he would be a firm and faithful viceroy to King Edward'.[14] One anecdote from the peace negotiations tells that Gruffydd and King Edward faced each other on opposing banks of the River Severn, each waiting for the other to make the first move. When Edward finally set out in a boat to cross the river, Gruffydd then walked into the water to meet him and carried the king to the shore on his shoulders.[15]

Unfortunately for Gruffydd, the peace was not to last, and his luck ran out in 1063. At Christmas 1062, Earl Harold had launched a surprise attack on Gruffydd's court at Rhuddlan, from which the king barely escaped with his life, taking to the sea to evade his attackers. In the summer of 1063, building on this success, Harold launched a two-pronged attack on Gruffydd, with Tostig invading Wales from Chester in the north and Harold advancing from the south. However, before he could face the English forces, Gruffydd was betrayed and killed by his fellow Welshmen, who sent his severed head to the English earls; Harold, in turn, sent the grisly trophy to King Edward.

In the *Brut y Tywysogion* Gruffydd was memorialised as 'the head and shield and defender of the Britons'.[16] Gruffydd left two young sons, Maredudd and Idwal, both of whom appear to have died by 1070. However, Gwynedd and Powys were not left to them, but given to the dead king's half-brothers, Bleddyn and Rhiwallon, who swore oaths of fealty to King Edward and gave hostages as proof of their good faith; they also agreed to 'pay tribute from the land as was paid long before to other kings.'[17] In the south, however, the old ruling family of Deheubarth was restored, thus once more dividing Wales and weakening its position against the English.

What happened to Ealdgyth immediately after her husband's death has gone unrecorded. However, given that she had no son to succeed her husband, and a young daughter to look after, it is likely that she returned to Mercia. Her father, Ælfgar, had probably died in 1062, which was the last time he appeared in the records, and so her brother Edwin was now Earl of Mercia. Ealdgyth's grandmother, Lady Godiva, was still living and may have helped her adjust to her new status as a widow. However, Ealdgyth was not destined to stay single for long, as she was from a powerful family and had been Gruffydd's queen and such a dual status made her a great marriage prize. She would soon make a dynastic marriage that would see her, once again, become a queen, but this time she would be queen of England.

Between 1063 and 1066, Harold's support of King Edward made him the most powerful man in the kingdom, after the king himself. When Northumbria rose in revolt against his brother, Tostig, Harold's refusal to support a military solution in support of his brother meant that Tostig lost his earldom and was exiled from England, fleeing to his wife's home country of Flanders. Earl Morcar was confirmed as the new earl of Northumbria. During the crisis, Tostig had accused Harold of allying with the rebels and helping to orchestrate his own brother's downfall. Harold swore in front of the king, and a room full of witnesses, that it was not so.

When King Edward died on 5 January 1066, it was Harold who he had named as his successor. The new king was crowned in Westminster Abbey on 6 January by Archbishop Ealdred of York, scant hours after King Edward had been laid to rest in his tomb in the abbey. The *Anglo-Saxon Chronicle* said of the old king:

> As soon as he had taken the reins of government, he made it his business to revoke unjust laws, and establish good ones; to become the protector of the churches and monasteries; to cherish and reverence the bishops, abbots, monks, and clerks; and to show himself kind, humble, and courteous to all good men, while to malefactors he used the utmost rigour. For he gave orders to his earls, ealdormen, vice-reeves, and all his officers, to arrest all thieves, robbers, and disturbers of the peace; and he laboured himself for the defence of the country by land and by sea.[18]

It is possible that Harold married Ealdgyth any time between Gruffydd's death in 1063 and the king's own death in October 1066. The wedding does not merit a mention in any of the chronicles of the time, and so the date of the event is open to speculation. However, once Harold was crowned king, he would have needed the support of Earls Edwin and Morcar, who as Earls of Mercia and Northumbria, respectively, guarded the eastern and norther borders of England. Given that Morcar was only confirmed as Earl of Northumberland in November 1065, it seems likely that a peace was brokered with the brothers sometime after this, with Harold's marriage to Ealdgyth sealing the agreement.

To King Harold, Ealdgyth was the ideal wife. She was the widow of King Gruffydd, daughter of Earl Ælfgar and sister of the earls of Mercia and Northumbria. She had already given birth to one child, and although it was a daughter, it was proof that she was fertile and so could provide Harold with an heir to secure the new dynasty. The marriage was a judicious one which gave Harold powerful allies in the guise of Ealdgyth's two brothers and also served to weaken the political ties of those same earls with the new rulers of north Wales, the half-brothers of Ealdgyth's late husband, King Gruffydd. As queen 'Ealdgyth would produce children who would unite the fortunes of the two formerly rival houses' and create a new royal dynasty.[19]

However, Ealdgyth was not the first woman in Harold's life, nor, indeed, the most important. For twenty years Harold had been living with the wonderfully named Eadgyth Swanneshals (Edith the Swanneck). History books label her as Harold's concubine, but Edith was no weak and powerless peasant, so it's highly likely the young couple had, at some point, gone through a handfasting ceremony – or 'Danish marriage' – a marriage, but not one recognized by the Church, thus allowing Harold to take a second 'wife'. Harold had met Edith the Swanneck at about the same time as he became Earl of East Anglia, in 1044, they had at least five children together, perhaps four sons, Godwin, Edmund, Magnus and possibly Ulf, and two daughters, Gytha, who married Vladimir Monomakh, Great Prince of Kiev, and Gunhild, who may have been intended to become a nun at Wilton Abbey in Wiltshire before eloping with a Breton knight.

Despite their twenty years and five children together, late in 1065 or in early 1066, Harold put aside his relationship with Edith Swanneck in order to strengthen his position as King of England. The marriage to Ealdgyth probably occurred in March or April 1066; although the *Anglo-Saxon Chronicle* does not mention a wedding, it does refer to a journey to York made by King Harold, from which he had returned at Easter (16 April) 1066.[20] This seems to have been the most likely time for Harold to finalise the agreement with Edwin and Morcar and marry their sister. He would have brought Ealdgyth back to London with him; as Harold's wife Ealdgyth was, therefore, for a short time, Queen of England, although there is no indication that she was ever given a coronation. King Harold was too busy defending his new realm.

There was, moreover, no honeymoon for the couple, as events in 1066 were to move rapidly towards that final showdown at Hastings in October. Following their return from York at Easter, a comet appeared in the sky. Staying visible for a week it was seen as a portent of great change, possibly of impending disaster. Halley's Comet was at the time known as 'the long-hair'd star'.[21] Shortly after the comet's journey across the skies, Harold's brother Tostig appeared on the Isle of Wight with a large fleet, which he then sailed around the Kent coast. Harold mustered an army and navy and departed for Sandwich to face his errant brother. Before he got there, Tostig had left, sailed north and eventually reached Scotland. Relief was non-existent, however, as Harold had also received news that Duke William was preparing an invasion fleet, and so the army spent the summer guarding the south coast, with Harold based on the Isle of Wight, watching and waiting. The army was on high alert the whole summer but, with supplies running low, Harold was forced to disband it in the first week of September. He returned to London to receive the news that Tostig had invaded the north with his new ally, Harald Hardrada, King of Norway. As King Harold gathered an army and marched his men the 200 miles to York in just four or five days, Harald and Tostig fought and defeated Harold's brothers-in-law, Edwin and Morcar, at Fulford, on the outskirts of York, on 20 September. Although the brothers escaped with their lives, their army was destroyed, and they were unable to join the king when he faced the Norwegian army at Stamford Bridge five days later.

Within days of the victory over Tostig and his Norwegian allies, at Stamford Bridge, Harold received news that Duke William had landed at Pevensey, on the south coast, and the king was forced to march his tired forces south. In order to move quickly, Harold disbanded his foot soldiers, knowing they would slow him down, and marched south with just his mounted forces, his housecarls. After arriving in London, he had a conference with his mother and brothers, in which his brother Gyrth offered to face Duke William on Harold's behalf, knowing Harold had sworn oaths to William during his visit to Normandy. Harold refused, however, and having resolved to face Duke William himself, he marched his forces southward. The opposing armies faced each other just north of Hastings, in Sussex, the English taking position at the top of a hill, with the Normans, therefore, forced to attack uphill. The rest we know.

Despite his marriage to Ealdgyth, it seems Edith Swanneck remained close to Harold and it was she who was close by when the king faced William of Normandy at Senlac Hill. She awaited the outcome alongside Harold's mother, Gytha. Sources say that Gytha was unable to identify her sons amidst the mangled bodies. As mentioned earlier, it fell to Edith to find Harold, by undoing the chain mail of the victims in order to recognise certain identifying marks on the king's body – probably tattoos.

Harold's mother, Gytha, eventually fled into exile on the Continent, taking Harold and Edith's daughter, another Gytha, with her, possibly arranging her marriage to the prince of Smolensk and – later – Kiev. Edith and Harold's sons fled to Ireland, all but one living into the 1080s, though the dates of their eventual deaths remain uncertain. Harold and Edith's daughter, Gunhild, remained in her nunnery at Wilton until sometime before 1093, when she became the wife or concubine of Alan the Red, a Norman magnate. Whether or not she was kidnapped seems to be in question but when Alan died in 1093, instead of returning to the convent, Gunhild became the mistress of Alan's brother and heir, Alan Niger. Alan Rufus held vast lands in East Anglia – lands that had once belonged to Eadgifu the Fair and, if this Eadgifu was Edith the Swanneck, it is possible that Alan married Gunhild to strengthen his claims to her mother's lands. After 1066 Edith's lands had passed to Ralph de Gael before eventually falling into the hands of Alan the Red. Of Edith Swanneck, there is no trace after Harold is interred at Waltham Abbey, she simply disappears from the pages of history.

Ealdgyth, on the other hand, can have spent little time with her husband. Their marriage probably lasted no more than six or seven months, before he met his death at Hastings. Ealdgyth had awaited the outcome of the campaign against William in London, the 'earls Edwin and Morcar, who had withdrawn with their troops from the battle on hearing that he was dead, went to London, and sent off their sister, queen Elgitha [Ealdgyth], to Chester.'[22] Edwin and Morcar, their forces still not fully recovered from the battle at

Fulford, probably never reached the battlefield at Hastings and, as soon as they heard of Harold's defeat and death, made for London to see to their sister's safety. They sent Ealdgyth under escort to Chester where, before the end of the year, it is possible she gave birth to Harold's posthumous son, Harold. Little Harold grew up in exile on the Continent and died sometime after 1098. It may be that Ealdgyth gave birth to twin boys, as another son, Ulf, has sometimes been attributed to her, although whether Ulf was the son of Ealdgyth, or of Edith Swanneck, is still hotly debated by historians. Ulf was held hostage during the reign of King William, but was released by his son, William II Rufus and is recorded as being alive in Normandy in 1087, but he disappears from the chronicles after this.[23] The same can also be said for young Harold. It may be that Ealdgyth never had any children by King Harold, we just do not know.

Ealdgyth's brothers continued the fight against the Normans, initially supporting the claims of Edgar Ætheling – which adds weight to the suggestion that Ealdgyth was childless by King Harold. However, they submitted to King William at Berkhamsted and accompanied the king on his return to Normandy in 1067. They were confirmed in their earldoms by William, but their positions were undermined by William's creation of several other earldoms, such as the appointment of Roger de Montgomery as Earl of Shrewsbury in 1068.[24] They rebelled in that year, supposedly after King William's promise of his daughter's hand in marriage to Edwin did not materialise. They sought help from their Welsh allies but were reconciled with the king soon afterwards. However, fearing arrest and imprisonment, in 1071 the brothers fled King William's court.

Earl Edwin was murdered by his own men as they attempted to reach Scotland. Morcar then sought sanctuary with the rebel forces on the Isle of Ely, led by Hereward the Wake. He surrendered following the siege of Ely and was imprisoned for the remainder of the Conqueror's reign. He was released on the king's death but imprisoned again by William II Rufus, after which nothing more is heard of him.

Ealdgyth's own fate is also unknown. She disappears from the story once she arrives in Chester. It is possible she retired to a convent in the Auvergne, where an English Queen Edith is remembered as having financed the construction of dormitory buildings by the monks of La-Chaise-Dieu.[25] Despite the difference in spelling, it is possible that Queen Edith was Ealdgyth, but, as with much of Ealdgyth's story, this cannot be confirmed with any certainty.

PART THREE

CONQUEST

11

Griefs and Sufferings

The momentous year of 1066 was brought to a close where it had begun, at Westminster Abbey. Whereas the year had opened with the funeral of Edward the Confessor and coronation of Harold II on the same day, 6 January, it ended with the coronation of Duke William, now King William, on Christmas Day, 25 December 1066. However, although victory at Hastings and the death of King Harold had put William in a strong position, it did not mean that the crown was laid at his feet. The killing of King Harold had given Duke William an advantage, but the people of England were still in need of persuasion to accept the Norman as king. In London, Archbishop Ealdred led the support for Edgar Ætheling to take the throne, proclaiming him king, 'as was his right by birth'. [1]

One of the main focuses of opposition for the English people, Edgar the Ætheling was the only son of Edward the Exile and his wife, Agatha. Edward the Exile, in turn, was the son of Edmund II Ironside, King of England in 1016; Edward's grandfather was, therefore, Æthelred II (the Unready) and his uncle was Edward the Confessor, England's king from 1042 until 1066. After his father's death in 1016, Edward and his younger brother, Edmund, were sent into exile on the Continent by England's new king, Cnut. It is thought that Cnut intended that they would be killed, but the boys were protected by the King of Sweden and sent on to safety in Kiev, at the court of its prince, Yaroslav the Wise.

Around 1043 Edward married Agatha, whose origins are obscure, but she was most probably the daughter of Liudolf, margrave of

West Friesland and a relative of Holy Roman Emperor Henry III. Margaret, the eldest of three children, was born in either 1045 or 1046; her sister, Christina was born around 1050 and her brother Edgar, the Ætheling, was born sometime between 1052 and 1056.

The family might have spent their whole lives in European exile, were it not for Edward the Confessor lacking an heir to the English throne; although Edward was married to Edith Godwinson, the couple remained childless. Sometime in 1054 Edward sent an embassy to Edward the Exile to bring him back to England as ætheling, heir to the throne. The family could not travel immediately, possibly because Agatha was pregnant with Edgar, and only arrived in England in 1057, having journeyed by a ship provided by the Holy Roman Emperor. Just days after their return Edward the Exile was dead, whether by nefarious means or simply a twist of fate is uncertain. The suspicion has been raised that Edward's rival for the throne, Harold Godwinson – the future Harold II – may have taken the opportunity to remove his rival; however, there is no evidence of this, and no accusations at the time that Edward had met with a violent death, let alone murder, although poison is always a possibility.

Whatever the circumstances, the death of Edward the Exile was a blow for Edward the Confessor's dynastic hopes. Little Edgar, now the ætheling, was far too young to assume a political role. He and his sisters, with their mother, were now under the protection of King Edward. They continued to live at court and by January 1066, when Edward the Confessor died, Margaret was approaching her twentieth birthday, while Edgar could have been as young as ten and was probably no older than fourteen. Due to his tender years, and lack of powerful allies, Edgar was passed over as a candidate for the throne in preference for the older and more experienced Harold Godwinson, who was crowned as King Harold II. Following Harold's death at the Battle of Hastings in October 1066, however, Edgar was proclaimed king in London by some of his supporters, led by Archbishop Ealdred of York, his youth being offset by the fact that the crown 'was his proper due by birth'.[2] The earls Edwin and Morcar, brothers-in-law of Harold II, 'promised them that they would fight with them'.[3] Many in England saw Edgar as their king, the obvious successor to King Harold. Indeed, when Leofric, the Abbot of Peterborough, succumbed to his wounds after the Battle of Hastings and the monks chose their Provost, Brand, as his successor, it was to Edgar that they sent him to receive the king's assent, an act that incensed Duke William.[4]

After the October battle, William had waited at Hastings for some time, expecting the English leaders to come and submit to him, but when this failed to materialise, the duke 'ravaged all the country that he overran'.[5] At Romney 'he inflicted such punishment as he thought fit for the slaughter of his men who had landed there by mistake.'[6] The duke then moved on to Dover, where the town was burned despite the fact it had surrendered; William of Poitiers later claimed the burning was an accident. After this, Canterbury sent a delegation of citizens to surrender to the duke. The duke then sent a force to Winchester, to take control of the treasury and demand its submission. The city was part of the dower of Edith of Wessex, Edward the Confessor's queen, and submitted without bloodshed; as a consequence, Winchester was treated leniently. William required little more than their professed fealty and a promise of future rent, whereas elsewhere, large tributes would be demanded in payment.

After an initial reluctance to submit, the *Carmen de Hastingae Proelio of Guy,* apparently written by the Bishop of Amiens within months of William's coronation, was soon reporting: 'from all sides the English rush to dance attendance on the king. Nor do they come with hands empty of gifts. All bring presents, bow their necks to the yoke, and kiss his feet on bended knees.'[7]

According to John of Worcester, the Normans 'laid waste Sussex, Kent, Hampshire, Middlesex and Hertfordshire, and did not cease from burning townships and slaying men.'[8] Soon, the only effective opposition was mounted by London itself. When Norman soldiers appeared on the south bank, a sortie was mounted by the city's defenders, but proved unsuccessful. They retreated back within the safety of the city walls, as Duke William pursued a campaign of terror around them; his men burned all the buildings on the south bank of the river, then made their way towards the west, crossing the Thames at Wallingford, laying waste to everything around them as they went. William spent several days at Wallingford, possibly using the time to lay the foundations for the new castle there.

He also received the submission of Stigand, the Archbishop of Canterbury and one of the leading English figures of the day, who did homage to William.

Within days, the Norman army continued inexorably onwards, crossing the Thames and following their circuitous route around London, leaving devastation in their wake, until they reached Berkhamsted. The situation in London must have been getting increasingly desperate, the people powerless as they watched the ruin of the countryside beyond their walls. At some point the earls Edwin and Morcar 'withdrew their support and returned home with their army'.[9] Within the city, opportunities were missed as hope was lost, as the *Anglo-Saxon Chronicle* records; 'Always when some initiative should have been shown, there was delay from day to day, until matters went from bad to worse, as everything did in the end.'[10] As winter began to close in, the city surrendered. Edgar and a delegation of bishops and leading English magnates made the 30-mile journey to Berkhamsted, 'out of necessity, after most damage had been done – and it was a great piece of folly that they had not done it earlier.'[11] According to John of Worcester; 'Edgar the ætheling ... and some Londoners of the better sort, with many others, met him [Duke William] and, giving hostages, made their submission, and swore fealty to him; but, although he concluded a treaty with them, he still allowed his troops to burn and pillage the vills.'[12]

Edgar submitted to Duke William of Normandy in early December. William treated Edgar honourably, allowing him his life and a semblance of freedom, and giving him land, but keeping him close at hand. With Edgar's submission, London was open to the Normans and the crown was William's for the taking. William could now move on to the capital and to his coronation at Westminster Abbey. William was reluctant to have his coronation without his wife, Matilda of Flanders, beside him, and may also have wanted to stamp his authority on the whole of England before undergoing the ceremony; since his arrival in England, it was only the southern parts of the country that were under the Normans' control. Military necessity persuaded the Duke to hold his coronation sooner rather than later – 'he hoped that once he had begun to reign, any rebels would be less ready to challenge him and more easily put down.'[13]

The atmosphere in London itself was still tense, however; many of the survivors of Hastings had fled to the city after the battle, in addition to the relatives of those who had been killed in the fighting. When William's men entered the city, they were met with some resistance. As a result, the Duke's advanced guard were ordered to build a fortress within the city 'as a defence against the inconstancy of the numerous and hostile inhabitants'.[14] The coronation was conducted according to an English rite, emphasising William's belief that he was Edward the Confessor's designated and rightful heir. William swore the traditional oaths to govern well and justly, to defend the Church and its rulers and to establish and maintain law and order. It was attended by both English and Norman magnates and was conducted in English by Ealdred, Archbishop of York (who had started the year by crowning King Harold for the English) with the Norman bishop of Coutances repeating the ceremony in French.[15]

Security, however, was tight, and the guards were nervous. Shouted acclamations inside the abbey were misinterpreted by the guards outside. Fearing their duke was under attack, the guards apparently panicked and burned down nearby houses in an effort to subdue the non-existent rebellion. As Marc Morris argues, this explanation of nervous guards is probably a smoke screen for the continuing burning and pillaging being carried out in London at the time; if the guards had been worried about treachery, they would surely have rushed into the abbey, rather than burning down the buildings around it.[16] According to Orderic Vitalis, as the fire spread rapidly outside, 'the crowd who had been rejoicing in the church took fright, and throngs of men and women of every rank and condition rushed outside in frantic haste.'[17] Despite the exodus of the spectators, inside the abbey the coronation ceremony continued, with the anointing, crowning and enthronement of Duke William by the prelates; outside some were fighting the fires while others joined in the looting. In an era when portents were seen in comets and the timing of events, the fact that a riot had effectively broken out at the exact moment that William was accepted as King of England must have been seen as a warning that worse was still to come.

Almost immediately following the coronation, William began the distribution of rewards to his supporters. Those who had fought with him at Hastings were treated generously, but the greatest beneficiaries were the churches on the Continent, who had offered spiritual encouragement for his success and were rewarded with jewelled crosses, golden vessels and luxurious vestments, quite likely plundered from English churches. The major beneficiary was Pope Alexander, to whom was sent King Harold's banner, and 'more gold and silver coins than could be credibly told, as well as ornaments that even Byzantium would have considered precious.'[18]

As for his new English subjects, William refrained from making sweeping changes in his new kingdom, for the time being; there was no mass replacement of bishops and ecclesiastical offices and he made some attempts at conciliation with the Saxon nobles. William also issued a writ, confirming London's privileges as they had been during the reign of King Edward, written in Old English and following a traditional English style. A new coinage was issued, but again it followed the pre-1066 styles as William was keen to emphasise continuity with the regime of Edward the Confessor. On the other hand, according to the *Anglo-Saxon Chronicle,* he 'imposed a heavy tax on the country'.[19] In the new year of 1067, William met with the surviving English earls, Edwin and Morcar, and other English nobles. They all officially submitted to him and the Mercian brothers 'sought his pardon for any hostility they had shown him, and surrendered themselves and all their property to his mercy.'[20] William of Poitiers and the *Anglo-Saxon Chronicle* differ in the timing of the brothers' submission; English sources say they submitted to William at Berkhamsted, at the same time as Edgar, while the Norman chroniclers say the submission was at Barking in January of 1067. It is impossible, with the distance of time, to be certain which source is right. However, the fact that the brothers submitted in the new year would be understandable given John of Worcester's assertion that they had left London and returned to their own lands, before Edgar's own submission in December of 1066. With this in mind, a submission at Barking in January seems the more likely of the two versions.

William of Poitiers goes on to say that 'the king readily accepted their oaths, freely granted them his favour, restored all their possessions, and treated them with great honour.'[21] How freely the king restored their lands is debatable, given that the *Anglo-Saxon Chronicle* stipulates that they had to buy back their lands: 'Men paid him tribute, and gave him hostages, and then redeemed their lands from him.'[22]

William was able to reconcile with the surviving lords while still having resources to reward his own followers owing to the large number of fallen at the Battle of Hastings. The lands and property of the dead were declared forfeit; the king issued a writ demanding the surrender of 'all the land which those men held ... who stood in battle against me and there were slain.'[23] As some of the greatest landowners in England had fallen at Hastings, including Harold and his brothers Leofwine and Gyrth, this meant a large swathe of English soil was available for distribution to William's loyal supporters. The county of Kent was given to his half-brother Odo, while William fitz Osbern received the Isle of Wight and lands in Hampshire. William de Warenne was given Lewes in Sussex and the Honour of Conisbrough, formerly belonging to King Harold, in Yorkshire. The bulk of the forfeited land, however, William kept for himself.

By March 1067 the Anglo-Norman regime was established and William felt the need to return to Normandy, leaving two of his staunchest allies in charge of England. His half-brother Odo, Bishop of Bayeux and now also Earl of Kent, and one of his most ardent supporters, William Fitz Osbern, now Earl of Hereford, his jurisdiction equivalent to the old earldom of Wessex, were in overall control of England, although many of the sheriffs under them had been retained after the Conquest and were native Englishmen. To further guarantee the security of his new conquest, the king took many of the English nobles with him to Normandy, those whose loyalty and power he still felt were suspect. Indeed, he kept most of the leading magnates of Anglo-Saxon England with him at court throughout 1067 and into 1068, ostensibly as hostages, 'so that the general populace, deprived of their leaders, would be less capable of rebellion.'[24]

William spent much of the year in Normandy; reunited with his family, he attended celebrations for the success of his English venture and distributed gifts to the churches and abbeys of his homeland. To his own foundation of St Stephen's at Caen, the Abbaye aux Hommes, he gave gifts so valuable 'that they deserve to be remembered until the end of time.'[25] William's stay in Normandy coincided with the expansion of Norman control over England, motte and bailey castles were being built in various strategic locations, such as Pevensey, Windsor, Dover and London. The *Anglo-Saxon Chronicle* lamented the fact that that Bishop Odo and William fitz Osbern 'built castles widely throughout this nation, and oppressed the wretched people; and afterwards it always grew very much worse.'[26] Moreover the king had 'imposed a heavy guild on the wretched people; but notwithstanding, let his men always plunder all the country that they went over.'[27] Even given the possibility that the *Anglo-Saxon Chronicle* is exaggerating to some extent, the worsening situation in England meant that the people were ripe for encouragement to rebellion, which came in the form of the Godwinson family at Exeter.

There had been several minor insurrections in 1067. Edric the Wild fought with the castle builders at Hereford, uniting with the Welsh successors of King Gruffydd to ravage the town. The men of Kent sent to Eustace of Boulogne for his aid in taking the castle at Dover. Despite their past, the count was happy to help, but after two days of siege, the Norman defenders were able to mount a counterattack and the besiegers fled. Further unrest arose in Northumberland, where William had split the earldom between Morcar in the south and Copsig, a former lieutenant of its previous earl, Tostig, in the north. Copsig was ambushed and murder by Oswulf, a rival claimant to the earldom and the nephew of Gospatric, whose murder, supposedly on the orders of Edith of Wessex, had caused the rebellion of 1065. Oswulf himself would meet an untimely end within months, killed by a robber.[28] None of these uprisings, however, necessitated William's return from Normandy; but a conspiracy unearthed towards the end of the year saw the king returning to England and besieging the city of Exeter.

The conspiracy was focused around the surviving members of the Godwinson family, in particular King Harold's mother, Gytha, and his sons by his handfast wife, Edith Swanneck. It was from Exeter that messages were being sent to other cities, urging rebellion. It appears that Gytha planned a Godwinson revival with the sons of Harold and Edith Swanneck. In their late teens or early twenties, the boys had fled to Ireland after the death of their father and were now plotting to return with an invasion fleet. However, before the rebellion could take hold, William arrived and demanded that Exeter give him its fealty, but the city refused. As the king's army surrounded Exeter, the town played for time, saying they would open their gates, while at the same time preparing to resist. The resulting siege was hard fought on both sides, the town's inhabitants withstanding the Conqueror's attempts to storm it or mine underneath the walls. After eighteen days of siege, the city surrendered.

The Norman chroniclers suggest that the inhabitants were worn down by William the Conqueror's relentless assaults, or that the city wall partially collapsed; while the English Chroniclers argue that the surrender came about after the Godwin clan deserted the cause. According to John of Worcester, 'the countess Gytha, mother of Harold, king of England, and sister of Sweyn, king of Denmark, escaped from the city, with many others, and retired to Flanders; and the citizens submitted to the king, and paid him fealty.'[29] Earl Godwin's widow, Countess Gytha escaped the city before its surrender, taking a boat into the Bristol Channel and landing on the island of Flat Holme, possibly to await the arrival of her grandsons from Ireland. It is possible that Edith of Wessex, King Edward's widow, who held land in the area, interceded with King William to achieve favourable terms for Exeter, including protecting the city from subjection to post-siege plundering and a promise that the city would pay the same amount in tax as it had done under King Edward.[30]

With the failure of the Exeter conspiracy, William was able to redistribute more land; that forfeited by Countess Gytha. Moreover, he awarded the earldom of Northumbria, vacant since the death of the murderous Oswulf, to Gospatric, a member of the ancient house of Bamburgh, in return for the payment of 'a great sum'.[31] By Easter 1068, William felt secure in his kingdom, enough to proceed with the coronation of his queen, Matilda of Flanders; she was crowned at Whitsuntide in Westminster Abbey.

However, the dispossession of the property of those who died at Hastings had caused an underlying resentment in the surviving relatives that festered and grew into open rebellion. The steady erosion of the authority of the surviving English leaders, such as Earls Edwin and Morcar, who saw their earldoms reduced and divided among the victorious Normans, meant that those who had been appeased in the aftermath of the Conquest were now becoming increasingly disaffected with the new regime. For Edwin in particular, his actual position after the Conquest fell far short of what he had apparently been promised. According to Orderic Vitalis, William had granted Edwin 'authority over his brother and almost a third of England, and had promised to give him his daughter in marriage.'[32] Moreover, his position in Mercia was being undermined by the insertion of Norman veterans, such as William fitz Osbern, Earl of Hereford, and Roger of Montgomery, Earl of Shrewsbury, into key lands within Mercia.

Fuelled by the fact that a projected marriage between Edwin and a daughter of King William had never materialised, the brothers therefore rose in rebellion in 1068. They were supported by their traditional Welsh allies, including King Bleddyn, successor to Gruffydd ap Llywelyn. The rebellion spread into Northumbria and took root; it was joined by Edgar Ætheling, who had been endowed with land by King William, but now provided the rebels with a legitimate cause to restore the English royal line. According to the *Anglo-Saxon Chronicle*, 'the king was informed that the men of the north were gathered and meant to make a stand against him if he came.'[33] William made his way north with his army to deal decisively with the insurrection. Edwin and Morcar were the first to surrender, following the king's establishment of a new castle at Warwick; Nottingham fell soon afterwards, prompting York to submit to William, sending hostages and the keys to the city. As William reached the ancient northern capital, he commenced the building of a new castle, the remains of which, Clifford's Tower, still watch over the city. The rebels disbanded and fled, the majority of them making for their way north to Scotland.

Edgar Ætheling was among the fugitives who fled to the court of Malcolm III Canmore, taking his mother and sisters with him. The family was warmly received at Dunfermline by Scotland's king.

At the time, Malcolm was married to Ingebiorg and the father of two sons, Duncan and Donald. Whether Ingebiorg died or was put aside seems uncertain, but her sons were exiled from court; although Duncan would eventually reign as Duncan II, he was killed at the Battle of Monthechin in 1094. Despite the fact Ingebiorg's fate is unknown, we do know that in 1069 Malcolm asked Edgar and his mother for Margaret's hand in marriage; and, by all accounts, it seems to have been a happy and successful marriage.

William's campaign in the north provided an opportunity for the sons of King Harold. Godwine, Edmund and Magnus landed in Somerset and made for Bristol. Although their campaign failed to take the city, they returned to Ireland with considerable plunder after raiding along the Somerset coast. Within a year, two of Harold's sons were back again (although John of Worcester does not specify which two); they sailed from Ireland in the summer of 1069, landing in Devon, near Barnstaple, with a force of sixty-four ships. The local lord, Brian, Count of Brittany, 'came unawares against them with a large army and fought with them, and slew there all the best men that were in the fleet; and the others, being small forces, escaped to the ships: and Harold's sons went back to Ireland again.'[34] No longer welcome in England, the brothers eventually went into exile, making their way to the court of their cousin, King Swein Estrithson, in Denmark.

In 1069, William's choice of Earl of Bamburgh, Robert de Commines, was murdered after the house he was lodging in was set alight; he was killed trying to escape the flames. This was the spark for yet another northern rebellion and soon afterwards, Edgar was back in northern England at the head of the Northumbrian rebels who entered York and fortified Durham:

> In a certain place in one county, rendered inaccessible by water and by forest, they built a castle with a most powerful rampart, which they called in their own language Durham. From there they made various attacks and then returned home to await the arrival of Swein, king of the Danes, to whom they had sent messages requesting aid. They also sent to enlist the people of York to their cause... Once united with them, they furnished the city with an abundance of arms and money, prepared themselves for a strong

resistance, and chose as their king a certain boy, nobly descended from the stock of King Edward.[35]

However, Edgar again met with defeat when William came to face him and he fled back to Scotland. This repeat insurrection prompted the king to build a second castle in York, to more closely control the city. When a Danish fleet, sent by King Swein Estrithson, arrived in the Humber, Edgar returned to lead the Northumbrians yet again. The army captured both Norman castles at York and killed the garrison. During the winter, Edgar narrowly evaded capture when he raided into Lincolnshire with a ship from the Danish fleet. King William marched north for a third – and final – time. The Danish fleet fled before his arrival, leaving the north to the mercy of the Norman's wrath. Determined that this would be the final uprising against his new regime, William brought the full force of his fury down on the north, systematically and brutally crushing the rebellion and devastating the country. The king 'went northward with all the force that he could collect, despoiling and laying waste the shire.'[36] The Harrying of the North stripped the region of everything it needed to sustain its people; with crops and livestock destroyed and villages laid waste, as many as 100,000 may have died of famine.[37] Orderic Vitalis, an Anglo-Norman writing in the latter part of the eleventh century, condemned William's tactics:

> My narrative has frequently had occasion to praise William but for this act which condemned the innocent and the guilty alike to die by slow starvation, I cannot commend him... I would rather lament the griefs and sufferings of the wretched people than make a vain attempt to flatter the perpetrators of such infamy.[38]

Edgar fled from King William's ire, while others, including Gospatric, and Waltheof, son of Earl Siward of Northumbria, who had twice been passed over as earl himself, submitted to William. Both were pardoned and restored to their lands. By 1074 Edgar Ætheling was in exile in Flanders. Later, he returned to Scotland, and on the advice of his brother-in-law, Malcolm III, submitted to William I and was established at his court. According to William of Malmesbury, he remained at court 'for many years, silently sunk into contempt through his indolence, or more mildly speaking, his simplicity.'³⁹ Domesday Book records that Edgar held two estates in Hertfordshire in 1086; Barkway and Hormead. He became close friends with two of the Conqueror's sons; Robert Curthose and William Rufus. In 1086, he was sent to Apulia, another land under Norman rule, with a force of 200 knights, although the nature of his mission is unknown, the mission itself is testament to the high regard in which the Normans held him. Edgar then joined Robert Curthose, duke since his father's death in 1087, in Normandy, but was expelled from there in 1091 following a treaty between Robert and his brother, William II of England.

Scotland suffered a great tragedy in November 1093, when Malcolm and Margaret and their eldest son, Edward, died within a few days of each other. In 1095 Edgar campaigned with William Rufus against the rebellious earl of Northumbria, Robert de Mowbray, and in 1097, as guardian for his nephew, Edgar, in Scotland, he 'went with an army, with the king's support, into Scotland, and conquered the country in a severe battle' making his nephew and namesake king of Scotland.⁴⁰ Edgar the Ætheling seems to have been only a minor player in the politics and upheaval following the Norman Conquest. Despite his impeccable royal lineage, his political isolation meant that few took his claim to the English crown seriously. While his participation in military actions and in relations with Scotland are mentioned in various documents, his death passed without notice – or remark. William of Malmesbury wrote of him in 1125, that 'he now grows old in the country in privacy and quiet.'⁴¹ Nothing is mentioned of him thereafter; nor is it ever noted that he had a wife or children. If he had only been a few years older in that crucial year of 1066, his story could have been very different. Instead, he simply slips from the pages of history, remembered only as England's king-that-never-was.

The revolt of 1069–70 was the most serious of William's reign, and the last major insurrection; after its suppression there were no more general risings led by English nobles. It also persuaded William to take every opportunity to replace the old Saxon aristocracy with his Norman affinity: 'So very stern was he … that no man durst do anything against his will. He had earls in his custody. Bishops he hurled from their bishoprics, and abbots from their abbacies and thegns into prison.'[42] And, after the Harrying of the North, there was only one last act in the revolt that needed to be played out: Ely. The last vestiges of English defiance were led by Hereward the Wake, a native of Lincolnshire who is remembered as a hero by many; his story is shrouded in the mists of legend. Hereward's origins are not entirely clear; he was a nobleman who was already an outlaw when he made his appearance in the historical records of 1070. Supported by the invading Danish, under Earl Asbjørn, brother of King Swein Estrithson, who had seized the town of Ely, Hereward infamously plundered Peterborough Abbey, in retaliation for it being given to a Norman abbot. The abbey treasures were taken, supposedly to save them from being stolen by the avaricious Normans and much of the town itself reduced to ashes.

At some point after the raid on Peterborough, however, William offered terms to the Danish king, who was moored in the Humber while his brother operated in East Anglia. Aware that he would be unable to conquer England with his depleted fleet, Swein accepted and withdrew with his forces to Denmark: 'The Danes left Ely taking all the aforementioned [Peterborough] treasures with them.'[43] The remnants of English resistance were now on their own. With the Danes gone, William believed he had destroyed the threat and was soon back in Normandy, dealing with issues there. However, the monks at Ely, fearful that they would be faced with Norman reprisals and having Norman rulers forced upon them, gathered about them the discontented from throughout England. As the *Gesta Herewardi* says, 'Fearing subjection to foreigners, the monks of that place risked endangering themselves rather than be reduced to servitude, and, gathering to themselves outlaws, the condemned, the disinherited, those who had lost parents, and suchlike, they put their place and the island in something of a state of defence.'[44]

Exiles and outlaws from all corners of the country converged on Ely; Æthelwine, the outlawed Bishop of Durham who had been involved in the northern risings, was one such, returning from Scotland to join the new insurrection. They were also joined by Morcar, the erstwhile earl of Northumbria; the two Mercian brothers had become disaffected with William's court and the erosion of their authority within their earldoms and had escaped the court to raise rebellion. A failure to attract support saw Edwin making his way to Scotland, although he was murdered by his own men en route, while Morcar joined the rebels at Ely in the Fens. The brothers' disaffection caused King William to take notice of the new uprising and he returned to England from his Normandy domains to deal with it. At that time, Ely was an island, completely surrounded by marshes, accessible only at certain points by bridges and walkways. We have few details of the fight for Ely, with sources offering conflicting narratives of Hereward and his men seeing off the numerous assaults of the Norman forces, and of William personally mounting a successful attack and putting the rebels to flight. What is certain is that the siege of Ely ended in an English surrender; Morcar and Æthelwine among them: 'The king took their ships, and weapons, and many treasures; and all the men he disposed of as he thought proper.'[45] Bishop Æthelwine was sent to the abbey at Abingdon, where he died the following winter. Morcar was imprisoned for the rest of his life. As for the rest, 'some he [William] imprisoned, some he allowed to go free – after their hands had been cut off and their eyes gouged out.'[46] Hereward the Wake and several others who refused to surrender managed a remarkable escape through the fens; Hereward 'courageously led them out'.[47] We know nothing of the rebel leader's eventual fate.

Although William could not have known it, the siege of Ely was the last significant English threat to William's throne. It marked the final subjugation of a conquered country. There were, of course, still threats out there; the Godwinsons were in Denmark, the Saxon royal line continued in Scotland, where Edgar's sister Margaret was now queen, but none of them would materialise into any significant opposition to the new regime.

England had been conquered by the Normans.

Matilda of Flanders

Matilda of Flanders was the consummate duchess and queen. Born in the early- to mid-1030s, possibly around 1032, Matilda was the daughter of Baldwin V, Count of Flanders, and his wife Adela, who was a daughter of Robert II the Pious, King of France. The couple had married in 1028 and soon after, Adela had encouraged Baldwin to rebel against his father, Baldwin IV. However, peace was restored in 1030, and Baldwin eventually succeeded as Count of Flanders on his father's death in 1035. Adela was born around 1009 as the second daughter of Robert II, King of France, and his third wife Constance of Arles, who was the daughter of William I, Count of Provence. In January 1027 Adela was married to Richard III, Duke of Normandy, but the marriage was short-lived as Duke Richard died suddenly on 6 August of the same year. Too great a marriage prize to be a widow for long, she was married to Baldwin of Flanders the following year.

Matilda had two brothers who each became Count of Flanders in his turn; Baldwin (VI) of Mons became count on his father's death in 1067. However, his early death in 1070 meant the county passed to his son, Arnulf III, but he was killed in the Battle of Cassel in 1071, fighting against his uncle, Robert the Frisian, who was trying to wrest Flanders from his nephew. As a result, Robert was recognised as Count Robert I of Flanders. Matilda's aunt was Judith of Flanders, who was the daughter of Baldwin IV by his second wife, and only a toddler when her older brother became Count of Flanders in 1035. Judith and Matilda were of a similar age and may well have been raised and educated together. Judith had married Tostig Godwinson, Earl of Northumberland and younger brother of Harold, Earl of Wessex and later the king of England as Harold II. Flanders had close links with England; it had provided a safe haven for Emma of Normandy, when she had been exiled from England by her stepson Harold I Harefoot in 1037, and for Earl Godwin and his family when they, in turn, were exiled by King Edward the Confessor towards the end of 1051.

As is often the case with medieval women, we know very little of Matilda's early life and the first time she appears on the world stage is when her marriage is being discussed. There is a popular story of how Matilda refused to marry William, Duke of Normandy, stating that she was too high-born, as the grand-daughter of a king of France, to marry a man who was illegitimate, despite the fact that he was a duke. The story goes on to say that on hearing this, William was so infuriated that he rode to Flanders and confronted Matilda; he is said to have assaulted her, throwing her to the ground, pulling her braids and cutting her with his spurs. Matilda, unlikely as it seems, then accepted the proposal and they were married. There is little doubt that this story of rough wooing is a later invention, designed to highlight the masculinity of the Conqueror, perhaps, but it seems unlikely to have happened in reality. It makes sense that William was the one to propose the marriage; although he was a duke, the status of his illegitimacy would have meant his proposal to a niece of the King of France was audacious, to say the least.

William was the illegitimate son of Robert I the Magnificent, who was Duke of Normandy from 1027 until his death in Nicaea in 1035, whilst returning from his pilgrimage to Jerusalem. Before departing on pilgrimage, Robert had named William, then only seven or eight years old, as his heir. The origins of William's mother, Herleva, who died in 1055, are obscure. Her father was Fulbert, who has been frequently identified as a tanner of Falaise, but also as an undertaker, and the chamberlain of the ducal household. Despite the fact that not all marriages were blessed by the Church, and handfast, or *more Danico*, marriages were not uncommon, as we have seen with King Cnut the Great and King Harold II, there does not appear to have been any such arrangement with William's parents. Whereas King Harold's children by Edith Swanneck were recognised as legitimate despite the lack of a Christian marriage, William had no such privilege and was frequently described as *bastardus*, or illegitimate, in contemporary sources.[1] Sometime after William was born, possibly in or before 1030, Herleva was married to Herluin de Conteville, by whom she had at least two sons and two daughters, William's half-siblings. The two sons, Odo (died 1097) and Robert (died 1095), would benefit from their relationship with the duke and would rise to become Bishop of Bayeux and Count of Mortain, respectively. Herleva had two daughters: Adelaide, who may have been William's full sister, married three times, first to Enguerrand, Count of Ponthieu, then to Lambert of Lens and, finally, to Odo, Count of Champagne; Muriel married a Norman magnate, Eudo, Vicomte of the Contentin.[2]

Two tutors, Ralph the Monk and William, appear in the charters of Normandy in the late 1030s and early 1040s, which suggests William was given a literary education as a child, although we do not have any details. He was raised alongside three of his cousins, William fitz Osbern, Roger de Beaumont and Roger of Montgomery, all of whom would play prominent roles in the conquest of England. William himself appeared in charters during his father's reign as duke, suggesting that Duke Robert always thought of William as his heir, despite the question mark over his birth. This, of course, does not mean that William would not have been supplanted, had a legitimate heir arrived. However, it did mean that when Duke Robert died on pilgrimage, William was accepted as his father's successor. To guarantee this eventuality, before his departure for Jerusalem in 1035, Robert formally designated William as his heir and the Norman magnates swore fealty to him, with the French king, Henry I, as overlord of Normandy, adding his support to the arrangement. Although it would have been considered scandalous elsewhere, Normandy had a tradition of honouring the children of concubines, and allowing them to inherit, it had been 'the custom of this people ever since they first appeared in Gaul.'[3]

As William was only in his eighth year when his father died, guardians were appointed to rule for him, including Robert, Archbishop of Rouen, who was a great-uncle of William's and the son of Richard I, Duke of Normandy. It was these guardians who, in 1036, supported the expeditions to England of Edward and Alfred, the sons of Æthelred II and Emma of Normandy, who were eager to benefit from the uncertainty caused by the death of Cnut in 1035. Although both expeditions were unsuccessful, Edward was able to return safely to Normandy, whereas young Alfred was ambushed by the men of King Harold Harefoot; he was blinded and imprisoned at Ely, where he died in 1037. Normandy itself, however, became increasingly unstable following Archbishop Robert's death in 1037; one story tells of Herleva's brother hiding the young duke in the cottages of peasants at night, for his safety.[4] Squabbles for control of the child duke – and for personal gain – among the Norman aristocracy, led to the deaths of several of William's guardians: Alan of Brittany and Gilbert of Brionne were killed in 1040, and William's tutor, Turold, was murdered in 1041; one of the stewards of the ducal household, Osbern, was murdered as William slept in the same room.[5] The duchy had descended into aristocratic feuding and anarchy.

As he turned fifteen years old, William was knighted; this significant event meant he was now old enough to take control of his duchy, he had come of age. William now surrounded himself with his own supporters, such as William fitz Osbern and Roger of Montgomery, men loyal to him. However, his troubles were far from over; in 1046 his own cousin, Count Guy of Brionne, supported by various counts and viscounts, challenged his right to the Duchy of Normandy. William sought the support of King Henry I of France, and with his own army and that of King Henry, William was able to defeat Count Guy at the Battle of Val-ès-Dunes near Caen, in 1047. It was a 'happy battle, that in one day ruined so many castles of criminals and houses of evil-doers.'[6] The battle not only crushed the rebellion but established William as a force to be reckoned with within Normandy.

William could now turn his thoughts to the future, and a wife. According to William of Jumièges his 'magnates urgently drew attention to the problem of his offspring and the succession.'[7] A country was always subject to unrest when the succession was uncertain. As a consequence, a marriage alliance with Flanders, Normandy's powerful neighbour, was decided upon. Unlike the 'rough wooing' story of later generations, the actual arrangements for the marriage of Matilda and William probably started in 1048, but were a long, drawn-out affair, marred by papal and political machinations. Indeed, the Synod of Rheims, of 3 and 4 October 1049, issued a decree instructing Count Baldwin not to allow the marriage of his daughter to Duke William. Although no reason was given for the prohibition, historians have speculated that this was possibly due to consanguinity; that the couple were related within the prohibited seven degrees. Historian Teresa Cole has done a detailed study of the lineage of the couple and found no connections, except that William's aunt, Eleanor of Normandy, became the second wife of Matilda's grandfather, Baldwin IV; however, there was no blood relationship as Matilda's father was the son of Baldwin IV's first wife, Orgive of Luxembourg, not his second.[8] The only other close family connection would be in Matilda's mother, Adela, having been married for a short time – eight months – to William's uncle, Richard III, Duke of Normandy.

It seems more likely that the basis of the prohibition was politically motivated. Baldwin V had recently backed the failed Lotharingian rebellion against the Holy Roman Emperor and it may well be that the new pope, Leo IX, a German who was elected through the backing of the Holy Roman Emperor, was being loyal to his imperial supporters by forbidding a marriage that would strengthen an anti-German alliance. However, although the pope's decree probably delayed the marriage, it failed to prevent it, and it may have taken place as early as 1050, when Matilda first appeared as witness to a Norman charter, but had certainly happened by 1053 at the latest. It was by this date that the pope was effectively a prisoner of those Normans who had established themselves in the southern Italian states; as he was in no position to continue his opposition to the marriage, there was an informal withdrawal of the prohibition, although it was only officially lifted by the new pope, Nicholas II, in 1059. A penance was imposed on the couple, for their disobedience in marrying against papal prohibition. Each was to establish an abbey; William founded the Abbaye-aux-Hommes, or St Stephen's Abbey, in his Norman capital of Caen, while Matilda founded the Abbaye-aux-Dames, or Holy Trinity Abbey, in the same city. The two abbeys still stand to this day.

Matilda was a few years younger than William and, reportedly, beautiful. The marriage between Matilda and William proved to be a strong and trusting relationship; William is one of very few medieval kings believed to have been completely faithful to his wife. No known lovers or illegitimate children have ever been uncovered, although that did not stop rumours of such in later generations. William of Malmesbury related one story of a mistress, the daughter of a priest. Matilda is said to have ordered her to be hamstrung and disinherited; in revenge, Matilda was beaten to death by a horse bridle, supposedly on William's orders. Malmesbury himself was sceptical of the story and, given Matilda's death resulted from a short illness in 1083, it does seem rather far-fetched.[9]

Matilda and William had a relatively large family, with four sons and at least four daughters. Their eldest son, Robert Curthose, who inherited Normandy, was followed by Richard, who was killed during a hunting accident as a youth; then William, known as Rufus, who became King William II; and the youngest son was the future King Henry I of England. Of the four or five daughters, Cecilia was given to the Convent of Holy Trinity – the abbey her mother founded in penance for her irregular marriage to William – as a child and Constance married Alain Fergant, Duke of Brittany. There are suggestions of two other daughters, Matilda and Agatha, though evidence for their existence is extremely limited. The couple's eldest daughter Adelida, or Adeliza, eventually became a nun following a series of failed marriage plans, which included to Herbert II, Count of Maine, two kings of Spain and, possibly, Harold Godwinson. It has been speculated that during his visit to Normandy in 1064, Harold promised to marry one of William's daughters, and that the proposed daughter was Adelida, though the evidence is far from convincing. Archbishop Anselm's prayers and meditations were probably dedicated to her, who he addresses as 'venerable lady of royal nobility'.[10] She died some time before 1113.

A final daughter, Adela, married Stephen of Blois; their son, another Stephen, would succeed Henry I as King of England. Although most sources give Adela's date of birth as about 1061/2, recent research argues that she was born after the Norman Conquest, as a contemporary poet, Godfrey of Reims, suggests she was born as the daughter of a king, with the lines; 'The royal virgin obtained by fate that her father would be king. In order for Adela to be the daughter of a king, the Fates allowed the father to establish himself as king.'[11] Given her high level of literacy, and her patronage of poets in adulthood, it is likely that Adela was very well-educated as a child; either through tutors or possibly through residence in a convent, as happened with many daughters of the nobility at that time. As a child, it seems, a marriage was arranged between Adela and Simon Crispin, Count of Amiens; however, when Crispin chose to take monastic vows, Adela was betrothed to Stephen of Blois, son of Count Theobald III, Count of Blois and Champagne. Stephen was about twenty years Adela's senior. The formal betrothal took place at Bourgueil and was later followed by a lavish wedding ceremony in Chartres Cathedral in either 1081 or 1082, although it may have been a few years later, as the first charter in which Adela appears is 1085.[12] Poetry from the time of her wedding describes Adela as valorous, learned and generous. The Archbishop of Dol praised her 'beauty, dignity and grace', saying she had 'the brilliance of a goddess'.[13]

Adela and Stephen would have about eleven children in all, with at least two sons born before Stephen succeeded his father as Count of Blois and Champagne in 1090. Adela paid particular attention to their education, ensuring all her children were well versed in their studies. Adela and Stephen's eldest son, Humbert, Count of Virtus, died young, and their second son, William, survived into adulthood but appears to have been disinherited at an early age. Described as an 'idiot' by some, William was married to Agnes, the daughter of Giles, Lord of Sulli, and was given the titles Count of Chartres and Lord of Sulli, but was not allowed to inherit the richer County of Blois, which went to his younger brother, Theobald. Theobald, who was knighted in 1107, became Count of Blois and Champagne and married Matilda, the daughter of Ingelbert II, Duke of Carinthia. Another son, Stephen, named after his father, was born around 1096/7 and was created Count of Mortain sometime before 1115; he became Count of Boulogne in right of his wife, Matilda of Boulogne, before 1125.

On the death of Henry I, King of England, Stephen claimed the throne ahead of his cousin, Matilda, the Countess of Anjou and former Empress of Germany. He was crowned at Westminster

Abbey on 26 December 1135, his actions plunging England into a civil war that lasted almost twenty years, which became known as The Anarchy. Stephen and Adela's youngest son, Henry, was born around 1099 at Winchester, England. He was given to the priory at Cluny, in France, as a child and had a highly successful career in the Church. He later transferred to Bermondsey Abbey, just outside London, where he eventually became abbot, before being elected abbot of the prestigious abbey at Glastonbury, Somerset, in 1126. He was consecrated Bishop of Winchester on 17 November 1129; he died in August 1171, and was buried in Winchester Cathedral. He was a great support to his older brother, Stephen, when he claimed the throne of England on his uncle Henry's death in 1135.

Of Stephen and Adela's five daughters, Matilda married Richard d'Avranches, 2nd Earl of Chester. The couple drowned in the disaster of the White Ship, in 1120; a tragedy which also deprived Henry I of England of his only son and heir, William the Ætheling. Another daughter, Eleanor, married Raoul, Count of Vermandois and died in 1147. Of three other daughters, Agnes married Hugh III de Puisset, Alice married Reginald III, Count of Joigni, and an Adela (or Lithuise) married Miles de Brai, Viscount of Troyes and Lord of Montlheri, but the marriage was later annulled.

Adela was a lot like her mother, not only in character and appearance, but also in her political acumen. She seems to have been a great asset to her husband, who included her in charitable donations and even in his early judicial rulings. She developed a cordial relationship with Bishop Ivo of Chartres, which worked well to maintain the peace between the laity and the clergy in the county. William of Malmesbury said she was 'a powerful woman with a reputation for her worldly influence'.[14] In 1095, when Stephen of Blois took the cross and became one of the leaders of the First Crusade, Adela was left as head of the family and regent of his domains. Letters that the count sent home to his wife indicate a great degree of affection and trust; Adela was given charge of the family's finances as well as their lands. However, Stephen's return from crusade appears of have been less than happy. He returned home as the siege of Antioch was still in progress, and before he had fulfilled his vow to reach Jerusalem.

Adela was highly critical of the fact that he had not satisfied his crusader's vow and her reproach may have been a contributing factor in his return to the Holy Land in 1101. Stephen was killed in combat in the Holy Land during the siege of Ramallah in May 1102. He was succeeded as Count of Blois by his second surviving son, Theobald. Theobald was knighted in 1107, by which time his older brother, William, had already been removed from the succession to the county. William inherited the lesser title of Count of Chartres. Following Stephen's death Adela continued to act as regent until Theobald attained his majority and even after Theobald came of age, mother and son ruled jointly until Adela retired from public life in 1120. Adela was particularly close to her younger brother, Henry, who became King Henry I of England in 1100. She even supported him against their oldest brother, Robert, when Henry claimed the English crown.

An able administrator and negotiator, Adela settled many disputes among monasteries, and even between monasteries and laymen, in her own domains and beyond. Anselm, Archbishop of Canterbury during the reign of William II and Henry I, praised her skills as negotiator and peacemaker following her success at achieving a temporary truce between Anselm and her brother in 1105. Anselm described her as an ardent supporter of papal reform and enjoyed her hospitality during his exile from England.[15] Adela hosted many other Church dignitaries, including Archbishop Thurstan of York and Pope Paschal II. Her family's prestige and power were bolstered by her friendships with the leading ecclesiastic figures in both France and England. An avid patroness of the arts, Adela corresponded with such dignitaries as Hildebert, Bishop of Le Mans and Abbot Baudri of Bourgeuil – later Bishop of Dol – who both wrote poems dedicated to the countess. The book *Ecclesiastical History Together with the Deeds of the Romans and the Franks*, written by Hugh of Fleury, was dedicated to Adela.[16]

An active ruler, Adela regularly toured the family's domains, both as regent and mother of the reigning count. She also maintained links with the Anglo-Norman and Capetian kings. In 1101 Adela sent knights to help Philip I of France's son, Louis, battling against rebels north of Paris. However, by 1107 her son Theobald had joined the revolt and relations with France were to deteriorate further in 1113, when the allied forces of Theobald, Henry I and Adela defeated a Capetian-Angevin army. After more conflict in 1118 Adela used her wealth and diplomatic skills to benefit her family. Theobald's two sons, Henry and Theobald, would later marry Marie and Alice, the two daughters of Louis VII of France by his first wife, Eleanor of Aquitaine. Theobald's daughter, Adela, as Louis VII's third wife, would be the mother of Louis' long-desired son and heir, Philip II Augustus.

In 1120 Adela stopped using the title of countess and retired to the Cluniac Priory of Marcigny; it was the same year that her daughter Matilda died in the White Ship disaster off Barfleur in Normandy. She continued to be active in political affairs and lived to see her son, Stephen, claim the throne of England, in 1135; although she did not witness the twenty years of conflict that ensued. Aged almost seventy, and having been a widow for half of her life, this most remarkable woman, Adela of Normandy, former Countess of Blois and Chartres, died in 1137, possibly on 8 March. Although later tradition has her buried with her mother at Holy Trinity in Caen, the Abbaye-aux-Dames, contemporary sources say she was buried at Marcigny.

William trusted Matilda to act as regent in Normandy during his many absences on campaign or in England. Their relationship was more of a partnership than most medieval marriages; as Duchess and, later, Queen Matilda, she was witness to thirty-nine pre-Conquest and sixty-one post-Conquest charters. Matilda supported her husband's proposed invasion of England and promised a great ship for William's personal use; called the *Mora*, the ship had a mast topped with a cross. The *Mora's* stern bore the head of a lion, while the figurehead on the prow was a statue of a small boy, whose right hand pointed to England and left hand held a horn to his lips. It also flew the pope's flag as a sign that the expedition had the blessing of God and the papacy. According to Elisabeth van Houts, the ship's name derives from 'Morini', the name of the ancient people of Flanders and was a reminder of Matilda's origins.[17]

William's expedition to England arose from his claim that Edward the Confessor had promised the crown to him during his visit to England in 1051, a visit recorded by the *Anglo-Saxon Chronicle*: 'Then soon came Duke William from beyond the sea with a great retinue of Frenchmen, and the king received him and as many of his companions as it pleased him, and let him go again.'[18] If Edward did offer William the succession in 1051, it would have been to spite his most powerful noble, and father-in-law, Earl Godwin. At that time, his relationship with the Godwin family was at its lowest point and he owed a debt of gratitude to the Normans for taking him in when England was overrun by the Danes. It may also be that Edward was trying to tempt the young duke away from too close an alliance with Flanders, a country that had frequently harboured fugitives from English justice, by dangling the English crown in front of the ambitious duke. That Edward changed his mind on his deathbed, and named Harold as his successor in January 1066, may have been forced on the dying king when it became apparent that the English would not be willing to accept the Norman as their king.

Before leaving for England on his expedition of conquest in September 1066, William spent the summer preparing for war, gathering ships and men and organising the administration of his duchy for what could be a prolonged absence. He accompanied Duchess Matilda to the consecration of her foundation, Holy Trinity Abbey – the Abbaye-aux-Dames – in Caen. At the same time, he arranged for her to act as regent in his absence, in the name of their fourteen-year-old son, Robert, with the help of his loyal counsellors, Roger of Beaumont, Roger of Montgomery and Hugh d'Auranchin.[19] Matilda's regency proved very effective; the duchy was faced with no major challenges, which meant that William could concentrate on subduing the English population. Following his victory at Hastings, William made his way to London, where he was crowned on Christmas Day, 1066. The Duke may have wanted to delay the coronation, so that he and Matilda could be crowned together, but he was persuaded that his consecration as king would help to subdue the people and establish his authority over the country.

As we have seen, the Conquest was not without problems; William was able to return to Normandy for a time in 1067, taking many English nobles with him as hostages and to guard against them inciting unrest in England while he was away. However, he had to return to his new kingdom within months, when Exeter, encouraged by King Harold's mother, Gytha, rose against him. The city submitted after a short siege, but it was not until 1068 that William thought that the country was safe enough for him to bring Matilda over from Normandy for her coronation. Matilda was crowned Queen of England in Westminster Abbey, by Archbishop Ealdred of York, on 11 May 1068. The *Anglo-Saxon Chronicle*, as usual, was economical with the details, simply recording; 'And soon after that the Lady Matilda came here to the land, and Archbishop Aldred consecrated her queen in Westminster on Whit Sunday.'[20] The coronation ceremony included a crowning and anointing with holy oil. The wording of the coronation ceremony was changed slightly for Matilda, making queenship more constitutional than customary. The inserted phrases included: *regalis imperii ... esse participem*, 'the queen shares royal power', and *laetatur gens Anglica domini imperio regenda et reginae virtutis providential gubernanda*, 'the English people are blessed to be ruled by the power and virtue of the Queen.'[21]

At the time of her coronation, Matilda was six months pregnant. Her fourth and youngest son, Henry, would be born at Selby, Yorkshire, in September. He was the only child of William and Matilda to be born in England and arrived as a new northern uprising was gathering steam. The severity of this new uprising in the north soon saw Matilda, with baby Henry, returned to the relative safety of Normandy, where she resumed her duties as regent for her absent husband. Although Matilda's primary focus would always be Normandy, she did have some interests in England. She had trusted men in England to help manage her estates, grant charters and manors. She founded a market at Tewkesbury and granted the manors of Felsted in Essex and Tarrant Launceston in Dorset to her abbey of Holy Trinity in Caen, to provide the nuns with wardrobes and firewood.[22]

Matilda proved to be a strong and capable regent in Normandy. She was one of the most active of medieval queens, standing in as an able administrator during her husband's absences; hearing land pleas and corresponding with great personages such as the pope, who is known to have asked her to use her influence over her husband, on occasion. Indeed, Pope Gregory VII encouraged her: 'Urge your husband, do not cease to suggest useful things to his soul. For it is certain that, if the infidel husband is saved by a believing wife, as the apostle says, a believing husband can be made better by a believing wife.'[23] She also retained her interest in her homeland of Flanders and when trouble brewed there, she joined forces with the King of France to try to rectify the situation. When her brother, Baldwin VI, died in 1070, he was succeeded by his son Arnulf, who was still a child, with Arnulf's mother, Richildis, as regent. However, Matilda and Baldwin's brother, Robert, saw an opportunity in his brother's death and invaded Flanders. As Flanders was a vassal of the French crown, it was up to the King of France to send aid to young Arnulf. Matilda sent an Anglo-Norman force, under the command of William fitz Osbern, to help the French army. The combined forces of France, Normandy and those Flemings loyal to young Arnulf were roundly defeated at the Battle of Cassel on 22 February 1071. Arnulf had taken part in the battle himself and was killed by his uncle's forces. Matilda's commander, and William I's loyal friend, William fitz Osbern, was also killed. The French then accepted Robert as the new Count of Flanders and Matilda was forced to acquiesce to the arrangement, but it can't have been easy for her.

Matilda was very close to her family, especially her eldest son, Robert, whose later antics were to cause problems between his parents. William and Robert, father and son, were often at loggerheads, with Robert in open rebellion against his father as a young adult. Matilda was constantly trying to play the peacemaker and was so upset by one quarrel that she was 'choked by tears and could not speak'.[24] Even during a period of exile imposed on Robert, Matilda still supported her son as best she could; not known for his thrift, Matilda would send Robert vast amounts of silver and gold through a Breton messenger, Samson. On discovering Samson's complicity, William threatened to blind the messenger and it was only through Matilda's intervention that the Breton escaped punishment.

Matilda was the driving force in holding her family together, keeping relations as cordial as possible, even with the rebellious Robert. And it may well be her own strength of character, as the centre of the family, which meant that none of her sons was married until after her death. Although the problems with Robert, their oldest son, caused considerable tensions within the marriage, Matilda and William's relationship is one of the most successful of the medieval period. Their partnership as rulers, and as husband and wife, was strong and appeared to be one built on mutual trust and respect. One contemporary remarked that 'The queen adorned the King and the king the queen.'[25] Said to have a happy and loving marriage, their trust in each other was demonstrable. It was remarked upon when William fell seriously ill during a stay at Cherbourg sometime between 1063 and 1066. Matilda prayed for his recovery at the altar; the monks commenting on her informal appearance as a sign of the distress her husband's illness was causing her. In correspondence between them, William addresses Matilda warmly:

> William, by the grace of God king of the English, to queen Matilda, his dear spouse, perpetual health/greeting. I want you to know that I grant to St. Martin at Marmontier the church of Ste. Marie des Pieux and the lands that depend on it, free of all rents, as priest Hugh held them on the day of his death. Furthermore, I charge you to render, as is just, all the land in Normandy belonging to St. Martin, free and secure from all those who would wish to burden it, as well as from the demands of the foresters; above all forbid Hugolin de Cherbourg to meddle further with the affairs of this house.[26]

Matilda's piety was renowned. Although founding the Abbaye-aux-Dames in Caen was a penance for her irregular marriage to William, her constant and repeated donations to religious houses demonstrate her dedication to her faith. There is, however, one black mark against her name when she is said to have demanded that the monks of Abingdon send their abbey's most precious ornaments to her, so that she could choose those she would like for herself; although it has to be noted that the veracity of the story is questionable as it comes from an English source in the 1130s and is used as an example of post-Conquest Norman bullying tactics. Among Matilda's many donations, she gave the monks of Marmoutier a new refectory and a cope, and to the monks of St Evroult she gave £100 for the building of a refectory, a mark of gold, a chasuble decorated with gold and pearls, and a cope for the chanter. To St Corneille at Compiègne she gave a vase decorated with gold and precious stones and to the abbey of Cluny a chasuble 'that was so rigid because of the metal that it could not be folded.'[27] The nuns of her abbey at Holy Trinity, Caen, received a substantial bequest from Matilda's will, written the year before her death. As well as her crown and sceptre, they were given a chalice, a chasuble, a mantle of brocade, two golden chains with a cross, a chain decorated with emblems for hanging a lamp in front of the altar, several large candelabras, the draperies for her horse and all the vases 'which she had not yet handed out during her life'.[28]

In July 1083, as the relationship between her husband and son soured once more, Matilda fell ill. She, William and Robert were together for the last time at Caen, on 18 July, and Robert left court shortly thereafter.[29] Matilda had drawn up her will in the previous year, so it is possible that she was aware of her illness long before her last summer. The continuing worry over the rift between her husband and beloved son cannot have helped her health and the arrival of winter saw her gravely ill. Matilda died on 2 November 1083, having 'confessed her sins with bitter tears and, after fully accomplishing all that Christian custom requires and being fortified by the saving sacrament...'[30] Her husband was with her throughout the final days of her illness, and he '... showed many days of the deepest mourning how much he missed the love of her whom he had lost.'[31] The chronicles of the time report her death in the briefest of terms: 'Queen Matilda died in Normandy on Thursday the fourth of the nones [the 2nd] of November, and was buried at Caen.'[32] She was buried at her own foundation of Holy Trinity, Caen, after a funeral that lasted two days and was attended by a host of monks, abbots, bishops and nuns; and 'a great throng of people' came to pay homage to the late, respected duchess and queen.[33] There is no record of which of her children attended the funeral, although her daughter Cecilia was most likely in attendance, as she had been a nun at the abbey since childhood. The original tombstone still survives; it has an inscription carved around the edge, emphasising her royal descent on her mother's side.

Matilda's height has been frequently discussed by historians, with some claiming that she was a dwarf. The casket, containing her bones, was opened in 1961 and supposedly revealed a woman of about 4ft 2in tall.[34] However, recent studies have argued against this finding. Had Matilda really been so short, she would have had much difficulty giving birth to any child, let alone the nine children she is known to have had. Professor Dastague, from the *Institut D'Anthropologie* at Caen, who was present at the original dig confirmed to Sir Jack Dewhurst, president of the Royal College of Obstetricians and Gynaecologists, who was writing an article on royal confinements, that it had been calculated that Matilda was in fact 152cm, about 5ft, in height.[35] Matilda's actual height cannot be given with certainty, however, as the skeleton which was examined was incomplete.

The queen's grave had been destroyed in the sixteenth century, during the French Wars of Religion, and much of her remains never recovered. What we do know is that her childbearing record precludes any idea that she was a dwarf.[36]

Following her death William became increasingly isolated; Robert deserted him, leaving his brother William to support his father. William the Conqueror followed his wife to the grave four years later, in 1087. In many aspects of her life, Matilda is clearly seen as the ideal medieval wife and mother. Ever supportive of her husband, he relied heavily on her to administer Normandy in his frequent absences. She was seen by many as a conduit to the king, as seen in the pope's letters encouraging her to be a good influence on her husband. Even when disobeying William, in her support of their eldest son Robert, she was still trying to be the embodiment of the medieval female ideal, playing the peacemaker between warring members of her family. She was the first Queen of England of the new Norman dynasty, a worthy successor to Emma of Normandy and Edith of Wessex, her predecessors.

St Margaret

The story of St Margaret, Queen of Scotland as the wife of King Malcolm III Canmore, started far away from the courts of Scotland and England, in Eastern Europe. St Margaret had an impeccable Saxon pedigree; she could trace her ancestry directly to Alfred the Great, King of Wessex, and his forebears. She was the daughter of Edward the Exile and his wife, Agatha.

Edward the Exile was the son of Edmund II Ironside, King of England in 1016; Edmund was the son of Æthelred II and his first wife, Ælfgifu of York. Edward's grandfather was, therefore, Æthelred II (the Unready) and his uncle was Edward the Confessor, England's king from 1042 until 1066. Edward the Exile's mother, Ealdgyth, was the widow of Sigeferth, a thegn from East Anglia, who had been betrayed in 1015, along with another thegn, Morcar, by Eadric Streona, who had lured them into his chamber during a great assembly at Oxford and killed them. After her first husband's murder, King Æthelred 'took possession of their effects, and ordered Elgitha [Ealdgyth], Sigeferth's widow, to be taken to the town of Malmesbury'.[1] Taking a stand against his father and Eadric, however, Edmund rescued Ealdgyth from Malmesbury and 'married her against his father's will', between the middle of August and the middle of September 1015. Edmund then rode into the territories of Sigeferth and Morcar, in the Five Boroughs (The Five Boroughs were Derby, Leicester, Lincoln, Nottingham and Stamford), 'and seizing the lands of Sigeferth and Morcar, compelled the villeins to acknowledge him as their lord.'[2]

The couple, therefore, were probably married at the beginning of August. They would have two sons, Edward and Edmund, who may well have been twins or were born just one year apart. Edward was born in 1016, with Edmund being born no later than 1017. Their father spent the rest of 1015 and 1016 trying to encourage resistance to the constant Danish onslaught. As his father weakened and fell ill at Cosham, Edmund raised an army in the Midlands to confront Cnut. However, Eadric Streona then turned traitor and took forty English ships – and their men – with him as he submitted to Cnut. As a consequence, with the situation looking hopeless, the people of Wessex then submitted to Cnut and gave hostages, also providing horses for his army. One of the clearest aspects of England in this era was a distinct lack of unity; it was every man for himself, which meant mounting a concerted resistance to Danish invasion was virtually impossible.

In early 1016, Edmund raised another army but was forced to disband it when his father and the London garrison failed to join them. They needed the king as a figurehead for the sake of unity and without him, few were willing to make a stand. A second army, this time with King Æthelred at its head, however, failed to make inroads against the Danes. After this, Edmund, along with Earl Uhtred of Northumbria, ravaged the Danish held territories of Staffordshire, Shropshire and Cheshire. However, when Cnut attacked York, Uhtred was forced to withdraw north to protect his own lands; he was executed on the orders of Cnut, following his submission to the Dane.[3] King Æthelred died in London on St George's Day, 23 April 1016, 'after a life of severe toils and tribulations'.[4] He was buried in Old St Paul's Cathedral, London; his tomb was lost when the cathedral was destroyed in the Great Fire of London in 1666.

On Æthelred's death, according to John of Worcester, the leading men of England came together and, while electing Cnut as their new king, 'repudiated all the descendants of king Æthelred.'[5] However, the people of London and the south chose Edmund as king:

Raised to the royal throne the intrepid Edmund went without delay to Wessex, and being received with great joy by the whole population, he quickly brought it under his rule; and the people of many provinces in England, hearing this, gave him their voluntary submission.[6]

Edmund then spent the summer fighting a series of indecisive battles with the Danes. He managed to force the withdrawal of a Danish army besieging London, before defeating it at Brentford. However, when he was forced to withdraw to Wessex to raise more troops, the Danes invaded London again, only to be defeated once more when Edmund returned. As a testament to Edmund's personal courage, John of Worcester said Edmund 'fought desperately in the first rank at close quarters, and, while he superintended every movement, fought hard in person, and often struck down an enemy, performing at once the duties of a brave soldier and an able general.'[7]

It was possibly as a result of his successes, and a desire to be on the winning side, that Eadric Streona turned his coat yet again and rejoined the ranks of Edmund's allies. However, Edmund was defeated by Cnut in battle at 'Assundun' (possibly Ashdon or Ashingdon in Essex) on 18 October; in the heat of the battle, the treacherous Eadric Streona again turned and fled with his men. The English suffered heavy losses. Following a possible further battle in the Forest of Dean, Cnut and Edmund met at Alney in Gloucestershire and a compromise was reached, whereby Edmund would rule all lands to the south of the River Thames and Cnut would rule everything to the north, with the longest surviving inheriting the lands of the other.

This understanding, however, was cut short when Edmund died on 30 November, probably having succumbed to wounds received during the summer of vicious fighting, rather than the later story of murder with a sword or arrow into his bowels whilst visiting the latrines.[8]

With Edmund's death, and with his two sons being only toddlers, there was no further organised opposition to Cnut and the Dane was able to take possession of the entire country. As soon as he had control, Cnut sent Edmund's infant sons to the court of the King of Sweden, Olof Stötkonung, apparently with instructions to have them killed. However, the Swedish king was understandably squeamish about murdering two toddlers and eventually sent them on to the relative safety of the court of the Grand Prince of Kiev, Yaroslav the Wise, and his wife – Olof's daughter, Ingegerd. As young adults, Edward and Edmund later made their way to Hungary and helped in the restoration of the exiled Andrew of Hungary. Edmund is said to have married a Hungarian princess but died sometime before 1054. Around 1043 Edward married Agatha, whose origins are extremely obscure. She may have been a daughter of Yaroslav and Ingegerd of Kiev but was more likely the daughter of Liudolf, Margrave of West Friesland and a relative of Holy Roman Emperor Henry III. The couple had three children: Margaret, the eldest, was born in either 1045 or 1046; her sister, Christina was born around 1050 and her brother Edgar, the Ætheling, was born at some time between 1052 and 1056.

The family could have spent their whole lives in European exile, were it not for Edward the Confessor's failure to produce a legitimate heir by his wife, Edith of Wessex. In 1054 Edward, having realised that he needed to settle the question over the succession, sent an embassy to Eastern Europe in search of his brother Edmund's children. Ealdred, Archbishop of York, spent several months at the court of Holy Roman Emperor Henry III, but was initially unsuccessful in arranging Edward the Exile's return to England. A second embassy in 1056 managed to persuade the prince to return to his homeland and he arrived back in England in 1057, forty years after he was sent into exile. We do not know whether his family travelled with him or arrived later. However, just days after his return Edward the Exile was dead, before he even saw the king, his uncle, and was buried in St Paul's Cathedral, London. Whether his death was caused by nefarious means is uncertain. As we have seen, the suspicion has been raised that Edward's rival for the throne, Harold Godwinson – the future Harold II – may have taken the opportunity to remove his rival; although it was likely that it was Harold who had escorted Edward back to England, as he was on the Continent at that time, so, surely, had he intended murder, he would have done it sooner and far from English soil.

Whatever the circumstances, the death of Edward the Exile was a blow for Edward the Confessor's dynastic hopes. Little Edgar, now the Ætheling and accepted heir, was much too young to assume a political role. He and his sisters, with their mother, were now under the protection of King Edward. They continued to live at court, Edgar was adopted by Queen Edith, who raised him and saw to his education. Margaret and Christina were probably sent to the nunnery at Wilton, where the queen had been schooled, to continue their education. By January 1066, when Edward the Confessor died, Margaret was approaching her twentieth birthday, while Edgar could have been as young as ten and was probably no older than fourteen. Due to his tender years Edgar was passed over as a candidate for the throne, in preference for the older and more experienced Harold Godwinson, who was crowned as King Harold II the day after King Edward's death. Following Harold's death at the Battle of Hastings, Edgar was proclaimed king by some of his supporters, including Archbishop Ealdred of York, but was hardly capable of mounting any real challenge to William the Conqueror and by December had come to terms with him at Berkhamsted.

By 1068 Edgar the Ætheling had become involved in the opposition to Norman rule, which had been festering in northern England. However, when events turned against him he fled to Scotland, taking his mother and sisters along with him. The family was warmly received at Dunfermline by Scotland's king, Malcolm III Canmore. Malcolm III Canmore was the son of Duncan I and Sybilla of Northumbria. His father had been killed by Macbeth, of Shakespearean fame, in August of 1040. Malcolm himself had defeated King Macbeth in battle at Lumphanan in August 1057 and Macbeth's son Lulach in March 1058, to take the throne. By 1069 he was well established as king and had two sons by his first wife, Ingeborg. Ingeborg was the daughter of Fin Arnasson, friend of Harald Hardrada and Jarl of Holland. The couple had three sons, Duncan, Malcolm and Donald. In 1069 Malcolm asked Edgar and his mother for Margaret's hand in marriage:

> Then began Malcolm to yearn after the child's [Edgar] sister, Margaret, to wife; but he and all his men long refused; and she also herself was averse, and said that she would neither have him nor anyone else, if the Supreme Power would grant, that she in her maidenhood might please the mighty Lord with a carnal heart, in this short life, in pure continence. The king, however,

earnestly urged her brother, until he answered Yea. And indeed he durst not otherwise; for they were come into his kingdom... The prescient Creator wist long before what he of her would have done; for that she would increase the glory of God in this land, lead the king aright from the path of error, bend him and his people together by a better way, and suppress the bad customs which the nation formerly followed: all which she afterwards did. The king therefore received her, though it was against her will, and was pleased with her manners, and thanked God, who in his might had given him such a match.[9]

What happened to Malcolm's first wife, Ingebiorg, seems uncertain, we do not know whether she died or was put aside in favour of this new marriage to a descendant of Alfred the Great. Her death seems most likely, however, making Malcolm free to find another wife, though whether it was of natural causes, or murder, would be another question for which the answer is elusive. Margaret was reluctant to agree to the marriage, she was more inclined to a religious life and had hoped to become a nun.[10] Nonetheless, with pressure from Malcolm, her brother and, possibly, her own sense of obligation to the king who was sheltering her family, she eventually accepted his proposal. They were married at Dunfermline sometime in 1069 or 1070 and, by all accounts, it seems to have been a happy and successful marriage and partnership.

The first ever wife of a Scottish king to be recognised as Queen, Margaret was a strong figure; she was pious but also worldly wise.[11] Having grown up on the Continent, she was familiar with many of the courts of Europe and had met some of its leading churchmen. A modernising queen, Margaret brought luxury to the Scottish court and into the lives of the nobles of her new country. She was averse to the Celtic traditions of the Scottish court, associating the Gaelic language with the irregularities of the Scottish Church. As a result, Margaret introduced a more rigorous attention to etiquette than had previously been seen in the rough-and-ready Scottish court, no longer encouraging the use of bards, and druidic old men to recite the ancestry of Malcolm and Scotland's kings.[12] She introduced ceremony and luxury, not only to the court, but to the magnates throughout the kingdom.

A life of St Margaret was commissioned by her daughter, Matilda, when she was Queen of England as wife of Henry I. It was written sometime between 1100 and 1107 by Turgot, Margaret's former chaplain and then prior of Durham. The biography emphasises the queen's compassion for children and the poor and stresses her piety, pointing to the severity of her self-denial and her frequent fasting. However, it also tells us that she had a love of etiquette and formality, and a fondness for fine clothes and jewellery.[13] Margaret enjoyed a high reputation among the Anglo-Norman world, even in her own lifetime; Orderic Vitalis described her as 'eminent from her high birth, but even more renowned for her virtue and holy life.'[14]

Margaret was a 'strong, complex and interesting character, as well as beautiful and notably religious'.[15] According to Nigel Tranter, Margaret carried with her, everywhere, a piece of the true cross, on which Christ was crucified. It is from this relic, which became known as the Black Rood of Scotland, that the Palace of Holyrood, in Edinburgh, takes its name. Her life as queen of Scotland did not prevent her pursuing an active religious life; indeed, her position gave her a unique opportunity to influence the practice of Christianity in Scotland. Margaret strived to bring the Church of Scotland into conformity with the practices of western Catholicism, and away from the tenets of the Celtic, or Columban, Church, which held a lot of influence in the country and did not recognise the overlordship of the pope. The Columban Church celebrated Easter on a different day to the Catholic Church, as it included Sundays in its forty days of Lent, unlike the Roman Catholic Church. They also shared bread and wine among their congregation during communion, unlike the Catholic Church, which gave bread to the congregation, but only reserved the wine for the celebrant and priests.

Having been raised on the Continent, amid the splendour of the churches in the Holy Roman Empire, Margaret believed that the wearing of beautiful vestments by the clergy was done for the glory of God; as far as she was concerned, the rough, homespun habits of the Columban clergy, were not. She also believed in the strict hierarchy of the Church, from the pope, through cardinals, archbishops, bishops, abbots and the parish priests. The two churches even differed in the tonsures of their clergy; Roman priests shaved the crowns of their heads, whereas the Columban, or Celtic, priests, shaved their foreheads.[16] Queen Margaret encouraged the Scottish clergy, and its people, to receive communion more than once a year at Easter, to refrain from working on a Sunday and to observe the Lenten fast from Ash Wednesday, rather than the following Monday, and so bringing it in line with the practice of the Roman Catholic church. Margaret also urged the clergy to celebrate mass with a common ritual and sought to forbid marriage between a man and his stepmother or sister-in-law, a practice forbidden in the Roman Catholic Church but permitted within the Celtic Church.

Margaret was supported in all her reforms by her husband; indeed, if Malcolm III had not given his support it is doubtful that Margaret's influence would have achieved much, if anything at all. His role in her attempts at religious reform is vague, although Malcolm did arrange a conference for the clergy to introduce a number of reforms. Margaret was present and embarrassed some of the clerics by knowing more about the proper procedures of the Church than they did. She even had the papal manuals to quote from. It may well be that Malcolm was needed to facilitate the interactions between queen and clergy, as Margaret's biographer claimed the queen's first language was English, whereas Malcolm was fluent in English and his native Gaelic and could have acted as translator for his wife.[17]

The queen founded a monastic community at Dunfermline, building the first major stone church in Scotland; and arranged with Lanfranc, Archbishop of Canterbury, with whom she corresponded often, to populate the abbey with monks from the cathedral monastery at Canterbury, to become its first community. Although it started as a priory, it was elevated to an independent abbey in 1128, at the instigation of Margaret's son, David I.[18] The Queen's Ferry crossing on the Firth of Forth, for which Margaret had persuaded her husband to remit the charges for genuine pilgrims going further north to St Andrews, was named for Queen Margaret. As well as her foundation at Dunfermline Abbey, which became the burial site of many of Scotland's kings and queens, Margaret also rebuilt in stone the abbey on Iona, which had been burnt down. And at Edinburgh Castle, she built the small chapel which still bears her name.

Queen Margaret was therefore instrumental in forcing through the reforms of the Scottish Church. However, she suffered one reverse when King Malcolm appointed their fourth son, Æthelred, to the position of lay Abbot of Dunkeld, and thus the primacy of the Columban Church, a position which had also been held by the boy's great-grandfather, Crinan, from a similar early age. Æthelred fully embraced the Celtic Church, becoming a priest of the Church and marrying without his parents' permission; a married priest was not permitted within the Roman Catholic Church. His wife was the daughter of the late King Lulach (d. 1058). It may well be that these actions were the cause of Æthelred being barred from the succession, although he wasn't disowned by his family, as it seems he was with his mother when she died in 1093. Margaret and Malcolm would have a large family, with six sons and two daughters growing to adulthood. Margaret took great care in educating them, ensuring they were given the essentials for their future royal careers. Their eldest son, Edward, died in 1093 in his early twenties, within days of his father. As we have seen, another son, Æthelred, who may have been styled Earl of Fife, became Lay Abbot at Dunkeld and died around 1097.

Following their father's death and the succession dispute between Malcolm III's brother, Donald III, and his oldest son by Ingeborg, Duncan II, Margaret's youngest son, David, had fled to England with his brothers, Edgar and Alexander. Donald had initially usurped the throne on Malcolm's death, but was himself deposed by Duncan in May 1094. When Duncan was killed at the Battle of Monthechin in November of the same year, Donald again seized the throne. Margaret and Malcolm's son, Edmund, moreover, had sided with his uncle in order to become co-ruler. Edmund ruled south of the Forth/Clyde boundary, while Donald ruled the north, although there is no indication that he was ever crowned. Donald and Edmund were both deposed in 1097 in favour of Edmund's brother, King Edgar, who had the backing of William II Rufus of England. Edmund became a monk at Montacute Abbey, Somerset, and died there, having never married. Edgar died on 8 January 1107. Unmarried and childless, he was succeeded by his brother,

Alexander I, who had been married to Sybilla, an illegitimate daughter of King Henry I of England, but died without a legitimate heir in April 1124.[19]

Margaret's youngest son, David I, succeeded Alexander as king. As the sixth son, David would never have expected to succeed to the throne. After he and his brothers fled to England, he had served in the household of King Henry I of England. In 1113 he married Maud de Senlis, daughter Judith of Lens, niece of William the Conqueror, and Earl Waltheof of Northumbria, and therefore the granddaughter of Siward, the pre-Conquest Earl of Northumbria who had helped to establish Malcolm III on his throne. David and Maud had four children together, two sons and two daughters. One son, Malcolm, tragically died in infancy, murdered by a deranged Scandinavian priest of his father's household.[20] A second son, Henry of Huntingdon, married Ada de Warenne, by whom he had several children, including the future kings Malcolm IV and William the Lion, but predeceased his father. Their two daughters, Claricia and Hodierna, died young and unmarried. On his marriage, David acquired the Honour of Huntingdon, English lands stretching from South Yorkshire to Middlesex. David was bequeathed a swathe of lands in southern Scotland by his brother, King Edgar, and needed English help to wrest control of these lands from his brother, King Alexander. Once he had control, David instituted a policy of religious reform. When Alexander died in 1124, he succeeded to the Scottish throne, ruling until 1153, instituting political and religious reforms and extending Scottish territory further south than any Scots king had done before him. He died while at prayer in Carlisle on 24 May 1153 and was succeeded by his grandson, Malcolm IV the Maiden. (The name is not pejorative, suggestng weakness or effeminacy; it refers to his young age.)

Malcolm and Margaret also had two daughters: the oldest, Edith, changed her name to Matilda on marrying King Henry I of England, and was the mother of Empress Matilda, whose attempts to claim the crown on her father's death were thwarted by her cousin, King Stephen. Margaret's second daughter, Mary, married Eustace III, Count of Boulogne, and was the mother of Matilda of Boulogne, wife of Stephen, King of England.[21] Matilda and Mary were educated at Wilton Abbey, in the charge of Margaret's sister,

Christina. Edith/Matilda was unhappy in her aunt's care: 'I ... went in fear of the rod of my aunt Christina ... and she would often make me smart with a good slapping and the most horrible scolding, as well as treating me as being in disgrace.'[22] Christina's treatment of Matilda included forcing the girl to wear a veil, supposedly to hide her beauty from visiting men. This caused controversy when she married King Henry I, as it raised the question of whether she had ever taken her vows – or been veiled – as a nun. At the inquiry into this question in 1100, Matilda insisted she had not, saying; 'that hood I did indeed wear in her presence, chafing and fearful ... but as soon as I was able to escape out of her sight I tore it off and threw it in the dirt and trampled on it. This was my only way of venting my rage and hatred of it that boiled up in me.'[23]

Once married, Malcolm and Margaret continued to support Margaret's brother, Edgar the Ætheling; in 1075 he was welcomed 'with great honour' at the Scottish court on his return from Flanders. They gave him 'great gifts and many treasures ... and led him and all his sailors out of his domain with great honour.'[24] As King of Scots, Malcolm also had claims to Cumbria and Northumbria and in 1069/70, he made raids into Northumberland. King William I responded by sending an army north and the eventual peace treaty saw Malcolm's oldest son by Ingebiorg, Duncan, being sent south as a hostage and guarantee of his good faith. Duncan would eventually reign, briefly, as Duncan II, but was killed at the Battle of Monthechin in 1094. Malcolm made frequent raids into Northumberland, notably in 1079 and 1091, in attempts to gain control over the county. When a diplomatic mission, aided by his brother-in-law, Edgar the Ætheling, failed in 1092, he invaded northern England again in the follwing year, taking his eldest son by Margaret, Edward, with him. The resulting siege of Alnwick saw King Malcolm killed and his son, Edward, so seriously injured that he succumbed to his wounds just a few days later, at Jedburgh.

Many of the chroniclers of the time record Margaret's reaction to the news of the deaths of her husband and oldest son. John of Worcester told of Margaret's grief:

Margaret, queen of the Scots, was so deeply affected by the news of their death, that she fell dangerously ill. Calling the priests to attend her without delay, she went into the church, and confessing her sins to them, caused herself to be anointed with oil and strengthened with the heavenly viaticum; beseeching God with earnest and diligent prayers that he would not suffer her to live longer in this troublesome world. Nor was it very long before her prayers were heard, for three days after the king's death she was released from the bonds of the flesh, and translated, as we doubt not, to the joys of eternal salvation.[25]

The *Anglo-Saxon Chronicle* recorded: 'When the good Queen Margaret heard this – her most beloved lord and son thus betrayed she was in her mind almost distracted to death. She with her priests went to church, and performed her rites, and prayed before God, that she might give up the ghost, and drove out all the English that formerly were with King Malcolm.'[26] Margaret died just days after the battle, on 16 November, possibly as a result of receiving the news of the deaths of her husband and eldest son, although the fact her body was weakened by her frequent fasting and self-denial surely hastened her death. She was buried in the abbey she had founded at Dunfermline. Malcolm was initially buried at Tynemouth, but later moved to join his wife at Dunfermline.

The queen's personal piety was renowned; particularly for the severity of her fasting and self-denial. The story of her life, written by Turgot, emphasises her compassion for children and the poor. Her religious zeal may well have arisen from her childhood in Eastern Europe, which had only just been recently – and not entirely – been converted to Christianity. In the *Vita Sanctae Margaretae*, Turgot said of Margaret: 'She had a keen acuteness of intellect for judging whatever matter there was to be understood, a tenacity of memory for retaining many things, and a favoured facility for expressing things in words.'[27] The *Anglo-Saxon Chronicle* said: 'This queen aforesaid performed afterwards many useful deeds in this land to the glory of God, and also in her royal estate she well conducted herself, as was her nature.'[28] John of Worcester also recorded Margaret's piety:

For while she lived, she devoted herself to the exercise of piety, justice, peace, and charity; she was frequent in prayer, and chastened her body by watchings and fastings; she endowed churches and monasteries; loved and reverenced the servants and handmaids of God; broke bread to the hungry, clothed the naked, gave shelter, food, and raiment to all the pilgrims who came to her door; and loved God with all her heart.[29]

Margaret's sons honoured their mother's memory, encouraging the popular cult of St Margaret, which developed soon after the queen's death, in order to foster the idea that she should be made a saint. Such an honour would serve to enhance the political and religious status of their family. One of the miracles attributed to her was that in 1199, Scotland's king, William the Lion, was persuaded against launching an invasion of England after experiencing a vision while holding a vigil at Margaret's tomb at Dunfermline. Her canonisation came in 1250 and in 1673 Pope Clement X named her patroness of Scotland. Following the Reformation, the remains of both Margaret and Malcolm were removed to Spain by Philip II and reinterred in a chapel at the Escorial in Madrid.[30]

Margaret was a direct descendant of King Alfred the Great of Wessex; her Saxon royal blood guaranteed that she would not be allowed to enter a convent, she was too valuable on the marriage market. However, through her efforts to reform the Scottish Church, it could be said that she found a better way to worship God. Her legacy was cemented through the work of her son, David I, who continued her policy of Church reform; while her Saxon blood found its way back into the English royal family through her daughter Matilda's marriage to Henry I.

Quaint legends to our hearts endear
Ours sainted Scottish Queen:
Alone, unseen, oft strayed she here
In thoughtful mood, serene;
Thus oft from yonder ancient towers
She sought from pomp to dwell,
And pondered o'er life's fleeting hours
Beside her cherished well.[31]

Gundrada de Warenne

Gundrada de Warenne was the wife of one of William the Conqueror's most loyal knights, and one of the few men who it is known, beyond doubt, was with the Norman duke at the Battle of Hastings. William de Warenne was one of the many beneficiaries of the lands and titles handed out to Duke William's loyal Norman supporters in the years immediately after the Conquest.

William de Warenne, 1st Earl of Surrey, was a younger son of Rodulf, or Ralph, de Warenne, a minor Norman lord with lands in the Pays de Caux, and his wife Beatrix. Although William de Warenne's ancestry is far from clear, it is possible that his mother Beatrix was a niece of Duchess Gunnor, the wife of Duke Richard I of Normandy and the mother of Emma of Normandy, wife of both Æthelred II and King Cnut, and great-grandmother of William the Bastard, Duke of Normandy.

If this were true, it would mean that William was a distant cousin of the victorious Duke of Normandy, later to be known as William the Conqueror. The two families were certainly related in some way, as Anselm, Archbishop of Canterbury, would later forbid a marriage between William de Warenne's son, another William, and an illegitimate daughter of Henry I on the grounds of consanguinity (meaning the couple was too closely related by blood to be allowed to marry).[1]

The family name is probably derived from the hamlet of Varenne, situated just south of Arques in northern France and 13 miles from Bellencombre, on the river of the same name, Varenne. Varenne was part of the Warenne lands in the *département* of Seine-Inférieure, Normandy. William's older brother, Rodulf or Ralph, would inherit the greater part of the Warenne family estates in Normandy. It was suggested by Robert de Torigny, in his additions to the *Gesta Normannorum Ducum* of William of Jumièges, that William de Warenne was the brother of another Norman baron, Roger de Mortemer.[2] However, de Torigny's genealogies are rather confusing and it seems more likely that the two lords were cousins, as described by Orderic Vitalis, rather than brothers.[3]

William's father, Rodulf de Warenne I, who survived until 1074, is mentioned in a charter of Robert I, Duke of Normandy, father of William the Conqueror, which can be dated to sometime between 1030 and 1035 and confirmed the foundation of the abbey of St Armand at Rouen.[4] Another branch of the family may have descended from Roger, son of Ralph de Warethna, who held lands near Arques and was himself witness to a charter in favour of the abbey of St Wandrille sometime before 1045. There is no extant evidence of a familial link, but it is possible, given that Roger and Ralph were of the same generation, that they were cousins. The charter of Duke Robert demonstrates that Rodulf held lands in the vicinity of the abbey of the Holy Trinity at Rouen, which lay to the east of the city.[5] In 1053, the year by which William of Normandy had married Matilda of Flanders, Rodulf, described as '*quidam miles de Warenna, Radulfus nomine*', gave all his land in Vascœuil, in the Eure *département*, to the abbey of Pierre de Préaux. His wife Beatrix gave her consent to the gift, with his brother Godfrey being a witness on the charter.[6]

Sometime between May 1055 and 1059, Beatrix died and Rodulf married his second wife, Emma; in 1055 Beatrix was witness to the sale of lands to the abbey of Holy Trinity in Rouen. However, in 1059 Rodulf and new his wife, Emma, sold four churches in the *pays de Caux*, to the same abbey. Rodulf and Beatrix had at least three children. The oldest was Rodulf de Warenne II, who inherited the Warenne estates from his father. The fact that some of those estates are later found in the hands of the d'Esneval family suggests that Rodulf had at least one child, a daughter, who married into the d'Esneval family, taking with her the de Warenne lands she had inherited from her father. William de Warenne was the second son of the family; they also had a daughter, whose name is unknown. She married Erneis de Coulances and had two sons, Richard, and Roger, who became a monk at St Evroul.[7]

William's birth, as you might expect, is shrouded in the fog of time; a younger son of the minor nobility does not tend to get a mention until he does something remarkable or becomes someone notable. Although still young, by the mid-1050s William was considered a capable and experienced enough soldier to be given joint command of a Norman army. His first recorded military action is in the campaign against the French king, Henry I, who invaded Normandy in 1052. William de Warenne was among the Norman lords, under the leadership of Count Robert of Eu, who fought the French king's brother, Odo, at the Battle of Mortemer. After several hours of fierce fighting, the Normans proved victorious, even taking prisoner Guy, Count of Ponthieu, one of the French commanders.

William's own kinsman, Roger (I) de Mortemer had also fought on the side of the Normans in the battle. However, in 1054 he fell foul of Duke William when he played host for several days to one of the duke's enemies, Count Ralph. The fact that Count Ralph happened to be the father-in-law of Roger de Mortemer was insufficient excuse for Duke William, who exiled Roger from Normandy and confiscated all his possessions. As a consequence, William de Warenne was rewarded for his services against the French with some of the Mortemer lands, including the castle of Mortemer itself. When Duke William eventually forgave Roger de Mortemer and restored him to his estates, William de Warenne was able to hold on to the castles of Mortemer and Bellencombre. Bellencombre would become the capital of the de Warenne estates in Normandy. At about the same time, de Warenne received more rewards from the lands of William, Count of Arques, confiscated in 1053.

William de Warenne was one of Duke William's most loyal friends and supporters from the early 1050s onwards. The duke's confidence in him is demonstrated in the fact he was one of the barons consulted during the planning of the invasion of England in 1066. Sometime in the years either side of the Conquest, moreover, William de Warenne had married Gundrada. Gundrada's parentage has long been a subject of debate. For many years she was believed to be the daughter of William the Conqueror and his wife, Matilda of Flanders. It seems the misunderstanding arose with the monks at St Pancras Priory in Lewes, when a copy of their foundation charter claimed that she was the daughter of Matilda of Flanders. The claim was also made in a charter giving the monks of St Pancras the manor of Walton in Norfolk.[8] St Pancras was founded as a Cluniac monastery by William and Gundrada and it may be that the monks got carried away with the idea of their foundress having royal blood, or that there was an error when copying the charter from the original.

For whatever reason, the claims by St Pancras Priory at Lewes have caused controversy throughout the ensuing centuries. In the sixteenth century Leland believed that she was the Conqueror's daughter, while Orderic Vitalis had stated that she was 'Sister of Gherbode, a Fleming, to whom King William the First had given the City and Earldom of Chester'.[9] According to this theory, it was thought that Gundrada was not a daughter of the king but his step-daughter. It was claimed that she was the daughter of the queen, Matilda, by an earlier, forgotten marriage to a Flemish nobleman called Gerbod. Other suggestions have included that she was an adopted daughter, raised alongside William and Matilda's own children who were of a similar age. Alternatively, due to her Flemish origins, it has been argued that the confusion arose as she had joined Matilda's household at an early age; an assertion supported by Matilda's gift to Gundrada of the manor of Carlton in Cambridge – a manor Gundrada later gave to Lewes Priory. In 1888 in the *English Historical Review*, E.A. Freeman used the priory's original charter to conclude that there was no familial relationship between Gundrada and William the Conqueror. In it, while the king and William de Warenne both mention Gundrada, neither refer to her as being related to the king or queen. Freeman stated, 'there is nothing to show that Gundrada was the daughter either of King William or of Queen Matilda; there is a great deal to show that she was not.'[10]

It now seems more likely that Gundrada was a Flemish noblewoman, the sister of Gerbod who would be, for a brief time, Earl of Chester. Her father may also have been called Gerbod, or

Gherbode, and was the hereditary advocate of the monastery of St Bertin; a title which later will pass down through the de Warenne family.[11] Another brother, Frederic, had lands in England even before the Conquest, when two people named Frederic and Gundrada are mentioned as holding four manors in Kent and Sussex. It would indeed be a coincidence if there were two other related people, named Frederic and Gundrada, very distinctive foreign names, in England at that time. The brothers, it seems, were deeply involved in the border politics between Flanders and Normandy; indeed, it is thought that Gerbod resigned his responsibilities in Chester in order to return to the Continent to oversee the family's lands and duties there. Frederic, along with the count of Flanders, was a witness to Count Guy of Ponthieu's charter to the abbey of St Riquier in 1067.[12]

Marriage between William de Warenne and Gundrada was a good match on both sides. Although William was a second son, he had acquired lands and reputation through his military skills, while Gundrada, with her politically astute brothers and links to England even before the Conquest, would have been an attractive proposition as a bride. In 1066 William de Warenne joined his namesake the Duke of Normandy on his expedition to conquer England, probably leaving Gundrada in Normandy to look after their estates while he was away. De Warenne is one of the few named knights known to have fought in the Battle of Hastings on 14 October 1066 and is mentioned by both Orderic Vitalis and William of Poitiers.[13] He was one of William of Normandy's most trusted and experienced captains. De Warenne was rewarded with vast swathes of land throughout the country. Although they were not all acquired in 1066, according to the Domesday Survey, de Warenne's lands extended over thirteen counties stretching from Conisbrough in Yorkshire to Lewes in Sussex, with more than half of his property located in Norfolk.

His territories were acquired over the course of the reign of William I and elevated him to the highest rank of magnates. By 1086, his was the fourth richest man in the kingdom, his riches only surpassed by the king, by the king's half-brothers and his own kinsman, Roger de Montgomery.

Shortly after the Conquest, William de Warenne was given the Rape of Lewes in Sussex, which probably stretched from the River Adur on the west to the River Ouse on the east, and beyond the Ouse to the north. At Lewes, William had a castle built on the top of the hill with two mottes, rather than the usual one; St Pancras Priory would later be built at the base of the hill. The administration of the area was reorganised before 1073, with William giving seventeen manors to William de Braose to create a new rape to the west of Lewes and twenty-eight of his manors in the east were added to the Count of Mortain's Rape of Pevensey. William was compensated for these losses with new lands in East Anglia.[14] William also received the Honour of Conisbrough in South Yorkshire, previously owned by the last Anglo-Saxon king, Harold II Godwinson. Conisbrough was an ancient manor, its name probably derived from the term 'king's burgh', and guarded the ford of the River Don; it probably passed to William following the 1068 campaigns in northern England, the Harrying of the North. Other land that had previously belong to King Harold included Kimbolton and two manors in Lincolnshire.[15] William de Warenne's most important lands, however, were in Norfolk, in eastern England, where he was the largest landowner in the shire. His lands in East Anglia centred on Castle Acre, where William de Warenne built a stone manor house protected by a bailey, but no motte (a mound of earth on which Norman castles were normally built). The motte at Castle Acre was added later, probably for increased protection during the civil war between King Stephen and Empress Matilda.[16]

Throughout his career, William de Warenne acquired lands in numerous counties, sometimes by nefarious means. Much of the property, such as Conisbrough, had formerly belonged to the late king, Harold. In Norfolk he is said to have asserted lordship over freemen who were not necessarily assigned to him. He had disputes with neighbouring landowners in Conisbrough over which properties were sokelands, and he is said to have stolen lands from the Bishop of Durham and the Abbot of Ely. Regarding many of these disputes, details were recorded in Domesday Book. Some acquisitions were obtained peacefully, such as the manor of Whitchurch in Shropshire, which was left to him by his kinsman

Roger de Montgomery. William was an energetic and attentive landowner and improved the yield of most of his estates, more than tripling his sheep flock at Castle Acre and doubling the value of his Yorkshire estates in just twenty years (at a time when the county was recovering from the devastation of the Harrying of the North).[17] William did, however, share lands among some fifty of his supporters, many of whom had come over from Normandy with him, although it appears he kept the largest manors in Sussex for himself. He was not so close-fisted elsewhere, dividing much of his land in Norfolk among his supporters.[18]

William de Warenne's brothers-in-law had also joined the expedition to conquer England. As a consequence, Frederic was rewarded with the lands of a man named Toki, situated in Norfolk, Suffolk and Cambridgeshire and worth in excess of £100. However, Frederic was unable to enjoy his good fortune for long, as he was killed in the rebellion of Hereward the Wake in 1070. His lands, still known as 'Frederic's Fief' in 1086, were inherited by his sister, who retained control of them throughout her lifetime. One manor was given to the abbey of St Riquier, possibly by Gundrada in memory of her brother. Gundrada's other brother, Gerbod, was given command of Chester and possibly made its Earl but resigned his position in 1070 and returned to Flanders, which was in the midst of civil war after the death of Count Baldwin VI. Gerbod's return home was essential to guarantee the safety of the family's lands and interests. The former Earl of Chester's fate is uncertain, however; one report has him killed while another sees him imprisoned, and a third account claims that Gerbod accidentally killed his lord, Count Arnulf III, the nephew of Queen Matilda, at the Battle of Cassel in 1071. According to this last account, Gerbod travelled to Rome to perform penance and eventually became a monk at Cluny.[19] It seems that neither brother raised a family, as Gerbod's lands in Flanders were also inherited by Gundrada; the family interest in the abbey of St Bertin would eventually be passed on to Gundrada and William's second son, Reynold.

In 1067 William de Warenne was one of four prominent Normans appointed to govern England during William the Conqueror's absence in Normandy. Following the Conquest, he continued to support the king and – subsequently – his son, William II Rufus as a military commander for more than twenty years. In 1074 he is named along with his father, his father's wife, Emma, and his brother in a charter at the abbey of Holy Trinity in Rouen, in which the family gave to the abbey the tithes and church of Auzouville-l'Esneval.[20] In 1075, with Richard de Clare, his fellow justiciar, he was sent to deal with the rebellion of Earl Ralph de Gael of East Anglia. De Gael had failed to respond to their summons to answer for an act of defiance and so the two lords faced and defeated the rebels at Fawdon in Cambridgeshire, mutilating their prisoners afterwards. Ralph withdrew to Norwich Castle; he was besieged for three months before he managed to escape his attackers by boat, while the castle surrendered and was occupied by de Warenne. Earl Ralph's lands passed to Alan Rufus (Alan the Red), the son of the Count of Brittany who lived with, or married, Gunhild, the daughter of King Harold II and Edith Swanneck; Edith's lands had made up by far the greater part of Earl Ralph's barony in East Anglia and it is believed that Alan Rufus married Gunhild to strengthen his claim to her mother's lands.

As with so many nobles of the eleventh century, Gundrada and William were known for their piety. Either in 1077 or 1081–3 (the dates vary according to the sources) the couple intended to make a pilgrimage to Rome; although they never actually made it to Italy, owing to the outbreak of war between the pope and the Holy Roman Emperor. They did, however, visit the magnificent abbey of St Peter and St Paul at Cluny in Burgundy, where they were received into the fellowship of the monks. Their visit to the abbey at Cluny inspired the couple, they 'were so struck with the high standard of religious life maintained there that they determined to put their proposed foundation under Cluny, and accordingly desired the abbot to send three or four of his monks to begin the monastery. He, however, would not at first consent – fearing that at so great a distance from their mother-house they would become undisciplined.'[21] It was only after the De Warennes had the backing of the king that the abbot gave his consent and sent a monk named Lanzo to act as prior, with three other monks, to found the community. William gave them the church of St Pancras at Lewes, which had recently been rebuilt in stone, and the land surrounding it. A second priory, started by William but finished by his son, also William, was built on their lands at Castle Acre in Norfolk. St Pancras at Lewes was the first Cluniac house in England. All the churches on the de Warenne's vast estates were given to the priory, including endowments from the lands of Gundrada's brother Frederic in Norfolk.

Gundrada and William had three children: William, Reynold and Edith. Their eldest son, William, would succeed his father as Earl of Surrey and de Warenne. He married Isabel de Vermandois as her second husband. Isabel had the blood of kings flowing through her veins; her father was Hugh Capet, younger son of King Henry I of France, and her mother was Adelaide de Vermandois, a descendant of the ancient Carolingian dynasty. Isabel was one of her parents' nine surviving children; four boys and five girls. She was the widow of Robert de Beaumont, Earl of Leicester, who was thirty-five years her senior and had married her when she was only eleven years old.

Isabel and Robert had had nine children together; their first was a daughter, Emma, born in 1102. Twin boys followed in 1104; Waleran and Robert de Beaumont, earls of Worcester and Leicester, respectively. The brothers were active supporters of King Stephen during the conflict with Empress Matilda, popularly known as the Anarchy. While Robert would come to terms with Matilda's son, the future Henry II, in 1153, Waleran was distrusted due to his support of Louis VII of France. Another daughter, Isabel, was a mistress of Henry I before being married to Gilbert de Clare, 1st Earl of Pembroke. Through her son Richard de Clare, 2nd Earl of Pembroke, she would be the grandmother of Isabel de Clare, wife of the great knight and Regent for Henry III, William Marshal.

Young William de Warenne had been refused a royal bride for himself when he asked for the hand in marriage of Edith of Scotland (her name was later changed to Matilda), daughter of Malcolm III Canmore and his queen, St Margaret. Edith was later married to King Henry I of England while William is reported, by the chronicler Henry of Huntingdon, to have seduced Isabel de Vermandois whilst she was still the wife of Robert de Beaumont, suggesting they had a love affair which lasted for several years.[22] It is hard to blame a young woman of 30, in an arranged marriage to a man more than twice her age, for looking elsewhere for love and comfort. At one stage, William kidnapped Isabel, probably with her approval, but her husband refused to grant her a divorce. Robert de Beaumont died on 5 June 1118 and Isabel and William were married soon after.

The couple had several children; their son and heir, William, the future third earl, was born in 1119. He would die on Crusade in January 1148 at Laodicea, in Turkey, whilst fighting in the elite royal guard of King Louis VII of France. His only child, a daughter, Isabel, became the greatest heiress in England.

Young William II de Warenne had a chequered career; he supported the claims of Robert Curthose, Duke of Normandy, to the English throne against the duke's younger brother, Henry I. However, Duke Robert lost and was captured and imprisoned by Henry. Henry eventually forgave William, who fought for the king at the Battle of Brémule and was with Henry when he died in 1135.

Gundrada and William de Warenne had a second son, Reynold de Warenne, who led the assault on Rouen in 1090 for William II Rufus, in the conflict between the English king and his older brother, Duke Robert. However, by 1105 Reynold was fighting for the duke against the youngest of the Conqueror's sons, Henry I, defending the castle of Saint-Pierre-sur-Dives for the duke. He was captured by Henry the following year but had been freed by September 1106. It is possible he died shortly after but was certainly dead by 1118 when his brother issued a charter in which he gave six churches to Lewes Priory for the repose of the souls of deceased family members, including Reynold.[23]

A third child was a daughter, Edith, who married Gerard de Gournay, son of the lord of Gournay-en-Bray. Gerard also supported William II Rufus against Duke Robert and took part in the Crusade of 1096. Edith later accompanied him on pilgrimage back to Jerusalem sometime after 1104, where he died. Gerard was succeeded by their son, Hugh de Gournay, whose daughter Gundreda would marry Nigel d'Aubigny and be the mother of Roger de Mowbray, a Norman magnate who fought with King Stephen and was captured at the Battle of Lincoln in 1141. Edith married Drew de Monchy as her second husband, with whom she had a son, Drew the Younger.[24]

In 1083–85 William de Warenne fought with the king on campaign in Maine, where he was wounded at the siege of the castle of Sainte-Suzanne.[25] He was created Earl of Surrey shortly before his death in 1088; after he had helped King William II Rufus to suppress a revolt led by Bishop Odo of Bayeux and Robert, Count of Mortain. De Warenne was wounded by an arrow during the fighting and died a short time later, in the summer of 1088.[26] Meanwhile, poor Gundrada had died in childbirth at Castle Acre in Norfolk on 27 May 1085 and therefore never assumed the title of countess. She was buried in the chapter house of St Pancras Priory at Lewes; her husband would be buried beside her three years later. Around 1145 new monastic buildings were consecrated at St Pancras, Gundrada's bones were placed in a leaden chest and interred under a tombstone of black Tournai marble, 'richly carved in the Romanesque style, with foliage and lions' heads'.[27] The sculptor was trained at Cluny and would later work for Henry I's nephew, Henry of Blois, Bishop of Winchester and the brother of King Stephen. Following the dissolution of St Pancras Priory at Lewes in the sixteenth century, the tombstone was initially moved to Isfield Church. It was moved again in 1775 to the parish church of St John the Baptist at Southover in Lewes. The church is situated close to the grounds of the ruined priory and may once have been within the priory's precincts. The remains of Gundrada and William were discovered in two leaden chests in 1845 and finally laid to rest in the Gundrada chapel at the Southover church in 1847.[28]

William married again after Gundrada's death. His second wife was a sister of Richard Guet, who was described as '*frater comitissae Warennae*' when he gave the manor of Cowyck to Bermondsey Abbey in 1098.[29] Guet was a landowner in Perche, Normandy, but his sister's name has not survived the passage of time. All we know of her is that a few days after her husband's death she attempted to gift 100 shillings to Ely Abbey, from which William had stolen land. The monks refused the donation, apparently hoping that Warenne's departing soul had been claimed by demons.[30] When the newly created earl was badly wounded by an arrow at the siege of Pevensey Castle, East Sussex, in the spring of 1088, he was taken to Lewes, where he died of his wounds on 24 June of the same year.

Earl Warenne was buried beside his first wife, Gundrada, in the chapter house of the Priory of St Pancras at Lewes.

Gundrada may appear to be an anomaly in a book which has, until now, concentrated on the leading female political and dynastic figures of the Norman Conquest. However, she merits inclusion as she is a shining example of the Norman incomers who made up the new Anglo-Norman aristocracy that arose from the Conquest, which included, among others, the families of Roger de Montgomery, William fitz Osbern and Roger de Beaumont.[31]

The dynasty founded by William and Gundrada would continue to serve the crown until the death of John, the 7th and final de Warenne Earl of Surrey, in 1347.

The Mysterious Woman of the Bayeux Tapestry

There is one more lady associated with the Norman Conquest who deserves consideration in detail. However, she is quite an enigma. No one seems to be sure of her actual identity, which has caused a lot of discussion among historians over the centuries. She appears in one scene of the Bayeux Tapestry, under the name, or designation, of 'Ælfgyva'.

The Bayeux Tapestry is the most famous pictorial depiction of the Norman Conquest and of the events of the two years leading up to it. Commissioned in the 1070s, probably by Bishop Odo of Bayeux, rather than a woven tapestry, the work is in fact an embroidery. While it is at least 70 metres long (the end panels are missing, so the exact length of the tapestry, when it was intact, is impossible to determine), it is just 50 centimetres in width. Started within ten years of the Norman Conquest it is a near-contemporary narrative of the events that changed England forever. It is told from the viewpoint of the victorious Normans but, at times, with a sympathetic view of the English.

The tapestry tells the story from 1064, showing the build-up and preparations for the Norman Invasion, and ends with the Battle of Hastings; the missing end panels may have included King William's coronation. It begins with Harold's journey to Normandy, his meeting with Duke William and campaigning in Brittany, followed by the controversial oath-swearing; it then follows Harold's return to England and his coronation following the death of Edward the Confessor, before concentrating on William's preparations for invasion and the Battle of Hastings itself.[1]

As a prime example of how women have been given little or no part in the story of the Norman Conquest, out of 626 human figures, there are only three women who appear in the main narrative of the Bayeux Tapestry. One of these is easily identifiable as Edward the Confessor's queen, Edith of Wessex, attending her husband on his deathbed. Another scene, as the Normans land on the shores of England, shows a woman and her child fleeing from a burning house, set alight by the invaders.

The most intriguing woman in the Bayeux Tapestry appears in one scene when Harold is in Normandy. She is identified as 'Ælfgyva', the name sewn into the tapestry above her head. However, the scene does not appear to be related in any way to the scenes either before or after, and has therefore caused much discussion and theorising among historians.

Ælfgyva appears to be in a doorway, possibly as a suggestion that she was indoors, with a priest touching her cheek. Whether the touch is in admonishment or blessing is open to interpretation, some take it is a collaboration of some sort between the two.[2] The full inscription above the scene is, in itself, either incomplete or deliberately ambiguous. Written in Latin as *Ubi unus clericus et Ælfgyva,* it simply reads 'Here a certain cleric and Ælfgyva'. The phrase in itself is an anomaly, and the only incidence of an incomplete phrase in the tapestry.[3] It does not identify the priest, nor the context in which the two are together. In the borders, at Ælfgyva's feet, is a naked man, imitating the stance of the cleric, perhaps placed there to indicate some kind of scandal associated with the lady. Ælfgyva appears to be well dressed and, given that she is one of very few women in the whole tapestry, may well have been a lady of some significance. The name, Ælfgyva or a derivation such as Ælfgifu, was quite popular in the eleventh century, but could also be used to simply mean 'noble lady'.

As this is the only scene in the entire Bayeux Tapestry in which the woman is the leading character, and considering that she is only one of three women depicted in the entire embroidery, the story which is depicted must be of some significance to the narrative of the Norman Conquest. Much paper and ink, therefore, has been expended in attempts to identify the mysterious Ælfgyva and the story that the tapestry is trying to relate and why that story is so important to the events to merit inclusion in the work. Unfortunately, we are not without a substantial number of potential candidates who could be identified as Ælfgyva because Ælfgyva and its variants, Ælfgiva, Ælfgyfu, Ælfgifu and Elgiva, were popular names in England in the eleventh century; indeed, Emma of Normandy's name was changed to Ælfgifu on her marriage to Æthelred and, just to make matters more confusing, Æthelred's first wife was also called Ælfgifu. Many historians have their own favourite theories for the identity of Ælfgyva; the numerous possible candidates include Emma herself, a sister of King Harold and the first, handfast wife of King Cnut. Each possibility comes with her own reasons for being the mysterious Ælfgyva, and her own claim for inclusion in the tapestry that tells the story of the Norman Conquest.

Several theories can be easily discounted. Writing in the eighteenth century, Ducarel suggested that 'Ælfgyva' translated to mean 'queen' and the image was therefore of a clerk informing Queen Matilda that King William had promised one of their daughters as a bride for Harold of Wessex. Of course, in 1064, Matilda was not queen, and so 'Ælfgyva' would have to translate as 'duchess'.[4] In the nineteenth century, it was suggested that the scene depicted the daughter of Matilda and William being informed of her betrothal. This theory, of course, ignores the fact that Matilda and William did not have a daughter with the name Ælfgyva, nor indeed with any name closely related to, or sounding like, Ælfgyva, their daughters being Adelida, Cecilia, Adela and Agatha. Other theories claim that the lady was one of the English hostages held by Duke William, alongside Harold's brother and nephew, Wulfnoth and Hakon. This hostage is supposedly being informed of her impending release and the cleric is touching her cheek in blessing and absolution. A final, easily discounted theory is that the lady is Ealdgyth, Harold's future queen, receiving the news of Harold's rescue, either from the shipwreck or from the clutches of Count Guy of Ponthieu, by Duke William. This is meant to demonstrate Harold's dishonesty in agreeing to marry a daughter of Duke William while he has a betrothed waiting at home.[5] Of course, there is no evidence that Harold was betrothed to Ealdgyth any earlier than late 1065 or early 1066. In fact, we do not know when Harold and Ealdgyth were betrothed or married, but it is likely to have happened shortly before, or during his kingship, when he needed the support of the Earls Edwin and Morcar, Ealdgyth's brothers.

One person we can almost certainly rule out as a candidate for the mysterious Ælfgyva is the first wife of Æthelred II, Ælfgifu of York. Ælfgifu is a shadowy figure in history, with very little known about her. The monk Ailred of Rievaulx, writing in the 1150s, identified her as the daughter of Thored. Ailred had served in the household of David I, King of Scotland, who was a great-great-grandson of Æthelred II and Ælfgifu through his mother, Queen Margaret, and so Ailred was well placed to learn the ancestry of King David with some accuracy. Thored was Earl of Northumbria between about 975 and 992 and regularly attested charters by King Æthelred II during the 980s.[6] Such a marriage for King Æthelred would have helped to strengthen his influence over the north of England, an area notoriously independent of the royal administration in the south. Æthelred and Ælfgifu were married around 985, when he was in his early twenties; Ælfgifu may have been a little younger. The couple had a large number of children, including at least six boys and four girls. Their eldest son, Æthelstan, was named ætheling, but would die in June 1014, during the wars against Cnut. Their other sons included Ecgberht, Edmund, Eadred, Eadwig and Edgar; in April 1016 Edmund succeeded his father as King Edmund II Ironside but died in November of the same year. Eadwig was murdered in 1017, on the orders of the victorious King Cnut. Of their four daughters, Edith was married to the traitorous Ealdorman, Eadric Streona; Ælfgifu married Uhtred, Earl of Northumbria, who was murdered on Cnut's orders in 1016; Wulfhild married Ulfcytel, Ealdorman of East Anglia, who was killed in the fighting of 1016. A fourth unnamed daughter was abbess at Wherewell and died in the early 1050s.

Other than the children she bore, however, Ælfgifu of York has left very little imprint on history. She does not make it into the chronicles of the time and there is no evidence that she was crowned and anointed as queen, unlike her successor, Emma of Normandy. We know nothing of her, not her personality nor her actions during her time as Æthelred's wife, not even the date of her death, though it must have been before April 1002, when Æthelred married Emma of Normandy. The fact that Ælfgifu went through her life unremarked by the chronicles adds weight to the assumption that she is not the Ælfgyva of the tapestry as we have no knowledge of anything she did that would merit her inclusion. Moreover, she died at least sixty-four years before the Norman invasion so one can be fairly certain that nothing in her life could have had such an influence that it would merit inclusion in the story of the Conquest.

Æthelred II's second wife, on the other hand, is a candidate who does merit closer investigation. Emma of Normandy was the wife of Æthelred from the spring of 1002 until his death in 1016. In 1017, however, she married Æthelred's nemesis and eventual successor, Cnut. Emma had three children by her first husband: Alfred, Edward and Goda, or Godgifu. She had three further children by King Cnut: Harthacnut, Gunhilda and an unnamed daughter who died as a child, aged around eight, and is buried in Bosham Church, Sussex.[7]

Emma's name had been changed to Ælfgifu on her marriage to Æthelred and, unlike her predecessor, she was a prominent figure at the English court, having been crowned and anointed queen after the wedding ceremony. Emma gained even more prominence in the reign of King Cnut, who married her soon after he took the crown. Cnut appears to have trusted Emma a great deal and is known to have left his treasury with her, as did her son, Harthacnut.[8]

Emma was one of the most politically active queens of England during the medieval era and certainly before the Conquest. As Cnut's wife, she served to provide a link between Æthelred's ancient dynasty of Wessex, dating back to King Alfred and beyond, and the new Danish dynasty of Cnut. As Cnut's queen, until his death in 1035, her position appeared unassailable. When Cnut died and was succeeded by his own sons as co-regents, Emma was able to hold on to Wessex, for a time for their son, Harthacnut, who was fighting in Denmark at the time of his father's death. The rest of England was in the control of Cnut's son by Ælfgifu of Northampton, Harold I Harefoot.

In 1037 Harold I Harefoot was able to stamp his authority on England and claim the crown for himself and one of the first moves he made was against Emma. He rode to Winchester and seized from her the treasury of Cnut, which the deceased king had left in Emma's safekeeping. Emma herself was banished from England and sought refuge at the court of Count Baldwin of Flanders. She was only able to return to England after King Harold's death in 1040, when she and Harthacnut returned unopposed and Harthacnut finally claimed the crown. Emma took her rightful place as Queen Mother and was once again a notable figure in the realm. Her triumph was short-lived, however, as Harthacnut collapsed and died at a wedding in 1042, and was replaced as king by his older half-brother, Edward. Edward was also a son of Queen Emma, but his relationship with his mother was far less cordial. Having been exiled in Normandy for twenty-five years, while his mother sat beside Cnut on the English throne for much of that time, Edward held a great deal of resentment towards his mother.

Edward was crowned king at Winchester on Easter Day 1043 with great pomp and ceremony. One of his first acts as king was to do as Harold I Harefoot had done and reclaim the country's treasury from Emma at Winchester:

> And this year, fourteen nights before the mass of St. Andrew, it was advised the king, that he and Earl Leofric and Earl Godwin and Earl Siward with their retinue, should ride from Gloucester to Winchester unawares upon the lady; and they deprived her of all the treasure that she had; which were immense; because she was formerly very hard upon the king her son, and did less for him than he wished before he was king.[9]

Emma's lands and property were all taken from her. The Dowager Queen's close friend and advisor, Stigand, newly consecrated as Bishop of East Anglia, shared in Emma's disgrace and was stripped of office and 'they took all that he had into their hands for the king, because he was nighest the counsel of his mother; and she acted as he advised, as men supposed.'[10] From the *Anglo-Saxon Chronicle*, it seems that Edward thought that Stigand had encouraged Emma in her perceived maltreatment of her only surviving son. It was probably as a result of this incident that various legends arose over Emma's disgrace.

One story, appearing two centuries later, suggested that Emma's relationship with Bishop Stigand was far more than that of a queen and her advisor and that he was, in fact, her lover – although the legend did get its bishops mixed up and named Ælfwine, rather than Stigand, as Emma's lover. The story continues that Emma chose to prove her innocence in a trial by ordeal, and that she walked barefoot over white-hot ploughshares. Even though the tale varies depending on the source, the result is the same; when she completed the ordeal unharmed, and was thus proven guiltless, she was reconciled with her contrite son, Edward. Emma appears to have never recovered fully from the depredations placed on her. Both she and Stigand seem to have been reconciled, to some extent, with Edward's regime by 1044, but she never again enjoyed the status to which she had become accustomed during the reigns of Cnut and Harthacnut.[11]

If Emma were the Ælfgyva/Ælfgifu of the Bayeux Tapestry, this story could well explain her inclusion, especially if the touch of the cleric in the Ælfgyva scene is that of a tender lover, rather than an admonishing priest. However, there are several reasons for discarding Emma as the candidate. The first instance of the story of Emma and Stigand as lovers appears two or three hundred years after her death, and there is no contemporary evidence of an affair that would have been the scandal of the decade, if not the century. Given that many of the chroniclers of the time were not averse to including such stories, it seems strange that they were all silent on the subject, unless, of course, the whole incident was a fourteenth-century fabrication. Another argument against the theory is that Emma's affair with Bishop Stigand, even in the unlikely event that it happened, would have had little bearing on the Norman Conquest, and would therefore be unlikely to merit inclusion in the Bayeux Tapestry.

Another candidate who has been suggested is Ælfgifu or Elgiva, supposedly a sister of Harold Godwinson who was thought to have died around 1066. However, it seems likely that this sister is spurious and has been mistakenly added to the Godwinson brood.

It has been suggested that she was in the Bayeux Tapestry because she was being offered by her brother King Harold, then Earl of Wessex, as a bride for one of Duke William of Normandy's four sons. The confusion arises from the fact that Ælfgifu is mentioned in the Buckinghamshire folios of Domesday Book as 'Ælfgifu, sister of Earl Harold'.[12] According to Ann Williams, this Ælfgifu's inclusion in the Godwinson family has arisen from the mistaken identity of her brother. Although Harold Godwinson was the famed Earl of Wessex before the Norman Conquest, Ælfgifu was in fact the sister of a thegn called Harold, not the earl. Harold the thegn held land in Buckinghamshire, which included Moulsoe and a manor at Tyringham; his wife, also called Ælfgifu, held a second manor at Tyringham. This Harold's sister, Ælfgifu, was married to a man named Sibbi and had two sons, Sired and Særic, and they held lands at Waldridge in the hundred of Ixhill, in the south of Buckinghamshire. Ann Williams argues that the confusion arose from the habit of the Domesday scribes to include the pre-Conquest titles of landholders in their entries. As Earl Harold of Wessex was one of the largest landholders before the Conquest, the scribe made the mistake of assigning the land titles to him, rather that the thegn of the same name, accidentally adding the title *comitis* (earl) to the name *Heraldi* (Harold) in the entry for Waldridge, and thus assigning another sister to Harold of Wessex.[13]

If we can therefore discount this Ælfgifu as the sister of Harold of Wessex, then we can also rule out the theory that the scene depicts Harold promising his sister in marriage to one of William's sons. Although Harold did have a sister who may have been unmarried in 1064, her name was Eadgifu, rather than Ælfgyva, and it appears that she may have been dead by 1066, as her manor of Crewkerne was being administered by the king's reeve, Godwin, suggesting that the land had reverted to King Harold on his sister's death.[14]

A leading candidate for Ælfgyva is a woman of a different name, but whose story included a scandal that would have been relevant to Harold of Wessex and his hostages. This lady was Eadgifu, or Eadgyva, the Abbess of Leominster in 1046. Eadgifu's story is told in the *Anglo-Saxon Chronicle*, when she came under the power of Swein Godwinson, oldest son of Earl Godwin and

Countess Gytha. Swein had been given an earldom made up from lands in Herefordshire, Gloucestershire, Berkshire, Oxfordshire and Somerset in 1043. In 1046 he had been campaigning in south Wales alongside Gruffydd, King of Gwynedd, in north Wales. The military campaign had ended successfully, with Swein receiving hostages for the good faith of the Welsh. On his return homeward, Swein stopped at Leominster, where a vast estate was owned by the abbey of Leominster and administered by its abbess, Eadgifu. Swein 'ordered the Abbess of Leominster to be fetched him; and he had her as long as he list [liked], after which he let her go home.'[15] It is likely that Swein abducted Eadgifu in order to gain control of Leominster's vast estates in Herefordshire. However, the king refused to give his permission for Swein and Eadgifu to marry; the pious King Edward was understandably horrified at the idea of Swein marrying an abbess, a woman who had dedicated her life to God. Indeed, the Archbishop of Canterbury, Eadsige, and Lyfing, Bishop of Worcester, are said to have threatened to excommunicate Swein for this sacrilegious act (although the priests in question may have been confused with others, as Lyfing was dead before the Welsh campaign and the ageing Eadsige was in retirement by 1046).[16] Swein released Eadgifu after he had held her for some considerable time, possibly as long as a year.

As a result of his actions, which were considered not only criminal but sacrilegious in the eyes of the Church, Swein was forced to flee England. A few months later, Swein returned to England, but was exiled again for the murder of his cousin, Beorn Estrithson, but was once again forgiven and allowed to return home. When the feud between Earl Godwin's family and the king arose in 1051, Swein was already back in England. The dispute between Godwin and the king looked likely to escalate into civil war, until the king summoned his allies, Earl Leofric from Mercia and Earl Siward from Northumbria, to make a show of force against the Godwin clan. Earl Godwin and Swein were forced, at some point, to give up hostages to the king, each handing over a son, Wulfnoth for Godwin and Hakon for Swein. Rather than face the *witan*, Godwin and his family chose to go into exile at the end of 1051 and only returned to England in the spring of 1052, following a show of force and a reluctance on the part of the king's supporters to go to war. Swein never returned to England as he had left on a barefoot pilgrimage to Jerusalem and he died on his homeward journey. The two hostages were not returned to the family and are thought to have been sent to Normandy, either as a sign of good faith on Edward's part, as guarantee that William would eventually gain the crown, or as a way to guarantee the future co-operation of the Godwin family.

It is possible that the union between Eadgifu and Swein resulted in a son, Hakon. It is not entirely certain that Hakon was the son of Eadgifu, but it does seem likely, as no other wife or concubine of Swein's is mentioned in the chronicles. If he was the son of Eadgifu and Swein, the child would have been five or six years old when he was taken as a hostage to Normandy, probably by Robert Champart of Jumièges in 1052. If Eadgifu was the mother of Hakon it would not only explain her presence in the Bayeux Tapestry, but also the inclusion of Ælfgyva and her cleric in that part of the tapestry.

Although there is no direct mention of these hostages in the tapestry, the scene immediately before the Ælfgyva scene is that of Harold arriving at Duke William's court; and one of the possible reasons for Harold's presence at William's court was the recovery of the hostages, who included Eadgifu's son. Given the disgrace that Eadgifu must have faced, as an abbess having given birth to an illegitimate child, and the fact the child was only five years old when he was taken to Normandy as a hostage, it is not implausible that his mother accompanied him, and therefore is included in the tapestry. Hakon, no longer a valuable hostage given that his father had been dead for more than ten years, was allowed to return to England with Earl Harold.[17]

There is one major flaw in this argument, and that is the confusion of the name because although Eadgifu and Ælfgyva are somewhat similar, they are very different names and it is hard to imagine that someone would make such a big mistake on so important an undertaking as the Bayeux Tapestry. On the other hand, it is not implausible, given that Harold's brother, Leofwine, is identified as Lewine on another portion of the tapestry.[18] We do not know, moreover, that Eadgifu ever accompanied her son to Normandy, or visited him there while he was a hostage. However, Eadgifu's story, the scandal associated with her abduction by Swein and the presence of her son in Normandy, still makes her a contender. The scene with the cleric could well be him giving her a blessing on her return to England, or an admonition about her having had a child out of wedlock – and while she was an abbess who had given her life to God. Despite the disparity in names, the fact that she had links to Normandy through her son, and that her story was associated with Harold's visit to Normandy and the request for the hostages to be freed, gives her a relevance to the tapestry and makes her one of the most plausible candidates for Ælfgyva.

The final leading possibility for the identity of the Ælfgyva of the Bayeux Tapestry is Ælfgifu of Northampton. Ælfgifu was the first wife of King Cnut, whom he had married *more Danico*, in the Danish fashion, as a handfast wife. She was born around 990; her father was Ælfhelm, an ealdorman of southern Northumbria and her mother was Wulfrune. She was born into a prominent and influential Midlands family. However, in 1006, her father was murdered and her brothers, Ulfegeat and Wulfheah, were blinded, supposedly on the orders of King Æthelred himself.[19] The family were again under suspicion of treachery during the conquest of Sweyn Forkbeard in 1013–14, with more family members put to death by the English. Possibly in a love match, but also as part of King Sweyn's policy to establish himself in the midlands, Ælfgifu was married to Cnut sometime between 1013 and 1016, The couple had two sons, Swein and Harold Harefoot. Swein would later be sent by his father to rule Norway, with his mother as regent, but was driven out by the Norwegians following years of misrule. He died in Denmark and Ælfgifu returned to England. Harold I Harefoot would rule England jointly with his half-brother, Harthacnut, after his father's death in 1035, but would be crowned as sole king in 1037, whilst Harthacnut was fighting in Denmark.

If Ælfgifu is the woman in the Bayeux Tapestry, then she is probably there in reference to a scandal that was spoken about even in her lifetime. John of Worcester asserted:

Canute, king of England, before his death, gave the kingdom of Norway to Swein, who was reported to be his son by Ælfgiva of Northampton, the daughter of Ælfhelm the ealdorman, and the noble lady Wulfruna. Some, however, asserted that this Ælfgiva desired to have a son by the king, but as she could not, she caused the new-born child of a certain priest to be brought to her, and made the king fully believe that she had just borne him a son.[20]

The same is said of Ælfgifu's other son by Cnut, Harold I Harefoot, in the *Anglo-Saxon Chronicle*, which reported that 'some men said of Harold that he was son of King Cnut and Ælfgifu, daughter of Ealdorman Ælfhelm, but to many men it seemed quite unbelievable.'[21] John of Worcester gave even more detail:

> Harold also said that he was the son of king Canute and Ælfgiva of Northampton, although that is far from certain; for some say that he was the son of a cobbler, and that Ælfgiva had acted with regard to him as she had done in the case of Swein: for our part, as there are doubts on the subject, we cannot settle with any certainty the parentage of either.[22]

The scandalous stories arose after Cnut's death in 1035, when Ælfgifu was back in England, following her disastrous regency in Norway and the death of Swein, working to establish the rule of her son, Harold Harefoot, as king. These tales claimed that Ælfgifu was unable to produce children of her own and a monk helped her to pass off the illegitimate children of a serving maid as sons of her own by Cnut. Another variation has the monk fathering the children himself.[23] The stories may have been mere propaganda used to discredit Ælfgifu and cast doubts on the legitimacy of Harold and, therefore, his right to rule as Cnut's successor. In the end, the fact that Harthacnut did not return from Denmark to claim his English inheritance meant that Harold could claim the throne as Harold I, but not before Ælfgifu's reputation was almost utterly destroyed.

The main question arising from the theory that Ælfgifu of Northampton is the Ælfgyva of the Bayeux Tapestry would be the relevance of a scandal that had arisen more than thirty years earlier. It has been argued that both William and Harold would view the scandal as propaganda, to discredit any claims by the Norwegians, such as Harald Hardrada, to the English throne. The naked men in the margins of the scene, one of whom is swinging an axe, are used as further evidence that it was Ælfgifu's scandalous behaviour to which the tapestry is referring.[24] However, the fact that both of Ælfgifu's sons died without heirs and that, therefore, there were no claimants descended from her to contest the throne in 1066, makes Ælfgifu's inclusion – if, indeed it is Ælfgifu – rather redundant.

Despite the many possibilities and theories surrounding Ælfgyva and her cleric, their identities and the reason for their inclusion in the *Bayeux Tapestry*, no definitive explanation is forthcoming. It is not beyond reason that the Ælfgyva of the Bayeux Tapestry is none of the ladies I have suggested, but someone else entirely who, in the passage of nearly a millennium, has been lost to us. The story may well have been a familiar one at the time the tapestry was created, and no explanation beyond 'Here a certain cleric and Ælfgyva' may have been needed to identify the protagonists to viewers in the eleventh century.

Today, however, the story and the identity of the protagonists continues to elude us.

Epilogue

The lives recounted in this book are merely the tip of the iceberg. Many women played roles in the Norman Conquest, before, during and after, and I have been able to highlight only a handful. More research would need to be done to provide a complete picture and there is still much to learn.

It would be interesting, for instance, to pin down the life and origins of Agatha, wife of Edward the Exile and mother of St Margaret, Queen of Scotland. Her parentage is still uncertain, and it would be a fine thing to find her family links, and the royal and political connections she must have had with the courts of Germany and the east. It is easy to imagine that she must have found England a strange and confusing land compared with the lands of Eastern Europe, where she had her origins. One can only envisage how scared and confused she must have felt, arriving in a foreign country, leaning heavily on her husband as the only familiar figure, only for him to die suddenly, within days; leaving her with three children in a world full of strangers. That she managed to keep those children safe and give them a future, that her daughter became Queen of Scotland, is truly remarkable.

And there is St Margaret's sister Christina, who is said to have become Abbess of the great Abbey of Romsey, although that is disputed. She is known to have educated her sister's daughters, Edith and Mary, at the royal Abbey of Wilton, presiding over a centre of learning and culture. However, she was a severe taskmaster, according to Edith, who said that she 'went in fear of the rod of my aunt Christina ... and she would often make me smart with a good slapping and the most horrible scolding.'[1] And then there are many Anglo-Saxon women who I would have loved to include, such as Ælfgifu of York, first wife of Æthelred II, and her daughters, Edith, Ælfgifu and Wulfhild. It may have been interesting to look at Ælfgifu and all the sisters of Edward the Confessor, but I had to avoid being sidetracked and so only managed to include those who play a role in Emma's story.

There were many women I came across whose lives I could barely touch upon, such as the daughters of Gytha and Edith Swanneck, for whom there is very little extant information. However, their continued survival and that of their families into the next century are proof of their resilence, that of their families and, in a sense, of Anglo-Saxon England.

As we have seen, while the men dominated the conflict of the era, the women were not without their contributions to the story of 1066. Women have always of course been a necessity to continue the bloodline and produce heirs, but any husband, father or son will tell you that they contribute so much more. And in the tumultuous eleventh century, this was no less true. Their power and influence shines through in every aspect of the story, from those who created the Bayeux Tapestry to Queen Emma and Queen Matilda, whose strength and influence helped to direct their husbands and sons alike. There are stories of love and loyalty from Edith Swanneck, of piety from St Margaret; and stories that became legend, as with Lady Godiva.

I have tried to show that the women were not merely passive observers in the face of these great events. They were not merely pawns, or brood mares whose only purpose was to produce an heir. They had a role to play in the cataclysmic story of 1066, and that role was not insignificant. From this distance in time, we cannot know the exact extent of their contribution, but from the evidence left to us, we know that it was considerable. Evidence of this can be seen in the enigmatic figure of Ælfgyva in the Bayeux Tapestry. We know that she was significant enough to be included in the narrative, even if her identity and relevance to the story still eludes us; her influence was considerable enough to merit inclusion in a work in which only three women, in total, are represented. We do know that the actions of these women in the political arena, and their support behind the scenes, had a major part to play in the actions and decision-making of the men around them. They may not have fought in the battles, but they played vital roles in the war.

We do know that they could not fight with sword, shield, axe and spear, as their men did. However, these women found their own ways to contribute to the war effort, to fight for the survival of their families. Emma of Normandy used her political acumen to ensure her survival and the eventual success of her sons, Harthacnut and Edward; even if Edward did not appreciate it, his succession was probably due in no small part to his mother's influence on Harthacnut, the half-brother whom Edward barely knew. Gytha used her words of persuasion and encouragement to get Exeter to stand up to the Norman king; that her tactics eventually failed does not make her efforts any less remarkable. Edith of Wessex submitted to King William, an act that saved Winchester from the severe repercussions seen elsewhere. St Margaret, as Queen of Scotland, utilised her devotion to Christianity to bring a whole country into the Roman Catholic faith. And Matilda of Flanders, Queen of England and Duchess of Normandy, used her considerable skills and influence to rule Normandy as regent for her husband, in partnership with him.

Each remarkable woman provided a necessary component to the story, from the wives of Harald Hardrada, who followed their husband to war, to Edith and Gytha searching the battlefield of Hastings for the body of Harold, his lover and mother united in their grief for the fallen king. Their stories are, at times, heart-wrenching, while at other times infuriating. However, whatever the event or action, their expereinces provide a more rounded, accurate view of what life was like for the women *and* the men of that era.

It has been a pleasure and a privilege to examine the lives of some of the most incredible women of the eleventh century.

Notes

Introduction

1. *The Chronicle of Henry of Huntingdon. Comprising the history of England, from the invasion of Julius Caesar to the accession of Henry II. Also, the Acts of Stephen, King of England and duke of Normandy* Translated and edited by Thomas Forester.
2. *The Anglo-Saxon Chronicle* translated by James Ingram.

Chapter 1: The Battles for England

1. *The Chronicle of Henry of Huntingdon. Comprising the history of England, from the invasion of Julius Caesar to the accession of Henry II. Also, the Acts of Stephen, King of England and duke of Normandy* Translated and edited by Thomas Forester.
2. Simon Keynes, *Æthelred II [Ethelred; known as Ethelred the Unready] (c. 966x8-1016)* (article), Oxford Dictionary of National Biography, oxforddnb.com, 8 October 2009.
3. *The Anglo-Saxon Chronicle* translated by James Ingram.
4. *ibid.*
5. *A History of the Vikings* by T.D. Kendrick.
6. *The Anglo-Saxon Chronicles* edited and translated by Michael Swaton.
7. *The Anglo-Saxon Chronicle* translated by James Ingram.
8. *ibid.*
9. *ibid.*
10. *ibid.*
11. *Brewer's British Royalty* by David Williamson.
12. *Edward [St Edward; known as Edward the Confessor]* by Frank Barlow, (article), Oxford Dictionary of National Biography, oxforddnb.com, 26 May 2006.
13. *ibid.*

14. *The Anglo-Saxon Chronicle* translated by James Ingram.
15. *ibid.*
16. *ibid.*
17. *ibid.*
18. *The Anglo-Saxon Chronicles* edited and translated by Michael Swaton.

Chapter 2: Emma of Normandy

1. *Queen Emma and the Vikings* by Harriet O'Brien.
2. *ibid.*
3. *ibid.*
4. Ælfthryth by Pauline Stafford, Oxford Dictionary of National Biography.
5. *Anglo-Saxon Chronicle* quoted by Martin Wall in *The Anglo-Saxons in 100 Facts.*
6. *Anglo-Saxon Chronicle (E)* quoted in *Queen Emma and the Vikings* by Harriet O'Brien.
7. *The Chronicle of Henry of Huntingdon. Comprising the history of England, from the invasion of Julius Caesar to the accession of Henry II. Also, the Acts of Stephen, King of England and duke of Normandy* Translated and edited by Thomas Forester.
8. William of Malmesbury quoted in *Emma [Ælfgifu] (d.1052),* by Simon Keynes, Oxford Dictionary of National Biography.
9. *Britain's Royal Families; the Complete Genealogy* by Alison Weir.
10. *Anglo-Saxon Chronicle Texts C, D and E.* D. Whitelock, D. C. Douglas, & S. I. Tucker, eds. and trans., (1961).
11. *Massacre at St Frideswide's*, Oxford Today, The University Magazine, Michaelmas 2002.
12. *The Anglo-Saxon Chronicles [E]* edited and translated by Michael Swaton.
13. *ibid.*
14. *ibid.*
15. *ibid.*
16. *The Anglo-Saxon Chronicles [A]* edited and translated by Michael Swaton.
17. *Kings, Queens, Bones and Bastards* by David Hilliam.
18. *The Anglo-Saxon Chronicles [D]* edited and translated by Michael Swaton.
19. *The Anglo-Saxon Chronicles [E]* edited and translated by Michael Swaton.
20. *The Chronicle of Henry of Huntingdon. Comprising the history of England, from the invasion of Julius Caesar to the accession of Henry II. Also, the Acts of Stephen, King of England and duke of Normandy* Translated and edited by Thomas Forester.

21. *The Anglo-Saxon Chronicles [E]* edited and translated by Michael Swaton.
22. *The Anglo-Saxon Chronicles [C & D]* edited and translated by Michael Swaton.
23. *The Anglo-Saxon Chronicle* translated by James Ingram.
24. *Alfred Ætheling (d. 1036/7)* (article) by M.K. Lawson, Oxford Dictionary of National Biography.
25. *ibid.*
26. *The Anglo-Saxon Chronicle* translated by James Ingram.
27. *The Anglo-Saxon Chronicles* edited and translated by Michael Swaton.
28. *ibid.*
29. *ibid.*
29. *Queen Emma and the Vikings* by Harriet O'Brien.
30. *The Anglo-Saxon Chronicles* edited and translated by Michael Swaton.
31. *The Chronicle of Henry of Huntingdon. Comprising the history of England, from the invasion of Julius Caesar to the accession of Henry II. Also, the Acts of Stephen, King of England and duke of Normandy* Translated and edited by Thomas Forester.

Chapter 3: Lady Godiva

1. *Britain's Royal Families; the Complete Genealogy* by Alison Weir.
2. *Godgifu (d. 1067?)* (article) by Ann Williams, oxforddnb.com.
3. *Cartulary of Trentham Priory: Normancote*, in *Staffordshire Historical Collections, Vol. 11* edited by G. Wrottesley, and F. Parker.
4. *Godgifu (d. 1067?)* (article) by Ann Williams, oxforddnb.com.
5. *ibid.*
6. *ibid* and Stowminster.co.uk, *History* (article).
7. *ibid.*
8. *ibid.*
9. *The Ecclesiastical History of England and Normandy* by Ordericus Vitalis.
10. *Godgifu (d. 1067?)* (article) by Ann Williams, oxforddnb.com.
11. *ibid.*
12. *The Anglo-Saxon Chronicle* translated by James Ingram.
13. *The Anglo-Saxon Chronicles* edited and translated by Michael Swaton.
14. *The Anglo-Saxon Chronicle* translated by James Ingram.
15. *The Anglo-Saxon Chronicles* edited and translated by Michael Swaton.
16. *Godgifu (d. 1067?)* (article) by Ann Williams, oxforddnb.com.
17. *The Chronicle of Henry of Huntingdon. Comprising the history of England, from the invasion of Julius Caesar to the accession of Henry II. Also, the Acts of Stephen, King of England and duke of Normandy* Translated and edited by Thomas Forester. London, H.G. Bohn, 1807.

18. *Flores Historiarum* by Roger of Wendover, translated by Matthew of Westminster.
19. From the account of Richard Grafton (d. 1572), MP for Coventry, quoted in *Godiva: Her Literary Legend* (article) by Octavia Randolph, englishhistoryauthors.blogspot.co.uk, 9 September 2016.
20. Rev. John Moultrie, quoted in *The Romanticisation of Lady Godiva* (article), by Moniek Bloks, historyofroyalwomen.com, 7 February 2017.
21. *Godiva* by Alfred Lord Tennyson, 1842.
22. *Chronicles of the Kings of England, From the Earliest Period to the Reign of King Stephen*, by William of Malmesbury.

Chapter 4: Gytha of Wessex

1. *Gytha, Wife of Godwine* by Merceddes Rochelle.
2. *Godwine, earl of Wessex (d. 1053)* (article) by Ann Williams, Oxford Dictionary of National Biography, oxforddnb.com.
3. *The Anglo-Saxon Chronicles* edited and translated by Michael Swaton and *The Anglo-Saxon Chronicle* translated by James Ingram.
4. *The History of the Kings of England and of his Own Times by William Malmesbury*, translated by J. Sharpe.
5. *Godwine, earl of Wessex (d. 1053)* (article) by Ann Williams, Oxford Dictionary of National Biography, oxforddnb.com.
6. *On the Spindle Side: the Kinswomen of Earl Godwin of Wessex* by Ann Williams.
7. *Britain's Royal Families; the Complete Genealogy* by Alison Weir.
8. Quoted in *On the Spindle Side: the Kinswomen of Earl Godwin of Wessex* by Ann Williams.
9. *ibid.*
10. *Godwine, earl of Wessex (d. 1053)* (article) by Ann Williams, Oxford Dictionary of National Biography, oxforddnb.com.
11. *The Anglo-Saxon Chronicles* edited and translated by Michael Swaton.
12. *The Gesta Normannorum Ducum of William of Jumièges, Oderic Vitalis and Robert of Torigni* edited by E.M.C. van Houts.
13. *The Anglo-Saxon Chronicle* translated by James Ingram.
14. *The Gesta Normannorum Ducum of William of Jumièges, Oderic Vitalis and Robert of Torigni* edited by E.M.C. van Houts and *Encomium Emma Reginae*, edited by A. Campbell and S. Keynes.
15. *The Norman Conquest* by Marc Morris, p. 36.
16. *The Anglo-Saxon Chronicle* translated by James Ingram, p. 102.
17. *ibid.* p. 103.
18. *ibid.*
19. *The Chronicle of John of Worcester*, translated and edited by Thomas Forester, A.M.

20. *ibid.*
21. *ibid.*
22. *ibid.*
23. *ibid.*
24. *The Anglo-Saxon Chronicle* translated by James Ingram, p. 105.
25. *ibid.*
26. *ibid.*
27. *Godwine, earl of Wessex (d. 1053)* (article) by Ann Williams, Oxford Dictionary of National Biography, oxforddnb.com.
28. *Domesday Book*, 1.164, quoted in *Godwine, earl of Wessex (d. 1053)* (article) by Ann Williams, Oxford Dictionary of National Biography, oxforddnb.com.
29. *The Anglo-Saxon Chronicles* (C) edited and translated by Michael Swaton.
30. *The Chronicle of John of Worcester*, translated and edited by Thomas Forester, A.M.
31. *The Anglo-Saxon Chronicles* (D) edited and translated by Michael Swaton and *The Anglo-Saxon Chronicle* translated by James Ingram, p. 115.
32. *The Chronicle of John of Worcester*, translated and edited by Thomas Forester, A.M.
33. *Chartularium*, 275–6, quoted in quoted in *Godwine, earl of Wessex (d. 1053)* (article) by Ann Williams, Oxford Dictionary of National Biography, oxforddnb.com.
34. *The Norman Conquest* by Marc Morris.
35. *The Life of King Edward Who Rests at Westminster*, edited by F. Barlow.
36. *The Anglo-Saxon Chronicles* (E) edited and translated by Michael Swaton, p.172.
37. *The Anglo-Saxon Chronicle* translated by James Ingram.
38. *ibid.*
39. *The Life of King Edward Who Rests at Westminster*, edited by F. Barlow.
40. *The Chronicle of John of Worcester*, translated and edited by Thomas Forester, A.M.
41. *The Anglo-Saxon Chronicle* translated by James Ingram.
42. *The Anglo-Saxon Chronicles* (C) edited and translated by Michael Swaton.
43. *The Anglo-Saxon Chronicle* translated by James Ingram.
44. *ibid.*
45. *ibid.*
46. *The Anglo-Saxon Chronicles* (C) edited and translated by Michael Swaton.

47. *The Chronicle of John of Worcester*, translated and edited by Thomas Forester, A.M.
48. William of Malmesbury, quoted in *The Norman Conquest* by Marc Morris.
49. *The Norman Conquest* by Marc Morris.
50. *The Chronicle of John of Worcester*, translated and edited by Thomas Forester, A.M.
51. *The Anglo-Saxon Chronicles* (D) edited and translated by Michael Swaton.
52. *The Anglo-Saxon Chronicle* translated by James Ingram.
53. *The Chronicle of Henry of Huntingdon. Comprising the history of England, from the invasion of Julius Caesar to the accession of Henry II. Also, the Acts of Stephen, King of England and duke of Normandy* Translated and edited by Thomas Forester.
54. *Gesta Normannorum Ducum* by William of Jumièges, edited and translated by Elizabeth Van Houts.
55. *ibid.*
56. *The Chronicle of John of Worcester*, translated and edited by Thomas Forester, A.M.
57. *The Gesta Guillielmi of William of Poitiers*, edited by R.H.C. Davis and Marjorie Chibnall.
58. *The Ecclesiastical History of England and Normandy* by Ordericus Vitalis.
59. *The Chronicle of John of Worcester*, translated and edited by Thomas Forester, A.M.
60. *The Anglo-Saxon Chronicle* translated by James Ingram.
61. *The Ecclesiastical History of England and Normandy* by Ordericus Vitalis.
62. *The Chronicle of John of Worcester*, translated and edited by Thomas Forester, A.M.
63. *On the Spindle Side: the Kinswomen of Earl Godwin of Wessex* by Ann Williams.
64. *ibid.*
65. *A History of the County of Hampshire: Volume 4* edited by William Page, and, *A History of the County of Gloucester: Volume 11, Bisley and Longtree Hundreds* edited by N.M. Herbert and R.B. Pugh. british-history.ac.uk.

Chapter 5: Judith of Flanders

1. *The Penguin Atlas of World History, Volume One: From the Beginning to the Eve of the French Revolution* by Hermann Klinder and Werner Hilgemann.

2. *The Chronicle of John of Worcester*, translated and edited by Thomas Forester, A.M.
3. *The Anglo-Saxon Chronicles* (D) edited and translated by Michael Swaton.
4. *The Anglo-Saxon Chronicle* translated by James Ingram.
5. *Tostig, earl of Northumbria (c. 1029–1066)* (article), by William M. Aird, oxforddnb.com.
6. *The Anglo-Saxon Chronicle* translated by James Ingram.
7. *The Life of King Edward Who Rests at Westminster*, edited by F. Barlow.
8. *The Norman Conquest* by Marc Morris, p. 125.
9. *Vita Edwardi regis* quoted on pase.ac.uk. The pallium (a woolen cloak) is still bestowed on archbishops who are metropolitans by the pope as a symbol of jurisdiction bestowed.
10. *The Anglo-Saxon Chronicle* translated by James Ingram.
11. *The Life of King Edward Who Rests at Westminster*, edited by F. Barlow.
12. From the *Libellus de exordio atque procursu istius hocest Dunelmensis ecclesie* of Symeon of Durham, summarised in *Tostig, earl of Northumbria (c. 1029–1066)* (article), by William M. Aird, oxforddnb.com.
13. *Tostig, earl of Northumbria (c. 1029–1066)* (article), by William M. Aird, oxforddnb.com.
14. *The Anglo-Saxon Chronicle* translated by James Ingram.
15. *Vita Edwardi regis* quoted on pase.ac.uk.
16. *The Ecclesiastical History of England and Normandy* by Ordericus Vitalis.
17. *The Anglo-Saxon Chronicle* translated by James Ingram.
18. *ibid.*
19. *ibid.*
20. *ibid.*
21. *ibid.*
22. *The Chronicle of John of Worcester*, translated and edited by Thomas Forester, A.M.
23. *The History of the Kings of England and of his Own Times by William Malmesbury*, translated by J. Sharpe.
24. *Fulford: The Forgotten Battle of 1066* by Charles Jones.
25. *On the Spindle Side: the Kinswomen of Earl Godwin of Wessex* by Ann Williams.
26. *The Making of the Middle Ages* by R.W Southern.
27. *ibid.*
28. *Judith of Flanders, duchess of Bavaria (1030/5–1095)* (article), oxforddnb.com, by Elizabeth Van Houts.

Chapter 6: 1066

1. *The Chronicle of John of Worcester*, translated and edited by Thomas Forester, A.M.
2. *ibid.*

3. *Life in the Time of Harold Godwinson* (article) by G.K. Holloway.
4. *The Norman Conquest* by Marc Morris and *The Anglo-Saxons in 100 Facts* by Martin Wall.
5. William of Poitiers quoted in *The Norman Conquest* by Marc Morris.
6. *ibid.*
7. *The Norman Conquest* by Marc Morris.
8. *The Anglo-Saxon Chronicle* translated by James Ingram.
9. *The Anglo-Saxon Chronicle* translated by James Ingram, *The Chronicle of John of Worcester*, translated and edited by Thomas Forester, A.M., *The Anglo-Saxon Chronicles*, edited and translated by Michael Swaton.
10. *The Anglo-Saxon Chronicle* translated by James Ingram.
11. *ibid.*
12. *The Anglo-Saxon Chronicles*, edited and translated by Michael Swaton.
13. *The Anglo-Saxon Chronicle* translated by James Ingram.
14. *ibid.*
15. *ibid.*
16. *The Chronicle of John of Worcester*, translated and edited by Thomas Forester, A.M.
17. *The Norman Conquest* by Marc Morris.
18. *The Anglo-Saxon Chronicles*, edited and translated by Michael Swaton.
19. *The Norman Conquest* by Marc Morris.
20. *ibid.*
21. *The Gesta Guillielmi of William of Poitiers*, edited by R.H.C. Davis and Marjorie Chibnall.
22. *The Anglo-Saxon Chronicles*, edited and translated by Michael Swaton.
23. *The Anglo-Saxon Chronicles (D)*, edited and translated by Michael Swaton.
24. *The Chronicle of Henry of Huntingdon. Comprising the history of England, from the invasion of Julius Caesar to the accession of Henry II. Also, the Acts of Stephen, King of England and duke of Normandy* Translated and edited by Thomas Forester.
25. *ibid.*
26. *The Anglo-Saxon Chronicle* translated by James Ingram.

Chapter 7: Edith of Wessex

1. *The Anglo-Saxon Chronicles*, edited and translated by Michael Swaton.
2. *Godwine, earl of Wessex (d. 1053)* (article) by Ann Williams, Oxford Dictionary of National Biography, oxforddnb.com.
3. *ibid.*

4. *Life of King Edward* quoted in *Godwine, earl of Wessex (d. 1053)* (article) by Ann Williams, Oxford Dictionary of National Biography, oxforddnb.com.

5. William of Malmesbury, *Chronicles of the Kings of England, From the Earliest Period to the Reign of King Stephen,* c. 1090–1143.

6. *The Chronicle of Henry of Huntingdon. Comprising the history of England, from the invasion of Julius Caesar to the accession of Henry II. Also, the Acts of Stephen, King of England and duke of Normandy* Translated and edited by Thomas Forester.

7. *ibid.*

8. *The Chronicle of John of Worcester*, translated and edited by Thomas Forester, A.M.

9. *The Anglo-Saxon Chronicle* translated by James Ingram.

10. *Chronicles of the Kings of England, From the Earliest Period to the Reign of King Stephen*, by William of Malmesbury.

11. Osbert de Clare, quoted in *Edward the Confessor* by Peter Rex.

12. *ibid.*

13. *Edward the Confessor* by Peter Rex.

14. *The Lives of Edward the Confessor*, edited by Henry Richards Luard.

15. *Edward the Confessor* by Peter Rex.

16. *Godwine, earl of Wessex (d. 1053)* (article) by Ann Williams, Oxford Dictionary of National Biography, oxforddnb.com.

17. *ibid.*

18. *The Anglo-Saxon Chronicle* translated by James Ingram.

19. *The Chronicle of John of Worcester*, translated and edited by Thomas Forester, A.M.

20. *The Lives of Edward the Confessor*, edited by Henry Richards Luard.

21. *The Anglo-Saxon Chronicle* translated by James Ingram.

22. *The Anglo-Saxon Chronicles, (C),* edited and translated by Michael Swaton.

23. *The Chronicle of John of Worcester*, translated and edited by Thomas Forester, A.M.

24. *ibid.*

25. *Edith (Eadgyth) d.1075* (article), by Ann Williams, Oxford Dictionary of National Biography, oxforddnb.com.

26. *ibid.*

27. *The Chronicle of John of Worcester*, translated and edited by Thomas Forester, A.M.

28. *The Anglo-Saxon Chronicle* translated by James Ingram.

29. *The Lives of Edward the Confessor*, edited by Henry Richards Luard.

30. *La Vie de S. Edouard le Confesseur par Osbert de Clare*, edited by M. Bloch.

31. *The Gesta Normannorum Ducum of William of Jumièges, Oderic Vitalis and Robert of Torigni* edited by E.M.C. van Houts.
32. *The Lives of Edward the Confessor*, edited by Henry Richards Luard.
33. *ibid.*
34. *Edward the Confessor* by Peter Rex.
35. *Chronicles of the Kings of England, From the Earliest Period to the Reign of King Stephen,* by William of Malmesbury.
36. *The Lives of Edward the Confessor*, edited by Henry Richards Luard.
37. Quoted in *Edith (Eadgyth) d.1075* (article), by Ann Williams, Oxford Dictionary of National Biography, oxforddnb.com.
38. *The Anglo-Saxon Chronicle* translated by James Ingram.
39. *Brewer's British Royalty* by David Williamson.
40. *Edith (Eadgyth) d.1075* (article), by Ann Williams, Oxford Dictionary of National Biography, oxforddnb.com.
41. *Chronicles of the Kings of England, From the Earliest Period to the Reign of King Stephen,* by William of Malmesbury.
42. *Edith (Eadgyth) d.1075* (article), by Ann Williams, Oxford Dictionary of National Biography, oxforddnb.com.
43. *On the Spindle Side: the Kinswomen of Earl Godwin of Wessex* by Ann Williams.
44. Godfrey of Cambrai, prior of Winchester Cathedral (1082–1107), quoted in *Edith of Wessex, Queen of England* by Susan Abernethy and *Edith of Wessex, Queen of England* by Sharon L. Jansen.

Chapter 8: The Wives of Harald Hardrada

1. *A History of the Vikings* by T.D. Kendrick.
2. *The Chronicle of John of Worcester,* translated and edited by Thomas Forester, A.M.
3. *The Anglo-Saxon Chronicle* translated by James Ingram.
4. Bolverk, quoted in *Heimskringla. The Chronicle of the Kings of Norway,* by Snorre Sturluson.
5. *The Incredible Life of Harald Hardrada: The Last of the Great Vikings* (article) by Dattatreya Mandal.
6. *A History of the Vikings* by T.D. Kendrick and *Fulford: The Forgotten Battle of 1066* by Charles Jones.
7. Thiodolf, quoted in *Heimskringla. The Chronicle of the Kings of Norway,* by Snorre Sturluson.
8. William of Malmesbury, *Chronicles of the Kings of England, From the Earliest Period to the Reign of King Stephen,* c. 1090–1143.
9. Snorri Sturluson quoted in *Fulford: The Forgotten Battle of 1066* by Charles Jones.
10. *Prominent Russians: Anna Yaroslavna* (article), russiapedia.rt.com.
11. *ibid.*
12. Quoted in *Fulford: The Forgotten Battle of 1066* by Charles Jones.

13. *Heimskringla. The Chronicle of the Kings of Norway,* by Snorre Sturluson.
14. *ibid.*
15. *ibid.*
16. *Heimskringla. The Chronicle of the Kings of Norway,* by Snorre Sturluson.
17. *Fulford: The Forgotten Battle of 1066* by Charles Jones.
18. *The Anglo-Saxon Chronicle* translated by James Ingram.
19. *Heimskringla. The Chronicle of the Kings of Norway,* by Snorre Sturluson.
20. *ibid.*
21. *ibid.*
22. *ibid.*
23. *ibid.*
24. Adam of Bremen, quoted in *Tora Torbergsdottir,* Wikipedia.org.

Chapter 9: Edith Swanneck

1. *Eadgifu [Eddeua] the Fair [the Rich] (fl. 1066), magnate* by Ann Williams, oxforddnb.com, 2004.
2. *ibid.*
3. *Edith Swanneschals (c.1025–c.1086),* englishmonarchs.co.uk.
4. *The Anglo-Saxon Chronicle* translated by James Ingram.
5. *ibid.*
6. *ibid.*
7. *ibid.*
8. *ibid.*
9. *ibid.*
10. *ibid.*
11. *ibid.*
12. *Vita Edwardi regis.*
13. *Swein [Sweyn], earl* by Ann Williams, Oxford Dictionary of National Biography, oxforddnb.com, 23 September 2004.
14. *The Waltham chronicle* edited and translated by I. Watkiss and M. Chibnall.
15. *The Gesta Guillielmi of William of Poitiers,* edited by R.H.C. Davis and Marjorie Chibnall.
16. *Saxo Grammaticus* quoted in *On the Spindle Side: the Kinswomen of Earl Godwin of Wessex* by Ann Williams.
17. *Russian Primary Chronicle* quoted in *On the Spindle Side: the Kinswomen of Earl Godwin of Wessex* by Ann Williams.
18. *The Anglo-Saxon Chronicle* translated by James Ingram.
19. *Vita Wulfstani* of William of Malmesbury, edited by R.R. Darlington.
20. *Eadgifu [Eddeua] the Fair [the Rich] (fl. 1066), magnate* by Ann Williams, oxforddnb.com, 2004.
21. *The Latin and French Inscriptions of Lincoln Minster* by Nicholas Alldrit and David Tripp.

Chapter 10: Ealdgyth

1. Ælfgar, earl of Mercia (d. 1062?) (article) by Ann Williams, Oxford Dictionary of National Biography.
2. *The Chronicle of John of Worcester*, translated and edited by Thomas Forester, A.M.
3. *The Anglo-Saxon Chronicles* edited and translated by Michael Swaton.
4. *The Chronicle of John of Worcester*, translated and edited by Thomas Forester, A.M.
5. *ibid.*
6. *ibid.*
7. *ibid.*
8. *ibid.*
9. *The Gesta Normannorum Ducum of William of Jumièges, Oderic Vitalis and Robert of Torigni* edited by E.M.C. van Houts.
10. *The Anglo-Saxon Chronicle* translated by James Ingram.
11. *ibid.*
12. *Ealdgyth [Aldgyth] (fl. C. 1057–1066)* (article) by K.L. Maund, Oxford Dictionary of National Biography.
13. *Brutu: Penrith MS: 20,13* quoted in *Gruffudd ap Llywelyn (d. 1063)* (article) by David Walker, Oxford Dictionary of National Biography.
14. *The Anglo-Saxon Chronicle* translated by James Ingram.
15. Credited to Walter Map in *Gruffudd ap Llywelyn (d. 1063)* (article) by David Walker, Oxford Dictionary of National Biography.
16. *Brut y Tywysogion* quoted in *Brewer's British Royalty* by David Williamson.
17. *The Anglo-Saxon Chronicle* translated by James Ingram.
18. *The Chronicle of John of Worcester*, translated and edited by Thomas Forester, A.M.
19. *The Norman Conquest* by Marc Morris.
20. *The Anglo-Saxon Chronicles* edited and translated by Michael Swaton.
21. *The Anglo-Saxon Chronicle* translated by James Ingram.
22. *The Chronicle of John of Worcester*, translated and edited by Thomas Forester, A.M.
23. *The English and the Norman Conquest* by Ann Williams and *Britain's Royal Families; the Complete Genealogy* by Alison Weir.
24. *The English and the Norman Conquest* by Ann Williams.
25. *ibid.*

Chapter 11: Griefs and Sufferings

1. *The Anglo-Saxon Chronicle* translated by James Ingram.
2. 1066, Text D of *The Anglo-Saxon Chronicles* edited and translated by Michael Swaton.
3. *The Anglo-Saxon Chronicle* translated by James Ingram.

4. *ibid.*

5. *ibid.*

6. *The Gesta Guillielmi of William of Poitiers*, edited by R.H.C. Davis and Marjorie Chibnall.

7. *The Carmen de Hastingae Proelio of Guy, Bishop of Amiens* quoted in *The Norman Conquest* by Marc Morris.

8. *The Chronicle of John of Worcester*, translated and edited by Thomas Forester, A.M.

9. *ibid.*

10. 1066, Text D of *The Anglo-Saxon Chronicles* edited and translated by Michael Swaton.

11. *The Anglo-Saxon Chronicle* translated by James Ingram.

12. *The Chronicle of John of Worcester*, translated and edited by Thomas Forester, A.M.

13. *The Gesta Guillielmi of William of Poitiers*, edited by R.H.C. Davis and Marjorie Chibnall.

14. *ibid.*

15. *The Norman Conquest* by Marc Morris.

16. *ibid.*

17. *The Ecclesiastical History of England and Normandy* by Ordericus Vitalis.

18. *The Gesta Guillielmi of William of Poitiers*, edited by R.H.C. Davis and Marjorie Chibnall.

19. *The Anglo-Saxon Chronicle* translated by James Ingram.

20. *The Gesta Guillielmi of William of Poitiers*, edited by R.H.C. Davis and Marjorie Chibnall.

21. *ibid.*

22. *The Anglo-Saxon Chronicle* Text E, quoted in *The Norman Conquest* by Marc Morris.

23. *English Historical Documents* quoted in *The Norman Conquest* by Marc Morris.

24. *The Gesta Guillielmi of William of Poitiers*, edited by R.H.C. Davis and Marjorie Chibnall.

25. *ibid.*

26. 1067, Text D of *The Anglo-Saxon Chronicles* edited and translated by Michael Swaton.

27. *The Anglo-Saxon Chronicle* translated by James Ingram.

28. *The Norman Conquest* by Marc Morris.

29. *The Chronicle of John of Worcester*, translated and edited by Thomas Forester, A.M.

30. *The Norman Conquest* by Marc Morris.

31. Simeon of Durham quoted in *The Norman Conquest* by Marc Morris.

32. *The Ecclesiastical History of England and Normandy* by Ordericus Vitalis.

33. *The Anglo-Saxon Chronicle Text D 1068* quoted by Ann Williams in *The English and the Norman Conquest*.
34. *The Anglo-Saxon Chronicle* translated by James Ingram.
35. William of Jumièges quoted by Ann Williams in *The English and the Norman Conquest*.
36. *The Anglo-Saxon Chronicle* translated by James Ingram.
37. *The Battle of Hastings 1066* by M.K. Lawson.
38. *The Ecclesiastical History of England and Normandy* by Ordericus Vitalis.
39. *Chronicles of the Kings of England, From the Earliest Period to the Reign of King Stephen*, by William of Malmesbury.
40. 1097, Text E of *The Anglo-Saxon Chronicles* edited and translated by Michael Swaton.
44. *Chronicles of the Kings of England, From the Earliest Period to the Reign of King Stephen*, by William of Malmesbury.
42. *The Anglo-Saxon Chronicle* translated by James Ingram.
43. Text E of *The Anglo-Saxon Chronicles* edited and translated by Michael Swaton.
44. *Gesta Herewardi* quoted in *The Norman Conquest* by Marc Morris.
45. *The Anglo-Saxon Chronicle* translated by James Ingram.
46. *The Chronicle of John of Worcester*, translated and edited by Thomas Forester, A.M.
47. 1071, Text D of *The Anglo-Saxon Chronicles* edited and translated by Michael Swaton.

Chapter 12: Matilda of Flanders

1. *William I [known as William the Conqueror (1027/8–1087)* (article) by David Bates, Oxford Dictionary of National Biography, oxforddnb.com.
2. *Odo, Earl of Kent (d. 1097)* (article) By David Bates, Oxford Dictionary of National Biography, oxforddnb.com.
3. *Rodolfus Glaber, Historiarum Libri Quinque* edited by J. France, N. Bulst and P. Reynolds, pp. 204–5.
4. *William I [known as William the Conqueror (1027/8–1087)* (article) by David Bates, Oxford Dictionary of National Biography, oxforddnb.com.
5. *William I, England's Conqueror* by Marc Morris.
6. *Gesta Normannorum Ducum* by William of Jumièges, quoted in *the Norman Conquest* by Marc Morris.
7. *ibid.*
8. Teresa Cole, *The Norman Conquest: William the Conqueror's Subjugation of England* pages 157–9.
9. William of Malmesbury quoted by Elizabeth van Houts in oxforddnb. com, May 2008.

10. *Adelida [Adeliza] (d. before 1113)* (Article) by Elisabeth van Houts, Oxford Dictionary of National Biography, oxforddnb.com.

11. Tracy Borman, *Matilda, Wife of the Conqueror, First Queen of England*, p.107.

12. Lois L. Huneycutt, *Adela, countess of Blois (c.1067–1137)* (article).

13. Phyllis Abrahams, *Les Oeuvres Poétiques de Baudri de Bourgueil (1046–1130)*.

14. William of Malmesbury, *Chronicles of the Kings of England, From the Earliest Period to the Reign of King Stephen*, c. 1090–1143.

15. Robert Bartlett, *England Under the Norman and Angevin Kings, 1075–1225*, p. 403.

16. Lois L. Huneycutt, *Adela, countess of Blois (c.1067–1137)* (article).

17. *The meaning of 'Mora', the Flagship Matilda of Flanders gave William the Conqueror* (article) by Elisabeth Waugaman, thefreelancehistorywriter.com.

18. *The Anglo-Saxon Chronicle* quoted in *William I, England's Conqueror* by Marc Morris.

19. *Queens Consort* by Lisa Hilton.

20. Text E of *The Anglo-Saxon Chronicles* edited and translated by Michael Swaton.

21. Lois Huneycutt quoted in *Queens Consort* by Lisa Hilton.

22. *Queens Consort* by Lisa Hilton.

23. MGH, *Epistolae Selectae, Das Register Gregors VII*, ed. Erich Caspar (Berlin: Weidmann, 1920–23), ep.1.71, p.102–03, dated April 1074. Quoted by epistolae.ccnmtl.columbia.edu.

24. *Vita B Simonis*, col. 1219, quoted by Elizabeth van Houts in oxforddnb.com, May 2008.

25. P. Abrahams, editor, *Les Oeuvres Poétiques de Baudri de Bourgueil (1046–1130)*.

26. L. Couppey, "Encore Héauville! Supplément aux notes historiques sur le prieur, conventuel d'Héauville la Hague," *Revue catholique de Normandie*, X, 1900–01, p.348–49. Quoted by epistolae.ccnmtl.columbia.edu.

27. Musset *La Reine Mathilde* p.193, quoted by Elizabeth van Houts in oxforddnb.com, May 2008.

28. *ibid.*

29. Tracy Borman, *Matilda, Wife of the Conqueror, First Queen of England*, p.205.

30. *ibid* p. 206.

31. William of Malmesbury, *Chronicles of the Kings of England, From the Earliest Period to the Reign of King Stephen*.

32. *The Chronicle of John of Worcester*, translated and edited by Thomas Forester, A.M.

33. Ordericus Vitalis, *The Ecclesiastical History of England and Normandy*.
34. Peter Rex, *William the Conqueror: The Bastard of Normandy*, p. 258.
35. *A Historical Obstetric Enigma: How Tall was Matilda?* (article) by J Dewhurst *Journal of Obstetrics and Gynaecology*, 1981.
36. *Queen Matilda, wife of William the Conqueror, was NOT a Dwarf* (article) by Marc Morris, marcmorris.org.uk, 29 July 2013.

Chapter 13: St Margaret

1. *The Chronicle of John of Worcester*, translated and edited by Thomas Forester, A.M.
2. *ibid.*
3. *Edmund II [known as Edmund Ironside (d. 1016)* (article) by M.K. Lawson, Oxford Dictionary of National Biography, oxforddnb.com.
4. *The Chronicle of John of Worcester*, translated and edited by Thomas Forester, A.M.
5. *ibid.*
6. *ibid.*
7. *ibid.*
8. *Edmund II [known as Edmund Ironside (d. 1016)* (article) by M.K. Lawson, Oxford Dictionary of National Biography, oxforddnb.com.
9. 1067, *The Anglo-Saxon Chronicle* translated by James Ingram.
10. Symeon of Durham, *Vita Sanctae Margaretae Scotorum reginae, Symeonis Dunelmensis opera et collectanea*, ed. J. H. Hinde, Surtees Society, 1868.
11. *A Dangerous Saint: St Margaret of Scotland* by Claire Havrill, DangerousWomenProject.org.
12. *Scotland, History of a Nation* by David Ross.
13. Turgot's *Vita Sanctae Margaretae* quoted in *England in Europe; English Royal Women and Literary Patronage c.1000–c.1150* by Elizabeth M. Tyler.
14. Ordericus Vitalis, *The Ecclesiastical History of England and Normandy*.
15. *The Story of Scotland* by Nigel Tranter.
16. *ibid.*
17. G.W.S. Barrow, Oxforddnb.com *Margaret [St Margaret] (d. 1093), queen of Scots, consort of Malcolm III*, 2004.
18. *ibid.*
19. *David I (c. 1085–1153)* (article) by G.W.S Barrow, Oxford Dictionary of National Biography, oxforddnb.com.
20. *Brewer's British Royalty* by David Williamson.
21. *Britain's Royal Families, the Complete Genealogy* by Alison Weir.

22. *Christina (fl. 1057–1093)* (article) by Nicholas Hooper, Oxford Dictionary of National Biography, oxforddnb.com.
23. Eadmer, quoted in *Saint Margaret, Queen of Scotland* (article) by Susan Abernethy, thefreelancehistorywriter.com.
24. *The Anglo-Saxon Chronicles* edited and translated by Michael Swaton.
25. *The Chronicle of John of Worcester*, translated and edited by Thomas Forester, A.M.
26. *The Anglo-Saxon Chronicle* translated by James Ingram.
27. Turgot's *Vita Sanctae Margaretae* quoted in *England in Europe; English Royal Women and Literary Patronage c.1000–c.1150* by Elizabeth M. Tyler.
28. *The Anglo-Saxon Chronicle* translated by James Ingram.
29. *The Chronicle of John of Worcester*, translated and edited by Thomas Forester, A.M.
30. *Britain's Royal Families, the Complete Genealogy* by Alison Weir.
31. Thomas Morrison, quoted in *Saint Margaret, Queen of Scotland* (article) by Susan Abernethy, thefreelancehistorywriter.com.

Chapter 14: Gundrada de Warenne

1. *Warenne, William de, first earl of Surrey [Earl Warenne] (d. 1088)* (article) by C.P. Lewis, Oxford Dictionary of National Biography, oxforddnb. com.
2. *The Gesta Normannorum Ducum of William of Jumièges, Oderic Vitalis and Robert of Torigni* edited by E.M.C. van Houts.
3. *ibid.*
4. *Early Yorkshire Charters Volume 8* Edited by William Farrer and Charles Travis Clay and *William the Conqueror, the Norman Impact Upon England* by David C. Douglas.
5. *ibid.*
6. *ibid.*
7. *ibid.*
8. *Observations on the Parentage of Gundreda, the Daughter of William Duke of Normandy, and Wife of William de Warenne* by George Floyd Duckett, reprinted by Kessinger Legacy Reprints, originally published in Vol. III of the Cumberland and Westmoreland Archaeological Society.
9. *Early Yorkshire Charters Volume 8* Edited by William Farrer and Charles Travis Clay and *William the Conqueror, the Norman Impact Upon England* by David C. Douglas.
10. *ibid.*
11. *Warenne, Gundrada de (d.1085)* (article) by C.P. Lewis, Oxford Dictionary of National Biography, oxforddnb.com.
12. *ibid.*
13. *Early Yorkshire Charters Volume 8* Edited by William Farrer and Charles Travis Clay.

14. *Warenne, Gundrada de (d.1085)* (article) by C.P. Lewis, Oxford Dictionary of National Biography, oxforddnb.com.
15. *ibid.*
16. *Castle Acre and the Warennes* (article) by Marc Morris.
17. *Warenne, Gundrada de (d.1085)* (article) by C.P. Lewis, Oxford Dictionary of National Biography, oxforddnb.com.
18. *ibid.*
19. *Warenne, Gundrada de (d.1085)* (article) by C.P. Lewis, Oxford Dictionary of National Biography, oxforddnb.com.
20. *Early Yorkshire Charters Volume 8* Edited by William Farrer and Charles Travis Clay.
21. *A History of the County of Sussex: Volume 2* edited by William Page.
22. *The Chronicle of Henry of Huntingdon. Comprising the history of England, from the invasion of Julius Caesar to the accession of Henry II. Also, the Acts of Stephen, King of England and duke of Normandy* Translated and edited by Thomas Forester.
23. *Early Yorkshire Charters Volume 8* Edited by William Farrer and Charles Travis Clay.
24. *ibid.*
25. *Early Yorkshire Charters Volume 8* Edited by William Farrer and Charles Travis Clay.
26. *Early Yorkshire Charters Volume 8* Edited by William Farrer and Charles Travis Clay and *Castle Acre and the Warennes* (article) by Marc Morris.
27. *Warenne, Gundrada de (d.1085)* (article) by C.P. Lewis, Oxford Dictionary of National Biography, oxforddnb.com.
28. *ibid.*
29. 'brother of Countess de Warenne', *Early Yorkshire Charters Volume 8* Edited by William Farrer and Charles Travis Clay.
30. *Warenne, Gundrada de (d.1085)* (article) by C.P. Lewis, Oxford Dictionary of National Biography, oxforddnb.com.
31. *Companions of the Conqueror* (article) by C.P. Lewis, Oxford Dictionary of National Biography, oxforddnb.com.

Chapter 15: The Mysterious Woman of the Bayeux Tapestry

1. *A Historical Document* Pierre Bouet and François Neveux, bayeuxmuseum.com/en/un_document_historique_en.
2. *The Mystery Lady of the Bayeux Tapestry* (article) by Paula Lofting, annabelfrage.qordpress.com.
3. *Ælfgyva: The Mysterious lady of the Bayeux Tapestry* (article) by M.W. Campbell, *Annales de Normandie* and *The Bayeux Tapestry: The Life Story of a Masterpiece* by Carola Hicks.
4. A.C Ducarel, mentioned in *The Bayeux Tapestry, the Life Story of a Masterpiece* by Carola Hicks.
5. *ibid.*

6. *Æthelred II [Ethelred; known as Ethelred the Unready] (c. 966x8–1016)* (article) by Simon Keynes, Oxford Dictionary of National Biography, oxforddnb.com.
7. *Britain's Royal Families; the Complete Genealogy* by Alison Weir.
8. *Queen Emma and the Vikings: The Woman Who Shaped the Events of 1066* by Harriet O'Brien.
9. *The Anglo-Saxon Chronicle* translated by James Ingram.
10. *ibid.*
11. *The Bayeux Tapestry, the Life Story of a Masterpiece* by Carola Hicks.
12. *On the Spindle Side: the Kinswomen of Earl Godwin of Wessex* by Ann Williams.
13. *ibid.*
14. *ibid.*
15. *The Anglo-Saxon Chronicle* translated by James Ingram.
16. *Swein [Sweyn], earl* by Ann Williams, Oxford Dictionary of National Biography, oxforddnb.com, 23 September 2004.
17. *Ælfgyva: The Mysterious lady of the Bayeux Tapestry* (article) by M.W. Campbell, *Annales de Normandie.*
18. *ibid.*
19. *Ælfgifu [Ælfgifu of Northampton (fl. 1006–1036)* (article) by Pauline Stafford, Oxford Dictionary of National Biography, oxforddnb.com.
20. *The Chronicle of John of Worcester*, translated and edited by Thomas Forester, A.M.
21. *1036, E manuscript of The Anglo-Saxon Chronicles* edited and translated by Michael Swaton.
22. *The Chronicle of John of Worcester*, translated and edited by Thomas Forester, A.M.
23. *Ælfgyva – The Mystery Woman of the Bayeux Tapestry* by Paula Lofting, englishhistoryauthors.blogspot.co.uk 22 November 2017.
24. *Ælfgyva: The Mysterious lady of the Bayeux Tapestry* (article) by M.W. Campbell, *Annales de Normandie.*

Epilogue

1. *Christina (fl. 1057–1093)* (article) by Nicholas Hooper, Oxford Dictionary of National Biography, oxforddnb.com.

Bibliography

Primary Sources

Annales Monastici: Annales prioratus de Dunstaplia (A.D. 1–1297) Annales monasterii de Bermundesia (A.D. 1042–1432) Edited by Henry Richards Luard, London, Longmans, 1866.

Domesday Book: A Complete Translation, edited by A. Williams and G.H. Martin, 2002.

Eadmer's History of Recent Events in England, edited by G. Bosanquet, 1964.

Encomium Emma Reginae, edited by A. Campbell and S. Keynes, Cambridge, 1998.

Gervase of Canterbury *The Deeds of Kings* edited by W. Stubbs in *The Historical Works of Gervase of Canterbury*, Rolls Series, 1880.

Flores Historiarum by Roger of Wendover (d. 1236), translated by Matthew of Westminster c.1300–1320.

Gesta Normannorum Ducum by William of Jumièges, edited and translated by Elizabeth Van Houts, Oxford, 1992.

Godiva by Alfred Lord Tennyson, 1842.

Great Domesday Book: A Facsimile, edited by R.W.H. Erskine, London, 1986, fol. 164.

Heimskringla. The Chronicle of the Kings of Norway, by Snorre Sturluson, translated by Samuel Laing, London, 1844.

Historia Novorum in Anglia by Eadmer of Canterbury, edited by Martin Rule, London, 1866.

History of the Kings of England by Symeon of Durham, translated by J. Stevenson, facsimile reprint, Lampeter, 1987.

King Harald's Saga by Snorri Sturluson, edited by M. Magnusson and H. Pálsson, 1966.

La Vie de S. Edouard le Confesseur par Osbert de Clare, edited by M. Bloch, *Analecta Bollandiana*, 41, 1923.

Opera: S. Anselmi Opera Omnia by Anselm, edited by F.S. Schmitt, Edinburgh, 1938–61.

Rodolfus Glaber, Historiarum Libri Quinque, edited by J. France, N. Bulst and P. Reynolds, Oxford, Clarendon Press, 1993.

Roger of Wendover's Flowers of history, Comprising the history of England from the descent of the Saxons to A.D. 1235, volume II, by Roger of Wendover, edited by J.A. Giles, London, H.G. Bohn, 1849.

Sawyer, P.H. *Anglo-Saxon charters: an annotated list and bibliography, Royal Historical Society Guides and Handbooks* 1968.

Saxo Grammaticus Danonum Regum Heroumque Hiistoria Books X– XVI, edited by Eric Christiansen, 2 volumes, BAR International Series 84, 1980.

The Anglo-Saxon Chronicle, translated by James Ingram, London, 1823, reprinted by Dodo Press.

The Anglo-Saxon Chronicles, Swaton, Michael, edited and translated, London, Phoenix Press, 2000.

The Anglo-Saxon Chronicle. Whitelock, D., Douglas, D. C. & Tucker, S. I., editors and translators, London, 1961.

The Carmen de Hastingi Proelio of Guy, Bishop of Amiens, edited by Catherine Morton and Hope Muntz, London, 1972.

The Chronicle of Henry of Huntingdon. Comprising the history of England, from the invasion of Julius Caesar to the accession of Henry II. Also, the Acts of Stephen, King of England and duke of Normandy Translated and edited by Thomas Forester. London, H.G. Bohn, 1807.

The Chronicle of John Florence of Worcester with the two continuations, translated and edited by Thomas Forester, A.M., London, Henry G. Bohn, 1854.

The Chronicle of John of Worcester, edited by R.R Darlington and P. McGurk, 2 volumes, OMT, Oxford, 1995, 1998.

The Ecclesiastical History of England and Normandy by Ordericus Vitalis 1075–1143(?), London, Bohn, 1853.

The Gesta Guillielmi of William of Poitiers, edited by R.H.C. Davis and Marjorie Chibnall, OMT, Oxford, 1998.

The Gesta Normannorum Ducum of William of Jumièges, Oderic Vitalis and Robert of Torigni edited by E.M.C. van Houts, 2 volumes, Oxford, 1992–5.

The historie and cronicles of Scotland ... by Robert Lindesay of Pitscottie, 3 vols, Mackay, A. J. G., editor, Scottish Text Society, 42–3, 60 (1899–1911).

The History of the Kings of England and of his Own Times by William Malmesbury, Sharpe, J, translator, Seeleys, 1854.

The Life of King Edward Who Rests at Westminster, edited by F. Barlow, OMT, 2nd edition, London, 1992.

The Lives of Edward the Confessor, edited by Henry Richards Luard, London, Longman, archive.org., 1858.

The Waltham chronicle edited and translated by I. Watkiss and M. Chibnall, Oxford, Oxford University Press, 1998.

Vita Sanctae Margaretae Scotorum reginae, Symeonis Dunelmensis opera et collectanea by Symeon of Durham, ed. J. H. Hinde, Surtees Society, 1868.

Vita Wulfstani of William of Malmesbury, edited by R.R. Darlington, PR new series 40, 1928.

William of Malmesbury, *Chronicles of the Kings of England, From the Earliest Period to the Reign of King Stephen c. 1090–1143*, by William of Malmesbury, edited by John Sharpe and J.A. Giles, London, H.G. Bohn, 1847.

William of Malmesbury, *Chronicles of the Kings of England, From the Earliest Period to the Reign of King Stephen*, e-book, Perennial Press, 2016.

William of Malmesbury, *Gesta Regum Anglorum*, edited by R.A.B Mynors, R.M. Thomson and M. Winterbottom, OMT, 2 volumes, Oxford, 1998.

Secondary Sources

Abbott, Jacob, *William the Conqueror*, e-book, Timeless Classic Books, 2010.

Abernethy, Susan, *Edith of Wessex, Queen of England*, thefreelancehistorywriter.com, 5 June 2012.

Abernethy, Susan, *Saint Margaret, Queen of Scotland* (article), thefreelancehistorywriter.com, June 2012.

Adams, George Burton, *the History of England from the Norman Conquest to the Death of John*, e-book.

Aird, William M., *Tostig, earl of Northumbria (c. 1029–1066)* (article), Oxford Dictionary of National Biography, oxforddnb.com, 23 September 2004.

Aldritt, Nicholas and Tripp, David, *The Latin and French Inscriptions of Lincoln Minster*, The Honywood Press, 1990.

Andrews, Evan, *Who was Lady Godiva* (article), amphistory.com, October 2014.

Barlow, Frank, *Edward [St Edward; known as Edward the Confessor]* (article), Oxford Dictionary of National Biography, oxforddnb.com, 26 May 2006.

Barlow, Frank, *Edward the Confessor,* Berkeley and Los Angeles, University of California Press, 1984.

Barrow, J.S. (editor), *Prebendaries: Norton*, in *Fasti Ecclesiae Anglicanae 1066–1300: Volume 8, Hereford*, London, Institute of Historical Research, 2002, british-history.ac.uk.

Barrow, G.W.S., *David I (c. 1085–1153)* (article), Oxford Dictionary of National Biography, oxforddnb.com, 5 January 2006.

Barrow, G.W.S., *Margaret [St Margaret] (d. 1093), queen of Scots, consort of Malcolm III* (article), Oxford Dictionary of National Biography, oxforddnb.com, 2004.

Bartlett, Robert, *England Under the Norman and Angevin Kings, 1075–1225* Oxford, Oxford University Press, 2000.

Bates, David, *Odo, Earl of Kent (d. 1097)* (article), Oxford Dictionary of National Biography, oxforddnb.com, 1 September 2017.

Bates, David, *William I [known as William the Conqueror (1027/8–1087)* (article), Oxford Dictionary of National Biography, oxforddnb.com, 23 September 2004.

Bateson, Mary, *Medieval England 1066–1350*, Lecturable, e-book.

Baucero, Gianna, *Edith Swanneck* (article), giannabaucero.wordpress.com, 21 February 2015.

Bémont, Charles, *Medieval Europe, 395–1270*, Lecturable, e-book, 2012.

Bloks, Moniek, *Matilda of Flanders – Queen of the Conqueror* (article), historyofroyalwomen.com, 29 December 2017.

Bloks, Moniek, *The Romanticisation of Lady Godiva* (article), historyofroyalwomen.com, 7 February 2017.

Borman, Tracy, *Matilda, Wife of the Conqueror, First Queen of England*, London Vintage Books, 2012.

Bouet, Pierre and Neveux, François, *A Historical Document* (article), bayeuxmuseum.com/en/un_document_historique_en.

Brindle, Steven and Agnieszka Sadraei, *Conisbrough Castle, English Heritage Guidebook*, London, English Heritage, 2015.

Butler, Emily, *Emma of Normandy and the Women's Agency Between Conquests* (article), blogs.surrey.ac.uk, 12 December 2017.

Campbell, M.W., *Ælfgyva: The Mysterious lady of the Bayeux Tapestry* (article), Medievalists.net, 24 August 2014.

Campbell, M.W., *Ælfgyva: The Mysterious lady of the Bayeux Tapestry* (article), *Annales de Normandie* Vol. 34, no. 2, pp. 127–145, 1984.

Cannon, John, editor, *Oxford Companion to British History*, Oxford, Oxford University Press, 1997.

Carless Davis, H.W., *England Under the Normans and Angevins 1066–1272*, e-book, Lecturable.

Chambers, James, *The Norman Kings*, London, Weidenfeld and Nicolson, 1981.

Coe, Charles, *Lady Godiva: The Naked Truth* (article), Harvard Magazine (harvardmagazine.com) July–August 2003.

Cole, Teresa *The Norman Conquest: William the Conqueror's Subjugation of England*, Stroud, Amberley Publishing, 2016.

Courtney, Joanna, *The Queens of 1066*, joannacourtney.com

Crawford, Anne, editor and translator, *Letters of Medieval Women*, Stroud, Sutton Publishing, 2002.

Davis, William Stearns, *A History of France from the Earliest Times to the Treaty of Versailles*, Cambridge Massachusetts, The Riverside Press, 1919.

Dewhurst, J., *A Historical Obstetric Enigma: How Tall was Matilda?* (article), *Journal of Obstetrics and Gynaecology*, 1981.

Dockray-Miller, Mary, *Goscelin and Queen Edith: lexomics project* (article), blogs.surrey.ac.uk, 1 June 2016.

Douglas, David C., *William the Conqueror*, Yale University Press, 1999.

Douglas, David C., *William the Conqueror, the Norman Impact Upon England*, California, University of California Press, 1964.

Duckett, George Floyd, *Observations on the Parentage of Gundreda, the Daughter of William Duke of Normandy, and Wife of William de Warenne*, reprinted by Kessinger Legacy Reprints, originally published in Vol. III of the Cumberland and Westmoreland Archaeological Society, 1878.

Duducu, Jem, *Forgotten History: Unbelievable Moments from the Past*, Stroud, Amberley Publishing, 2016.

Duducu, Jem, *The Twice-widowed Queen* (article), facebook.com/historygems 1 February 2018.

Duruy, Victor, *History of the Middle Ages*, Lecturable, e-book, 2012.

Encyclopedia.com, *Elizabeth of Kiev (fl. 1045)*.

Englishmonarchs.co.uk, *Edith of Wessex (c. 1025– 18 December 1075)* (article).

Englishmonarchs.co.uk, *Edith Swanneschals (c. 1025–c.1086)* (article).

Evans, Kelly, Ælfgifu of Northampton and Emma of Normandy: Strong Women in a Man's World (article), kellyevans.com, 17 September 2015.

Farrer, William and Charles Travis Clay, editors, *Early Yorkshire Charters, volume 8: The Honour of Warenne*, Cambridge, Cambridge University Press, 2013 edition, first published 1949.

Fell, Christine, *Anglo-Saxon England* Vol. 3, Cambridge, Cambridge University Press, 1974.

Fleming, Robin, *Harold II [Harold Godwineson] (1022/3?–1066)* (article), Oxford Dictionary of National Biography, oxforddnb.com, 23 September 2010.

Floor, Liz Lea, *Near 1,000 years old, The Bayeux Tapestry is an epic tale and medieval masterpiece* (article), ancient-origins.net, 3 October 2015.

Fraser, Antonia, *The Warrior Queens: Boadicea's Chariot*, London, George Weidenfeld & Nicolson Ltd. 1993.

Freeman, Edward A., Hon. D.C.L., *The History of the Norman Conquest of England, its Causes and its Results Volume IV*, Oxford, Clarendon Press, 1871.

Frith, Matt, *Art, Allegory, and the Authorship of the Bayeux Tapestry* (article), thepostgradchroniclessite.wordpress.com, 23 January 2018.

Frith, Matt, *Danish Invasion, Viking Violence, and Cnut's Mutilation of Hostages at Sandwich* (article), thepostgradchroniclessite.wordpress.com, 5 May 2017.

Gardiner, Juliet and Wenborn, Neil, editors, *The History Today Companion to British History*, London, Collins & Brown Ltd, 1995.

Goubert, Pierre, *The Course of French History*, London, Routledge, 1991.

Graham, Henry Grey, *Margaret Queen of Scotland*, e-book, Leonaur, 2011.

Green, Mary Anne Everett Green, *Lives of the Princesses of England from the Norman Conquest*, Volume 2, London, Longman, Brown, Green, Longman, & Roberts, 1857.

H., Julia, *Harold Godwinson's Women* (article), thehistoryjar.com, 13 June 2016.

H., Julia, *King Harold's Children* (article), thehistoryjar.com, 15 July 2014.

H., Julia, *Alan of Brittany* (article), thehistoryjar.com, 14 April 2013.

Hasted, Edward, *The History and Topographical Survey of the County of Kent: Volume 1*, Canterbury, W Bristow, 1797. british-history. ac.uk.

Havrill, Claire, *A Dangerous Saint: St Margaret of Scotland* (article), DangerousWomenProject.org, 28 October 2016.

Herbert, N.M. and Pugh, R.B., editors, *A History of the County of Gloucester: Volume 11, Bisley and Longtree Hundreds*, London, Victoria County History, 1976. british-history.ac.uk

Hicks, Carola, *The Bayeux Tapestry: The Life Story of a Masterpiece*, London, Vintage, 2007.

Hicks, Leonie, *Norman Women: the power behind the thrones* (article), BBC History, historyextra.com, October 2016.

Hill, Justin, *The 1016 Danish Conquest that led to the Battle of Hastings* (article), historyextra.com.

Hilliam, David, *Kings, Queens, Bones and Bastards*, Stroud, The History Press, 1999.

Hilton, Lisa, *Queens Consort: England's Medieval Queens*, London, Phoenix, 2008.

Hindley, Geoffrey, *A Brief History of the Anglo-Saxons*, London, Robinson, 2015 edition.

Holloway, G.K., *Life in the Time of Harold Godwinson* (article), maryanneyarde.blogspot.co.uk, 5 March 2018.

Hooper, Nicholas, *Christina (fl. 1057–1093)* (article), Oxford Dictionary of National Biography, oxforddnb.com, 23 September 2004.

Hume, David, *The History of England*, volume 1, e-book.

Huneycutt, Lois L., *Adela, countess of Blois (c.1067–1137)* (article), *Oxford Dictionary of National Biography*, Oxford University Press, online edition, 2004.

Huneycutt, Lois L., *Margaret of Scotland; a Study in Queenship*, Woodbridge, The Boydell Press, 2003.

Bibliography

Hurlock, Kathryn, *Bayeux and Brexit: What the Tapestry says about the UK's shared European heritage* (article), ancient-origins.net, 6 February 2018.

Jansen, Sharon L., *Edith of Wessex, Queen of England* (article), monstrousregimentofwomen.com, 15 May 2015.

Jones, Charles, *Fulford: The Forgotten Battle of 1066*, Stroud, The History Press, 2013.

Jones, Terry, and Ereira, Alan, *Terry Jones' Medieval Lives*, London, BBC Books, 2005.

Keats-Rohan, Katharine, *Domesday People Revisited* (article), academia. edu, October 2011.

Kendrick, T.D., *A History of the Vikings*, New York, Dover Publications Inc., 2004.

Keynes, Simon, Æthelred II [Ethelred; *known as Ethelred the Unready] (c. 966x8-1016)* (article), Oxford Dictionary of National Biography, oxforddnb.com, 8 October 2009.

Keynes, Simon, ad Smyth, Alfred P., editors, *Chronicle D: Gendering Conquest in Eleventh Century England* (article) in *Anglo-Saxons* (journal), Portland, 2006.

Keynes, Simon, *Emma [Ælfgifu] (d.1052)* (article), Oxford Dictionary of National Biography, oxforddnb.com, 23 September 2004.

Klinder, Hermann and Hilgemann, Werner, *The Penguin Atlas of World History, Volume one: From the Beginning to the Eve of the French Revolution*, London, Penguin Books Ltd, 1978 edition.

Koenigsberger, H.G., *Medieval Europe 400–1500* New York, Longman, 1987.

Krag, Claus, *Harald Hardrada (1015–66)* (article), Oxford Dictionary of National Biography, oxforddnb.com, May 2006.

Lacroix, Paul, *Medieval Life: Manners, Customs and Dress During the Middle Ages*, London, Arcturus, 2011.

Laffin, John *Brassey's Battles: 3,500 Years of Conflict, Campaigns and Wars from A–Z*, London, Brassey's, 1995.

Lavelle, Ryan, *How England Rode the Viking Storm* (article), BBC History Magazine, November 2015.

Lawless, Erin, *Historical Heroines #34: Edith Swanneck* (article), erinlawless.wordpress.com, 5 August 2013.

Lawson, M.K., *Alfred Ætheling (d. 1036/7)* (article), Oxford Dictionary of National Biography, oxforddnb.com, 23 September 2004.

Lawson, M.K. *Edmund II [known as Edmund Ironside (d. 1016)* (article), Oxford Dictionary of National Biography, oxforddnb.com, 23 September 2004.

Lawson, M.K., *The Battle of Hastings 1066*, Stroud, The History Press, 2016.

Laynesmith, Joanna, *Who was the mysterious Ælfgyva in the Bayeux Tapestry* (article), Medievalists.net, 13 November 2012.

Lewis, C.P., *Companions of the Conqueror (act. 1066-1071)* (Article), Oxford Dictionary of National Biography, oxforddnb.com, 24 May 2007.

Lewis, C.P., *Warenne, Gundrada de (d.1085)* (article), Oxford Dictionary of National Biography, oxforddnb.com, 23 September 2004.

Lewis, C.P., *Warenne, William de, first earl of Surrey [Earl Warenne] (d. 1088)* (article), Oxford Dictionary of National Biography, oxforddnb. com, 23 September 2004.

Lewis, Michael, *Why is Harold a hero of the Bayeux Tapestry* (article), BBC History Magazine, March 2018.

Leyser, Henrietta, *Medieval Women, A Social History of Women in England 450–1500*, Phoenix, e-book, 2013.

Lofting, Paula, *Ælfgyva: The mystery Woman of the Bayeux Tapestry*, (articles) Parts I–VII, englishhistoryauthorsblogspot.co.uk, 2017–18.

Lofting, Paula, *The Mystery Lady of the Bayeux Tapestry* (article), annabelfrage.qordpress.com, 11 July 2017.

Lyon, H.R., *The Norman Conquest*, London, 1965.

Majda, *Who was Lady Godiva?* (article), historyreading.com 24 October 2017.

Mandal, Dattatreya, *The Incredible Life of Harald Hardrada: The Last of the Great Vikings* (article), realmofhistory.com, 5 September 2015.

Marlow, Joyce, *Kings & Queens of Britain*, (sixth edition) London, Artus Publishing, 1979.

Matthew, Donald, *King Stephen*, London, Hambledon and London, 2002.

Maund, K.L., *Ealdgyth [Aldgyth] (fl. C. 1057–1066)* (article), Oxford Dictionary of National Biography, oxforddnb.com, 23 September 2004.

McGrath, Carol, *Who was Edith Swanneck?* (article), 1066turnedupsidedown.blogspot.co.uk, July 2016.

McNulty, J. Bard, *The Lady Ælfgyva in the Bayeux Tapestry* (article), *Speculum* 55.4, pp. 659–68, 1980.

Morris, Marc, *Castle Acre and the Warennes* (article), marcmorris.org. uk, 30 June 2016.

Morris, Marc, *Queen Matilda, wife of William the Conqueror, was NOT a Dwarf* (article), marcmorris.org.uk, 29 July 2013.

Morris, Marc, *The Norman Conquest*, London, Windmill Books, 2013.

Morris, Marc, *William I, England's Conqueror*, London, Penguin Books, 2016.

Mount, Toni, *A Year in the Life of Medieval England*, Stroud, Amberley Publishing, 2016.

My-albion.blogspot.co.uk, *Harold Godwinson's Posthumous Reputation, 1066–c.1160* (article) 8 November 2013.

O'Brien, Harriet, *Queen Emma and the Vikings: The Woman Who Shaped the Events of 1066*, London, Bloomsbury Publishing, 2006.

Owen-Crocker, Gale R., *Bayeux unravelled: the scenes behind the threads* (article) historyextra.com, 17 January 2018.

Oxford Today, *Massacre at St Frideswide's* (article), The University Magazine, Michaelmas 2002.

The Prosopography of Anglo-Saxon England, pase.ac.uk, August 2010.

Page, William (editor), *A History of the County of Hampshire: Volume 4*, London, Victoria County History, 1911. british-history.ac.uk.

Page, William (editor), *A History of the County of Sussex: Volume 2*, London, Victoria County History, 1973. british-history.ac.uk.

Page, William (editor), *Houses of Benedictine monks: The abbey of Eynsham* in *A History of the County of Oxford: Volume 2*, London, Victoria County History, 1907. british-history.ac.uk.

Page, William (editor), *Houses of Benedictine monks: The abbey of Stow*, in *A History of the County of Lincoln: Volume 2*, London, Victoria County History, 1906. british-history.ac.uk.

Pelteret, David A.E., *Catalogue of English Post-Conquest Vernacular Documents*, Woodbridge, 1990.

Randolph, Octavia, *Godiva: Her Literary Legend* (article), englishhistoryauthors.blogspot.co.uk, 9 September 2016.

Randolph, Octavia, *Uncovering Lady Godiva* (article), englishhistoryauthors.blogspot.co.uk, 23 July 2013.

Rex, Peter, *Edward the Confessor, King of England*, Stroud, Amberley Publishing, 2013.

Rex, Peter, *Harold: The King Who Fell at Hastings*, Stroud, Amberley Publishing, 2017.

Rex, Peter; *William the Conqueror, the Bastard of Normandy* (third edition) Stroud, Amberley Publishing. 2016.

Richards, Julian D. and Hadley, Dawn, *The great Viking Terror* (article), BBC History Magazine, September 2016.

Rochelle, Mercedes, *Gytha, wife of Godwine* (article), mercedesrochelle.com, 9 March 2014.

Rochelle, Mercedes, *Return of Earl Godwine, 1052* (article), mercedesrochelle.com, 8 March 2012.

Rochelle, Mercedes, *The almost forgotten Edith of Wessex, Queen of England* (article), mercedesrochelle.com, 15 May 2015.

Rochelle, Mercedes, *The Children of Harold Godwineson* (article), mercedesrochelle.com, 15 March 2015.

Rochelle, Mercedes, *What Happened to Earl Godwine's Family?* (article), mercedesrochelle.com, 18 April 2010.

Ross, David *Scotland, History of a Nation*, Broxburn, Lomond Books Ltd, 2014.

Royal Historical Society, *An Account of the Bayeux Tapestry* (article), Vol. 5, Cambridge.org, December 1877.

russiapedia.rt.com, *Prominent Russians: Anna Yaroslavna* (article), russiapedia.rt.com/prominent-russians/the-ryurikovich-dynasty/anna-yaroslavna.

Salzman, L.F. (editor), *A History of the County of Sussex: Volume 7, the Rape of Lewes*, London, Victoria County History, 1940. british-history.ac.uk.

Salzman, L.F. (editor), 'The Domesday survey: The Text', in *A History of the County of Oxford: Volume 1*, London, Victoria County History, 1939. british-history.ac.uk.

Smurthwaite, David, *The Complete Guide to the Battlefields of Britain*, London, Michael Joseph Ltd, 1993.

Southern, R.W., *The Making of the Middle Ages*, 4th edition, London, The Folio Society, 1998.

Stafford, Pauline, Ælfgifu [Ælfgifu of Northampton (fl. 1006–1036) (article), Oxford Dictionary of National Biography, oxforddnb.com, 23 September 2004.

Stafford, Pauline, Ælfthryth (article), Oxford Dictionary of National Biography, oxforddnb.com, 23 September 2004.

Stafford, Pauline, *Queen Emma and Queen Edith: Queenship and Women's Power in Eleventh century England*, Oxford, Blackwell, 1997.

Starbuck, Lydia, *The Bayeux Tapestry and Matilda of Flanders* (article), historyofroyalwomen.com 8 February 2018.

Stephens, W.B. (editor), *The City of Coventry: The outlying parts of Coventry, Introduction*, in *A History of the County of Warwick: Volume 8, the City of Coventry and Borough of Warwick*, London, Victoria County History, 1969. british-history.ac.uk.

Stephens, W.B. (editor), *The City of Coventry: The legend of Lady Godiva*, in *A History of the County of Warwick: Volume 8, the City of Coventry and Borough of Warwick*, London, Victoria County History, 1969. british-history.ac.uk.

Stowminster.co.uk, *History* (article).

Sturdy, David *Alfred the Great*, London, Constable. 1995.

Thierry, Augustin, *History of the Conquest of England* (all volumes).

Tranter, Nigel, *The Story of Scotland*, e-book, 4th edition, Neil Wilson Publishing, 2011.

Tyler, Elizabeth M., *England in Europe; English Royal Women and Literary Patronage c.1000–c.1150*, Toronto, University of Toronto Press, 2017.

Undiscoveredscotland.co.uk, *King Malcolm III Canmore* (article).

Van Houts, Elizabeth, *Adelida [Adeliza] (d. before 1113)* (Article), Oxford Dictionary of National Biography, oxforddnb.com, 23 September 2004.

Van Houts, Elizabeth, *Judith of Flanders, duchess of Bavaria (1030/5–1095)* (article), Oxford Dictionary of National Biography, oxforddnb.com, 23 September 2004.

Van Houts, Elizabeth, *Matilda of Flanders (d. 1083) queen of England, consort of William I* (article), Oxford Dictionary of National Biography, oxforddnb.com, May 2008.

Walker, David, *Gruffudd ap Llywelyn (d. 1063)* (article), Oxford Dictionary of National Biography, oxforddnb.com, 23 September 2004.

Walker, Ian, *Harold, the Last Anglo-Saxon King*, Stroud, The history Press, 2016 edition.

Wall, Martin, *The Anglo-Saxon Age, the Birth of England*, Stroud, Amberley Publishing, 2015.

Wall, Martin, *The Anglo-Saxons in 100 Facts*, Stroud, Amberley Publishing, 2016.

Wall, Martin, *Warriors and Kings, The 1500-Year Battle for Celtic Britain*, Stroud, Amberley Publishing, 2017.

Ward, Emily Joan, *Anne of Kiev (c.1024–c.1075) and a reassessment of maternal power in the minority kingship of Philip I of France* (article), Institute of Historical Research, vol. 89, no. 245, August 2016.

Waugaman, Elisabeth, *The meaning of 'Mora', the Flagship Matilda of Flanders gave William the Conqueror* (article), the freelancehistorywriter.com, 12 September 2014.

Weir, Alison, *Britain's Royal Families; the Complete Genealogy*, London, Pimlico, revised edition 1996.

Whitehead, Annie, *1066 – The Mercian Perspective* (article), anniewhiteheadauthor.co.uk, 10 July 2016.

Whitehead, Annie, *Defining 'Nobility' in Later Anglo-Saxon England* (article), englishhistoryauthors.blogspot.co.uk, 26 April 2016.

Whitehead, Annie, *Did the Conqueror Build Upon Existing Foundations?* (article), englishhistoryauthors.blogspot.co.uk, 14 October 2016.

Whitehead, Annie, *Wealth, Power and Influence in Later Anglo-Saxon England* (article), englishhistoryauthors.blogspot.co.uk, 30 May 2016.

Williams, Ann, Ælfgar, earl of Mercia (d. 1062?) (article), Oxford Dictionary of National Biography, oxforddnb.com, 23 September 2004.

Williams, Ann, *Eadgifu [Eddeua] the Fair [the Rich] 9fl. 1066)* (article), Oxford Dictionary of National Biography, oxforddnb.com, 23 September 2004.

Williams, Ann, *Edith (Eadgyth) d.1075* (article), Oxford Dictionary of National Biography, oxforddnb.com, 23 September 2004.

Williams, Ann, *Godgifu (d. 1067?)* (article), Oxford Dictionary of National Biography, oxforddnb.com, October 2004.

Williams, Ann, *Godwine, earl of Wessex (d. 1053)* (article), Oxford Dictionary of National Biography, oxforddnb.com, 23 September 2004.

Williams, Ann, *Leofric, earl of Mercia (d. 1057)* (article), Oxford Dictionary of National Biography, oxforddnb.com, 26 May 2005.

Williams, Ann, *Morcar, earl of Northumbria (fl. 1065–1087)* (article), Oxford Dictionary of National Biography, oxforddnb.com, 23 September 2004.

Williams, Ann, *On the Spindle Side: the kinswomen of Earl Godwine of Wessex* (article), generously shared by the author, as yet unpublished.

Williams, Ann, *The English and the Norman Conquest*, Woodbridge, The Boydell Press, paperback edition, 2000.

Williamson, David, *Brewer's British Royalty*, London, Cassell, 1996.

Wissolik, R., *The Saxon Statement: Code in the Bayeux Tapestry* (article), *Annuale Medievale* 19, pp. 69–97, 1979.

Woodruff, Douglas, *The Life and Times of Alfred the Great*, London, George Weidenfeld and Nicolson Ltd and Book Club Associates, 1974.

Wrottesley, G. and Parker, F. (editors), *Cartulary of Trentham Priory: Normancote*, in *Staffordshire Historical Collections, Vol. 11*, London, Staffordshire Record Society, 1890.

Index